Energizing the Workplace:
A Strategic Response to Stress

Energizing the Workplace: A Strategic Response to Stress

Kim James and Tanya Arroba

Gower

Published by
Gower Publishing Limited
Gower House
Croft Road
Aldershot
Hampshire GU11 3HR
England

Gower
Old Post Road
Brookfield
Vermont 05036
USA

British Library Cataloguing in Publication Data
James, Kim
    Energizing the workplace : a strategic response
    1.Job stress 2.Job stress - Prevention 3.Stress management
    I.Title II.Arroba, Tanya
    658.3'14

ISBN 0 566 08022 2

Library of Congress Cataloging-in-Publication Data
James, Kim.
    Energizing the workplace : a strategic response to stress / Kim James and
    Tanya Arroba.
        p.   cm.
    ISBN 0–566–08022–2
    1. Job stress   2. Stress management.   I. Arroba, Tanya.
    II. Title.
    HF5548.85.J36   1999
    658.3'82–dc21   98–32252
                                                                            CIP

Typeset in 10 on 12pt Sabon by Wearset, Boldon, Tyne and Wear and printed in Great Britain at the University Press, Cambridge.

Contents

Figures

Acknowledgements

We are very aware of the number of people who have influenced our thinking over the years as well as all the managers with whom we have worked who have provided us with material from the world of organizations. We would like to thank all those people even though we are not able to thank everyone personally.

However, we would like to thank four people in particular for the role they have played in the, at times, lengthy and stressful process of bringing this book into being. A particular thank you goes to Clare Huffington of The Tavistock Consultancy Service for her support, encouragement and comments as we progressed to the final draft. We would also like to thank Paul Durham, Chief Executive of Chester City Council for his support and sharing his experience as a senior manager with us as well as for giving his comments. We would also like to thank Julia Scott for her editorial support and encouragement. Finally, special thanks to Ann Davies at Cranfield School of Management for her amazing skill at making sense of the manuscript and giving up a lot of time to help make the deadline.

Last, but far from least, we both want to thank our families and friends for their understanding and tolerance of our pre-occupation with our new approach to stress management. We hope we did not cause too much stress in the process!

KJ
TA

Introduction: this book and how to use it

We have heard so many times in the course of our work with organizations, that people have been asked to produce a way forward on organizational stress but felt uncertain and anxious about how to proceed. The task itself was a stress producer for many! This book is a response to that need. The purpose of this book is to explore the area of organizational stress and to provide guidelines on how to tackle this effectively. It is a distillation of the work we have done and what we have learned. It is a book on organizational stress; what it is, why it is increasing, how it comes about as a consequence of the working environment and the steps you can take to reduce stress in the organization. If you are interested in helping your organization address stress constructively, this book is for you.

Why is the book needed now?

The various methods which have been adopted to tackle stress are often expensive; training, counselling, fitness centres and so on all cost a great deal to run. Recognition of the detrimental effects of stress has risen and many organizations realize the importance of getting the most from their people, yet it is alarming that stress still seems to be rising in incidence rather than falling, despite the efforts to reduce it. This book explores this phenomenon and discusses what may be happening in our organizational lives where pressure levels become inappropriate and stress is all too frequently a fact of corporate life. If organizations want to make the most of their people's talents and skills they must understand and address the issues discussed in this book. Their actions in investing in people have to have a rationale and be pinpointed at the necessary areas. This book helps you to make positive, informed choices about your investment.

What is the focus of this book?

In the process of helping our clients with their stress management initiatives, we have learned a great number of lessons from the issues they have been tussling with, and from our involvement with them. Our experience over many years has confirmed the complexity of the issues surrounding the management of stress and organizations. What this book will do is to provide you with a map of the issues in stress management today and a guided process through which to take your organization. It will give you an understanding of what you need to address at each stage along the way and the options to consider in developing your own, tailored strategy which will meet the needs of your organization.

Our view is that because each organization has its own particular problems to deal with when looking at stress, the realistic and appropriate way forward is to understand the culture and needs of the organization you are in and work out what to do in that context. 'Uniqueness', such as a fiercely competitive environment, being in a public service, the vulnerability of the organization's clients or members, or complex and changing technology, are not reasons for inaction, but reasons for differentiated action. The company down the road may be doing a great job that you can learn from, but it will not have a solution which you can simply borrow. This book provides more than a simple checklist of things to do to reduce stress.

This book is not a self-help guide for people who are suffering from stress. There are many of these around and they can be very useful indeed. Our focus is on the organizational strategies and managerial actions for reducing organizational stress. As you will see, we believe that individuals do have a responsibility for, and need help and organizational support for, personal stress management. However, organizations also have a part to play in creating the conditions for stress as well as for providing methods for reducing it. The approach adopted here is to explore how stress is created organizationally, rather than just on how individuals can learn to survive. Making the jungle less dangerous is as important as learning to survive in it.

What informs our work and this book?

As we wrote this book we were learning more and more about the process described here. This is because the newer issues of organizational stress are still being understood and the new forms that organizations are developing are throwing up previously unexplored areas to consider. However, we did not come to these completely new. There is an extensive body of research on which this book rests. This comes from three main sources. Firstly, we are advocating a strategic approach to this issue. Strategy formation and implementation has been well researched and the process by which this can be achieved mapped. Secondly, there is a huge and burgeoning body of research on stress in the workplace on which we draw. Thirdly, there is a theoretical psychological understanding of organizational life as an emotional experience which has been developed over decades and which enables us to grasp the essential features of people's problems, needs and experiences. This body of thinking helps us to understand the organization as a living system, full of feeling and subjective thinking. By understanding that organizations are not just rational, objective vehicles for the attainment of goals, we believe we gain enormous insight into what is really going on at work and which leads to stress. This insight then informs our development of options and choices for dealing with stress and the implementation of the whole approach.

So is this a theory book? The answer to that is emphatically 'no'. We have combined our understanding of organizations as psychologists applying psychological principles to our work with clients, with our learning from our organizational consulting. This enables us to provide a practical approach for you to take. This book owes as much to our clients as it does to theory; the combination is the key. It is not a pure research book, nor is it 'just common sense'. The approaches are fine-tuned by experience and models and theories inform experience. Our aim in writing this book is to take ideas that you may not otherwise have access to, and turn these into an accessible read. We think that you will recognize many aspects of your own organization in what we say and in the examples we offer you from our work – even if we have never worked in your organization!

What the book covers

The book is in four parts. The first part describes a new approach to organizational stress. It discusses why we now need to tackle stress differently from the ways we have approached stress in the past. It looks at the current and predicted future organizational experience which leads to the conditions for stress. It looks at why the problem of organizational stress is set to increase. Unless we adopt more comprehensive methods for reducing stress it will become more serious. Comprehensive does not have to mean more expensive; instead of simply increasing the spend on stress management we need to rethink where that investment should be made.

We outline the importance of considering stress management as necessary for top performance in organizations. When stress is around, top performance is hard to achieve. We recognize the need for revitalized organizations in the wake of the many changes in organizational life in recent years and an uncertain future.

The second part of the book turns our attention to the need to recognize and understand how stress is manifested and how it comes about as a result of often unacknowledged anxiety within the workplace. We emphasize the need for an emotional focus to understand how stress is created. We also emphasize the need to look at the issue from a systemic perspective, looking at the organization as a whole system.

The third part of the book considers the options for creating a supportive environment. We see support as an essential factor in reducing stress levels. However, we argue that providing support is more than putting certain structures in place, such as a counselling scheme. We press for more consideration to be given to the processes needed to provide support. We look at the three levels of providing support: to the organization as a whole as well as at the managerial and personal level.

In the fourth part of the book we focus on the strategic aspect of organizational stress management; how to get an initiative off the ground which will be effective in your particular organization. We look at the steps needed to get it off the ground, the question of collecting data on stress in your organization and, finally, how to pull it all together in a co-ordinated strategic package.

We conclude with an endnote which summarizes how to put the new approach to organizational stress management into action.

Who is the book for?

We have worked with many senior managers over the years and are aware that managers from different backgrounds can express an interest in managing stress within their organization.

In writing this book we have in mind senior managers who are in a position to influence corporate strategy and have an interest in what managing stress can do to improve their organization's performance. We also recognize that human resources professionals, health and safety managers and lawyers will have a particular interest in the topic of stress management. This book will be useful to them as well.

How to use this book

We suggest that you read the whole book before you start taking steps to develop your own approach. Many of our points are illustrated in figures and there are also key points sections at the end of each chapter so that you can find the salient bits when you want to come back to them. The information we give you about the background to stress and the new approach will help you put your ideas together for presentation in your organization; use it to help you make the appropriate case in your organization. We are providing you with a process to use and, of course, yours will not happen exactly as we suggest here. For example, someone may have already done some data collection as part of a project so you may not start with a clean slate, or you may have already raised expectations with some training courses and feel that you have to do the next thing quickly to keep the momentum going. We understand that; we have often started in the middle! Use this book to help you do what you can, finding your way through to the best approach you can adopt. The best approach is the one that fits your organization.

So, if you want to find out what to put into a few seminars on stress so that you can say you have ticked the issue off your list, don't read on. If you think you want to take organizational stress seriously, that you want to 'make a difference', then this book will help you do that.

Part I
A New Approach to Organizational Stress Management

S trategic Approach
  for
T op Performance
  and a
R evitalized Organization
  depends on
E motional Focus
  with
S ystemic Thinking
  to develop a
S upportive Environment

In this part of the book we outline a new approach to organizational stress management. This approach is then explored in more depth throughout the rest of the book.

In Chapter 1 we look at why current approaches to stress management are not as effective as was hoped. We outline what elements we believe are needed for a more productive approach to organizational stress management.

In Chapter 2 we focus on why organizational stress management is needed and what you will gain from tackling it successfully. The aim is to ensure an organization capable of top performance with a revitalized and energetic staff.

A new approach to organizational stress management

There was probably no golden age in organizations during which stress was unknown. However there are some fundamental ways in which organizations have changed over the past few decades. During that time our understanding of stress at work has struggled to keep up with organizational requirements. Many organizations are struggling with the leanness which follows downsizing. Other organizations are trying to cope with the pressures of expansion. In both these scenarios, dealing with the feelings of the people who are in the organization, keeping the creative edge and managing with new structures are key to success. Stress management has struggled to keep up with these kinds of issues faced by organizations because in the past it has been focused on helping individuals to manage their own pressure levels. The issue of the organizational context has been largely ignored.

The development of approaches to stress management

Studies into stress began many years ago but the notion of stress in the workplace only started to be considered widely during the 1960s and 1970s. The impact of factors such as working patterns, roles at work and conditions of work on stress were explored. In addition research was undertaken on particular groups in organizations, such as workers in jobs which are paced by machine. The notion of executive stress began to catch people's imagination. An understanding of the physiology of stress was developing, although research still continues today to fathom out detailed mechanisms.

Because of work done in these areas in previous decades, and the newer findings then emerging, it became possible to develop training programmes on stress management, which could be presented in organizations. In those days it was unusual for organizations to be greatly committed to this. The usual reaction to the idea of stress was that it was 'oddballs and softies' who suffered. The most prevalent view was that one should watch out for these people and make provisions for them, but it need not be a mainstream activity.

Stress is taken seriously – for others!

By the 1980s the view was changing. More evidence of stress at work was rapidly emerging. In the early 1980s we were approached time and time again by organizations that wanted to run stress management training programmes for those who needed it. We were happy, like many others, to oblige! The overriding sense, though, was that it was always for the benefit of 'others' and managers usually attended so that they could help their staff rather than themselves. It was far too difficult to admit that 'it might be me'.

This was particularly brought home to us when we were brought in to help a group of directors who were described by the personnel manager as 'extremely stressed as a group'. They had just lost a colleague who had quite unexpectedly committed suicide. We were asked to work with them without mentioning or implying that any one of these directors could possibly experience stress personally. We were to teach them stress management skills as though we were simply doing it on behalf of their staff, who would in turn learn from them. To be fair to this group, this focus did shift once we were underway, but our brief speaks volumes about the 'not me' syndrome. It has lessened considerably in many organizations today, but by no means all.

Perhaps we all need to learn about stress

By the late 1980s and 1990s there was a considerable shift in many organizations as the realities of the massive organizational changes hit home. With fewer staff and high performance demands many organizations realized that a more encompassing approach was required. More acknowledgement of the impact of stress, public figures giving up career prospects to focus on home and family and the rising costs of absenteeism and stress-related illness, meant that organizations turned their attention to how to support staff through the pressures and changes. During this time organizations funded and supported more employee counselling schemes, fitness programmes and health screening, as well as stress management training programmes and stress awareness seminars for managers, than could have been foreseen two decades previously. Stress management had become mainstream.

Not all companies have embraced these developments and there is more to be done in creating awareness and action. Even in organizations where there are many stress management initiatives, realization is growing that current practice is not bringing about the desired results. The question is being raised as to whether current practice is sufficient. We need to build on the experience of the last two decades. It is not a case of throwing out the approaches that have been used. They will still be needed. Yet current experience has shown that there are problems still to be addressed. Stress in organizations has not disappeared despite all the efforts.

How do we know that the current practice of stress management is not working?

The main indicator telling us that stress continues to be a problem is the increase in reporting of stress-related illness and absence. Estimates are hard to verify, but figures of 90 million working days a year lost in the UK costing £7 billion have been suggested. Whilst some argue that the 'acceptability' of stress has led to greater reporting of its incidence, others argue that the real figures are hidden because many people still do not want their employers to know they feel stressed. In a recent survey over 80 per cent of human resource directors thought that stress was problematic in their organizations and trades unions have identified this as a growing issue for members. There is so much concern that a government enquiry into the incidence of stress has been set up.

One organization we know has provided for staff extremely well. It has offered all of the currently accepted support packages to staff: on-site fitness centre, health checks on site in company time, counselling for those who want it and regular stress management workshops to those who want to attend. However, their regular staff surveys show that high levels of stress are still an issue. In tackling this there is a real desire to treat staff well and an emphasis on being a good employer which can attract the best calibre of people and retain them. All of the senior managers have agreed that managing stress is a high priority in keeping their competitive edge. The problem is that they are at a loss as to what to do next.

Clearly, although much is being done, something is going wrong. We believe that there are four main areas to address to improve the effectiveness of the resources put into organizational stress management. These are:

■ a 'one-size-fits-all' philosophy which leads to a failure to design stress management initiatives strategically;
■ the lack of focus on the causes of stress which leads to a failure to view the organization as a whole system, that is systemically;
■ a difficulty in engaging with the emotional aspects of stress and its management;
■ a restricted view of providing support and a supportive environment.

Stress and a strategic approach: moving away from a 'one-size-fits-all' philosophy

It is tempting to search for the one solution to stress in the organization, whether this is training courses for everyone, or an on-site counselling service that everyone can use. Not that all stressed people want counselling or training, nor would it improve their situation if they did. Even providing more than one solution does not solve the problem, if it is assumed that patching up individuals is what is required.

An alternative is to take a blunderbuss approach: a bit of training, a bit of occupational health involvement, an occasional survey to see how we're doing and a tick can be placed in the organizational stress management box. This may provide a sense of achievement in that a lot is being done to address stress, but it still may not work. Effective stress management initiatives do not depend on the sheer volume of activity, but on whether the activity is based on a thorough understanding of the particular organizational context, a consideration of all options available and an explicit policy on the specific approach to be taken and why.

If the organization pays for a fitness training centre and works people too hard for them to use it, then it is more likely to raise blood pressure in resentment than it is to reduce it. This raises the question of following through consistently on good intentions. It may be recognized that improving fitness levels of staff will enable them to deal with pressure more effectively, but that is not enough. Nor is providing the latest in de luxe fitness equipment. To be effective all aspects need to be thought through. Failure to do so can make the situation worse. An organization we heard about became the focus for unwelcome, adverse media publicity after sending all their staff on a meditation course. The staff were incensed at the message they received from this well-intentioned initiative. As far as they were concerned, learning how to meditate was not going to solve the problems they faced in working for this particular organization. They viewed it as simply a patch-up and were resentful of this. As a result they notified the media who were happy to report on this organization's money-wasting venture, particularly as it was public money.

It is also not enough to focus on the initiative itself. It is vital to be very clear about the desired outcomes. Different outcomes will require different tactics. If you want the benefit of avoiding adverse litigation or reducing the costs associated with stress but are less interested in the good employer benefit, you need to adopt practices that will lead to the outcomes you want. If your main objective is getting top performance, that needs to inform your actions. These are strategic choices. The end objectives of any stress management initiative need to be clarified and inform any action.

Bringing all the actions together to address the needs of the particular organization in a co-ordinated way that is appropriate for the organization is the key to achieving the desired results. This is what we mean by taking a strategic approach.

Stress and systemic thinking: viewing the organization as a whole system

There is concern that stress management training has been rather like the job of MASH units portrayed in the movies about the US at war in Korea. Their job was to take wounded soldiers and patch them up so that they could return to the front. This is appropriate for an army unit, but should stress management training simply patch staff up to send them back to the battle zone?

Whilst casualties may be a fact of war, the armed services actively seek to reduce their casualties to a minimum. They do not only provide medical care and bury the dead, they develop strategies for having as few casualties as possible. What we are arguing for is that other organizations also view 'minimum casualties' as an approach to stress. In many cases, organizations still take the view that 'care for the wounded' is sufficient. Proactive rather than reactive stances are needed.

Many observers, indeed, have begun to comment on the cynicism, or even cruelty, of giving people the message that if they experience stress they and they alone must change their attitudes and behaviour. This cannot work unless some of the unnecessary pressures are also reduced. Single individuals cannot change the nature of their organization to make it more fit for human habitation. Organizations need to take a hard look at the causes of stress.

The lack of focus on the organizational causes of stress has led us to a fundamental shift in perspective. Early stress management focused on individuals. Now attention needs to turn to the organization as a whole. This gives a different focus to the consideration of stress management initiatives. It involves recognition that all the various parts of an organization impact on each other and create ripples, which resonate across the whole organization. This shift to observing the system as a whole is vital in moving to a broader and more effective view of stress management. What we now need is systemic thinking with regard to managing stress.

The dominant assumption that has operated for a couple of centuries in Western culture is that to change or create something, we fix the parts that are not working or add new parts. This is akin to the medical model of finding the cause of an illness and eradicating the bacteria, virus, gene or whatever causes it. It is a model of prediction and control and vital for the sick patient. However, this model is not so good at looking for the relationships between all the different body systems so that their interactions and balance are understood as the basis for health and well being. In medicine the 'both/and' perspective is taking hold.

Typically we run organizations in a way that focuses on fixing problems; a lot of forward planning is really the anticipation of problems that may arise. The aim is to control as much as possible. This can lead us to see problems as isolated events rather than a reflection of the whole organization in which the origins of a symptom may not even be in the part of the organization where it is observed.

Systemic thinking has been applied in the last few decades to most scientific fields: physics, biology, medicine, economics and psychology. To think systemically we have to move away from a localized cause-and-effect model. Systems thinking is more holistic. It recognizes the interplay between a system and the larger ones of which it is a part, and between the system as a whole and its parts. We can see systemic thinking in relation to our environment; even young children now understand the notions of habitat, food chains and so on. Even if politicians can't always act on the knowledge, we know that deforestation in one country can lead to far distant climate changes, and that as the life cycle of one species is affected the food chain and life expectancy of another is doomed.

This works in organizational management too. For instance, organizational cultures in a country will reflect some aspects of their national culture, in so far as they operate globally. In turn, what organizations do will, over time, affect national culture. Internally, what the management group does will impact on the organization's culture, but in turn, how the top team operates is also a reflection of the make-up of the organization as a whole. Any manager who has been successful in one environment but had little impact in another, has first-hand experience of how systems intertwine. In this case, for example, it may be the way their personal style is modified by the team dynamics which in turn will be influenced by the culture, so that their style worked in one environment, but not in another.

Thinking in this way forces us to recognize that to transform a system it is insufficient to tinker with one bit, however powerful that bit may be. Homeostasis – the pull to maintain stability – undoes the work. For example, we can put in a new chief executive with new ideals, but unless we change systems and processes at many levels the new mission statement will be forgotten before the copies come back from printing. The new structure may be in place but things will get done in annoyingly old ways. The expected culture change is elusive.

When looking at stress, we can see that it gets passed around from one part of the system to another or across the boundary into another system. A classic example is the home/work boundary. Some people feel that they can leave their home problems behind when they come to work. But it is not always your own problems that hit you; the boss's divorce becomes the team's bad day, your headache and someone else's grumpiness. What is more, when people pick up these circulating feelings, they can't figure out how they got to feel like that, which adds to the discomfort and difficulty of dealing with it. It's like a chain reaction in which recipients down the line have no idea why or what started it, but get the reaction anyway. By the time your boss has a go at you about something trivial, the source of the original reaction is long gone.

Engaging with the emotional aspects of stress

Organizations appear to be based on logic and rationality. They are designed, structured and run to produce products or services. Structures and processes are analysed logically to achieve targets, to promote efficiency and ensure effectiveness. This is the rationality of organizational life. But this is only the tip of the iceberg of organizational experience. Submerged emotions are the elements which have caused many an organization to sink. Navigating these seemingly irrational aspects of organizational life is the key to enabling people to produce their best. As organizations are made up of people and people are more than purely rational and logical beings, they experience emotions. They do not leave their emotional side at home when they come to work. The experience of work generates feelings and these emotions need to be acknowledged. It is the need to take account of, and to engage with, the emotional aspect of organizational life which has been lacking from many approaches to dealing with stress. There has been an attempt to consider stress as if it were purely a matter of logic. It is not. For example there has been much attention given recently to the issue of presenteeism, the need for employees to spend long hours in the workplace. Telling people to stop will not solve the problem. The reasons for working long hours are much more complex than the simple equation of amount of work and time. Many of the reasons why people work long hours have to do with anxiety to be seen as committed, loyal and hardworking, accompanied by fears if they do not conform. Many managers are frustrated when they explain to staff that there is no need for them to follow the managerial example of long hours, and the explanation goes unheeded.

Whenever stress is experienced or manifested in the workplace, emotion will be a component part. When considering the causes of stress from a systemic perspective emotion will feature largely. It is this often unspoken, unacknowledged aspect of organizational life which needs to be highlighted and brought to the forefront of awareness, and to play a key part in initiatives to manage stress.

Perspectives on the nature of a supportive environment

Support is not a structure. It is a process. Many organizations have put in structures which are designed to provide support for staff when they are stressed. These are frequently employee assistance or counselling schemes. The notion seems to be that the way to provide support for staff is to put a structure into place. This may well be helpful but it will not be enough.

If the intention is to provide support, it needs to be viewed as part of the whole working environment, rather than as just an add-on to the existing way of doing things. The way of doing things, which is assumed and taken for granted, is often part of the problem. People's willingness to question and explore aspects of the environment which have an impact on pressure levels, is a vital element of support. For this to work, it needs to be explicit in purpose and openly discussed. Unnecessary pressure in the organization will then be reduced. Cutting out unnecessary pressure is half of the stress management equation. The other half is practices and structures which help people to be resilient. Reducing unnecessary pressure and providing an environment which is conducive to resilience, is what we mean by support.

Let's look at an example of stress in an organization and how looking at the whole organization and considering the emotions of the staff, was the key to understanding how to move forward. Recently, a manager told us about a reorganization in his company. The company had split into two parts; one division was to own the new developments, the research and innovations, and was the key to the future. The other was formed to run the basic and existing product lines, which would fund these new developments. After the split the manager became aware of a lack of energy in the existing products division. He could not understand this. As far as he was concerned there was a logical reason for the new structure. He also recognized that stress levels were high and so was absenteeism. They had to find a solution to fix this low energy.

So far they had approached this as a problem of logic. They had introduced new incentive schemes, training programmes and away days. These did not solve the difficulty. It was not until there was recognition that this was about people's emotions that they were able to make progress. Taking this new view the management realized that despite all efforts, people in the existing products division were feeling like second class citizens. The management did not wish for this, on the contrary, they had as their strategic aim a high performing, energetic workforce in both new divisions. However, they were still unclear as to how to obtain this.

Systemic thinking offers some insights and points to a route forward. If we look at the whole of the organization and understand the symbolic meaning of the split to people, we get a different view. In the process of splitting, the picture of the new developments division was painted as sexy and exciting, the place to be. Those who got jobs in that division were clearly expected to be pleased and happy with their lot; there was no room for doubt. The other division was implicitly described as dull, stale and boring. In certain respects this was the reality and so no one was surprised when bad feeling arose within this division. However, the new developments division began to take on a slightly manic air; it was unheard of for people to complain, even though they were frantically busy and as one person described it, 'constantly working at the edge, close to burnout'.

In fact if you talked to people, there was considerable mixed feelings in both divisions. Old relationships had been severed and it was hard getting used to the new changes. Some people in the new developments division were finding it less exciting and more plain anxiety provoking than they had expected. But it was hard to talk about because they were supposed to be the lucky ones. In the existing products division, some people rather liked the familiarity of the processes and the sense of comparative calm and certainty. But again it was hard to talk about because it might appear as though they were of the old guard or lacking commitment and ambition. So the divisions were getting more polarized and frustrations between them increased.

Changing this situation needed a supportive environment in which staff in both divisions could explore together their reactions to the change, both positive and negative. This process could not be targeted at what had initially been seen as the problem division, it needed to involve both divisions.

A new approach to stress management

The new approach we are advocating leads on from current practice but incorporates ways of addressing the deficiencies in what is being done at the moment. Our approach is to recognize that organizational stress is experienced as a consequence of emotional turmoil at work. The turbulent emotional life of organizations is often an unconscious undercurrent and can best be understood by looking at what is going on in the whole system. The organization context, what is going on and how it is being managed is intimately involved with our experience of work. To help people we need to look at stress from the 'big picture'. Simply offering people 'sticking plasters' will not change their overall experience of their workplace. If organizations are to take this perspective then a coherent strategy is required; perceived support for the casualties of stress will not be sufficiently proactive. Without managing the whole system better, energy will be directed into defensive survival tactics and away from the work which is supposed to be done. The energy required to 'survive' emotionally drains the resources of everyone involved. For a really energized and vital organizational performance, stress needs a serious and concerted approach.

Therefore the key concepts on which the new approach is founded are:

■ a strategic approach;
■ systemic thinking;
■ focus on emotions; and
■ a supportive environment.

Taking these factors into account will meet today's organizational demand for:

■ top performance; and
■ revitalized organizational life.

To help you keep these factors clearly in your mind as you read the book and develop your own strategy for organizational stress management we have reordered these to form the word STRESS. This 'logo' reappears throughout the book, reminding you where you are in the conceptual thinking and why you are reading about it.

The complete model is shown in Figure 1.1.

Key points in Chapter 1

■ The STRESS model is the blueprint for a new approach to organizational stress management.
■ Approaches to stress management have changed over the years.
■ A new approach is required because the current practice of stress management is not reducing the incidence of stress in organizations.
■ The key elements of the new approach introduced in this chapter are a need for:
  − a strategic approach;
  − systemic thinking;

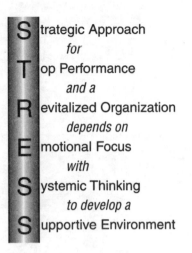

S trategic Approach
for
T op Performance
and a
R evitalized Organization
depends on
E motional Focus
with
S ystemic Thinking
to develop a
S upportive Environment

Figure 1.1 Key elements of successful organizational stress management

- focus on emotions; and
- a supportive environment.
In order to meet organizational requirements for
- top performance; and
- revitalized organizational life.

Managing for top performance and revitalized organizations

2

How managing stress is vital for top performance

At no point in our work have we ever encountered an organization in any sector which sets out to deliver less than optimum performance. We have never seen a statement which lists poor performance as an organizational goal. In contrast we have seen many vision or mission statements which clearly and unambiguously proclaim the wish to provide excellent service or products. That is an organizational given. Every organization wants to provide the best in order to be competitive and to foster pride in the organization's efforts.

And yet, while much is unclear, individualistic and subjective in the field of stress, one fact stands out with startling clarity. Whenever stress is present, performance will not be at its best.

Stress is what happens when there is a lack of balance between demands and resources, when the pressure level is inappropriate. As Figure 2.1 shows, when demands and resources are balanced and the level of pressure is at an optimum, then performance is at an optimum. This is the express desire of all organizations, to have staff working at their best as a prerequisite for top performance. In order for this to happen there needs to be a balance between demands and the ability to respond to those demands. If this is out of balance, if the pressure level is wrong, then stress will be present and performance will be below optimum. It is one of the few givens of understanding stress, that when stress is present then performance will be below optimum.

This link between the level of pressure and performance has been known for the best part of a century. Yet there appears to be a myth in many organizations which belies this fact. It is almost as if there is a belief that because performance is low when pressure is low then increasing the level of pressure will bring about a constant increase in the level of performance. Organizations act as if they believe in a direct line connection between pressure and performance. We have heard managers express this belief in words such as, 'pressure does them

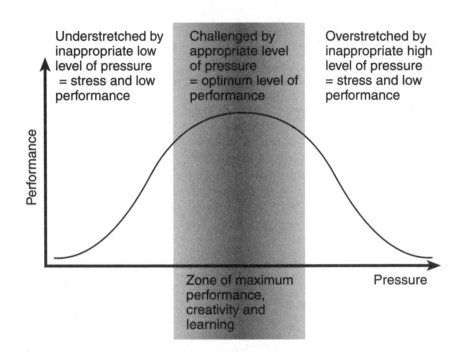

Understretched by inappropriate low level of pressure = stress and low performance

Challenged by appropriate level of pressure = optimum level of performance

Overstretched by inappropriate high level of pressure = stress and low performance

Performance

Pressure

Zone of maximum performance, creativity and learning

Figure 2.1 The relationship between pressure and performance

good', 'we need to keep the pace up'. It is true that too little pressure will not lead to top performance, but that does not mean that increasing the pressure indefinitely continues to lead to an indefinite increase in performance. If that belief is held, albeit not at an explicit level, then it is hardly surprising that organizations act as if constantly increasing pressure is a good thing.

As Figure 2.1 shows, this, however, is not the case. It is true that a very low level of pressure will result in a below par performance, but there comes an optimum level where pressure results in optimum performance. Any increase in pressure beyond that point will result in a decline in performance. Therefore the principle of increasing the pressure in the hope of obtaining even higher levels of performance will be in vain.

Another factor which can confuse the situation occurs where there is no clear understanding of the distinction between pressure and stress. Often these two words are used interchangeably as if they were identical. The distinction between these two words is necessary to gain an understanding of what it is that actually needs managing. Pressure is necessary. No one, individual, team or organization functions well in the absence of stimulation. On the other hand no one functions well when the pressure level is excessive.

Therefore the most basic reason why organizations need to have an effective strategy for managing stress, is simply to obtain top performance. However, there are other ways in which dealing with stress leads to top performance.

Effective stress management saves money

Stress in the workforce costs money. As the pressure grows for cost-effectiveness and increasing attention is given to efficiency, this emphasizes the need to be aware of costs. At the very least, a stressed person will not perform at their best. This will cost money. Absenteeism is linked to stress. Absenteeism costs money. The link between stress and ill health leads to sickness and this costs money. The final step of leaving the organization, whoever initiates it, will incur recruitment and selection and training costs and that will cost money.

These costs can be hidden and not immediately obvious. The cost of running a training programme in stress management or providing a counselling scheme may be more easily quantifiable. We have heard the argument raised that it is expensive to tackle stress. Our response is to draw attention to the fact that not doing something about stress in the organization can cost a good deal more. However many days are lost through stress-related problems, however many people are not able to give of their best because of the organizational conditions, these are costs which no organization can afford to bear. It may not appear on the annual accounts, nor have a budget head, but stress costs the organization money. This is a powerful argument. Instead of focusing on the costs of doing something about it, the response could be, could you afford not to do something about it?

Effective stress management demonstrates caring for staff

There are studies of good employers, organizations that are known to provide good conditions and care for staff. These league tables figure highly in individual choice of where to work. This is a factor which matters to people. The organizations of today and those of the future need good and highly skilled people to obtain top performance. The selection process is two-way and an organization will be sought after as an employer if they not only have a reputation as a good employer, but in reality do treat staff well.

Organizations need the commitment of staff. As the demands increase and the nature of work becomes even more exacting, the intangible factor of commitment becomes even more important. Commitment is more readily given when treatment is good and fair.

The notion of the psychological contract is one that is at the nub of this argument. Organizations vary in the degree of clarity they possess regarding the specific skills or competences they need in their staff, but again we have not encountered many places which set out to employ less than good and committed people. The organization has to provide something in return. Although a lot of emphasis is placed on financial rewards, the experience of working is more than simply the pay at the end of the month or week. We encountered a senior manager recently who is close to reaching the decision to leave her organization for the simple reason that 'this is not the sort of organization I want to be in, I do not like the way they treat people'. The pay was good but that was not enough to persuade this particular highly skilled and motivated senior manager to stay.

The psychological contract which used to be in place involved the employee offering the employer life-long commitment, unquestioning loyalty, trust, effort and obedience within the formal hierarchy. In return the employer offered the employee welfare, a career, training and development, and security. The new psychological contract involves the employee offering the organization high performance, high commitment and a willingness to seek training and development. The employer for its part offers the employee a job and high rewards for high perform-ance.

We are not proposing a return to nineteenth-century patriarchy, nor are we are proposing the emulation of Japanese practices. We are proposing that one argument for taking stress management seriously is that there is a basic principle involved: the principle of treating staff well. This is the basis of the good employer argument, that it matters to treat people well. There are often occasions when tough decisions have to be taken. That does not detract from the importance of a basic belief in treating staff with respect, good treatment and dignity. Putting staff under prolonged inappropriate pressure is not a way to treat staff well. Taking a long hard look at the whole system of the organization, identi-fying sources of stress, taking measures to do things differently as well as providing training and counselling; those are steps which back up a stated value in the importance of staff and their well-being. This is one element of the leadership needed for top performance.

Effective stress management as part of good leadership

We frequently hear the plea in organizations for strong leadership. However, there is room for different views of what strong leadership involves. Leadership involves more than counting the bottom line or setting performance targets, important though they are. For organizations to achieve their performance targets, leaders have to be concerned with values. It requires more than lip-service to demonstrate the value placed on people in the organization.

The early work on management as a discipline, in the days of scientific management, focused on the hard side of management. Measuring the time people take to do things, setting targets, clear monitoring and accountability, span of control and other elements of the harder, quantifiable side of management took precedence. Through the 1990s there has been a resurgence of interest in values, principles and even spirituality in organizations. This has been linked to the resurgence of interest in leadership as opposed to management. There is a need for principles to underpin organizational life and the principle of treating staff well is at the centre of this debate. The notion of empowerment of staff is one that figures largely in thinking on leadership.

Empowerment is a word that is used a great deal and is sometimes confused with delegation of responsibility. We hear people say, 'we have given them empowerment'. Empowerment is the process by which people are enabled to feel their personal power and can therefore take up the authority and responsibility that goes with their job. Staff who feel under pressure from a leadership which has simply abdicated responsibility downwards cannot feel empowered. Leaders who want to take the notion of empowerment seriously will include the issue of stress in their vision of the organization. Preventing the experience of stress can be a step towards empowering staff and setting a positive organizational culture. These are both elements of good leadership within an organization.

A final way in which the new approach to organizational stress management can aid top performance is by removing the threat of litigation.

Effective stress management reduces litigation

A recent development in the area of stress in the workplace has been the number of actions brought by employees for damages for stress resulting from conditions at work. The need to protect employees from dangerous conditions at work has been long enshrined in legislation. Legislation is designed to ensure that no employee is damaged as a result of being at work. The origins of this body of legislation were in the industrial sector of the nineteenth century. The belief that work should not be harmful to employees is well upheld by employers as well as enshrined in legislation.

The change which has occurred has followed well-publicized cases. Courts have been finding in favour of employees when it can be shown that employers have been responsible for causing stress. Damages are frequently awarded. These rulings have extended the scope of health and safety legislation so that emotional and psychological well-being is covered as well as physical well-being. Now it is clear that employers have a responsibility for the emotional well-being of their employees. The experience of being at work is not supposed to cause emotional difficulties. It is also very clearly stated that a lack of understanding of the area of stress is not a valid defence to a charge brought by a stressed employee. No longer can employers argue that they do not understand the elements of emotional well-being.

These rulings have highlighted the need for organizations to prevent stress. It is to this aspect of increasing understanding of the elements of emotional well-being and to preventing stress that we shall be turning our attention in this book. Employers can no longer rely on the fact that there is an employee counselling scheme or a stress management training programme as a defence. More proactive and preventive measures are needed. This increases the pressure for the organization, and each line manager as agent of the employer, to be aware of the issue of stress, to understand how it works in the workplace and to be aware of the impact of organizational demands and management style. This is a lot to ask, but it is what is now clearly required by legislation.

Following recent court rulings we received a flood of enquiries from organizations worried lest they be next in the queue for litigation. However, people were not asking for assistance in looking at stress management from a preventive point of view. Rather they were primarily requesting help with selection procedures. Specifically, the requests were for help in selecting people who would never succumb to stress. While there has been much research over the past decade into how some people appear to succumb to increased pressure more readily than others, there is no such person as a human being immune to stress. This work has shed light on what may help particular individuals maintain their resilience in the face of mounting pressure, but it is not claimed that we can find 'stress-proof' individuals, regardless of the situation they are in.

This immediate response to the legal situation reflects the common approach that stress is purely an individual matter, located within the person. It also reflects an element of the thinking that stress only happens to 'softies'.

Whatever values and beliefs each organization holds about stress, the legal position is now quite clear. Each organization has a legal responsibility to ensure the emotional well-being of its employees, by not causing stress. At the very least, this can act as an argument for protecting the organization against litigation. It also brings into sharp focus the need to take a proactive strategic approach which considers the organization as a whole, identifies sources of pressure and, by intervening in the system as a whole rather than just at the individual, remedial or training level, takes steps to remove causes of stress.

Revitalized organizations

The world of organizations has gone through major turmoil in the past few decades. It is tempting to think that this period of turmoil is coming to an end and that a time of stability is around the corner. Unfortunately we do not believe this to be the case. Some characteristics of organizations which we can expect to see in the future have already started to emerge. However, we cannot know exactly what organizations of the future will look like because new capabilities for producing products or services have yet to be developed. But if we extrapolate from recent experience we can see that new technological development can radically alter the ways in which organizations perform. Already we are talking about virtual organizations, for example. We are moving from an industrial era to the information age. This is a transition which will provide many exciting opportunities but will also require a great deal of psychological, emotional and social change. People will have to rethink what work and organizations actually are. A further confusing factor is that for some time to come we will be operating within assumptions which derive from the industrial era as well as from the information age. None of us will find this easy. It also means that we will be facing continuing and growing demands and this means a sapping of vitality.

This sapping of vitality lowers energy and performance. It highlights the need to revitalize organizational life. We will consider a few examples of the factors which contribute to the lowering of energy available for doing complex and creative work.

New technological capability

The impact of information technology (IT) has yet to be understood. Already IT capability exceeds the use to which it is put. Capacity for instant world-wide data sharing, virtual reality developments, cheaper video conferencing, digital television, purchasing through networks and so on, will offer more opportunity for pulling international virtual teams together and home working. New innovations will change the nature of the products and services which we can offer. There will be many new methods for creating and delivering them too. Our way of working is fashioned by old technology: the pen and face-to-face communication. New technology can enable us to have 'face-to-face' communication at a physical distance. This means that going to work becomes less necessary. Instead, work can come to you. Since more work is service oriented, there is less necessity for going to a particular place to make things.

New patterns of work

As organizations move towards different types of contracts of employment, fewer people can expect an organizational career. The notion of a
portfolio career will gain momentum. In this new world of employment,
being a core employee in an organization may take up fewer people's
lives, or for shorter periods. People may have shorter, renewable contracts, work for more than one employer at a time, be a contract
worker on specific projects and in support roles and put away pay for
those periods between work when, like the traditional actor, they can
expect to be 'resting'. New businesses will form, dissolve or merge as
markets change and product life cycles shorten. On negotiating work
we will concentrate on the skills we have rather than the positions we
have held.

New concepts of what forms an organization

Putting together the opportunities offered by new technologies and the
new patterns of working, will give a very different perspective on what
we imagine an organization to be. What its boundaries will look like,
what it means to be on the inside or outside will become much more
fluid. We have already begun to see this fluidity; for example, suppliers
working much more closely with their customers, having to conform to
customers' specifications about how they do what they do as well as
what is produced. Competitors now share more information on what
they are doing through the redesign of their processes and benchmark-
ing. The beginning and end of an organization's identity is less obvious
as mergers and reorganizations thrust separate and previously compet-
ing organizations under one umbrella. Other organizations contract out
work to new organizations staffed by people who were previously their
own employees. People leave full-time employment to be brought back
the next week as contractors.

New constraints and opportunities

In these new organizational forms, the competitive edge is the ability to
learn as a system, to change and to adapt. Above all, organizations need
to respond creatively to technological innovation and social change,
which will create different market opportunities or new service possibilities. Demographic changes in the age of the population will require differently organized public services. Environmental awareness will
constrain the wasteful or dangerous use of resources. Increased diversity

in the workforce will demand different assumptions about acceptable styles of management. The seeds of these developments are already present in our organizations.

These new innovations have had many positive benefits for Western society, but even positive change can be stressful. We have longer life expectancy and more leisure time. However, the effect of having to cope with rapid changes to our way of life has been described as 'an increase in health and a decrease in wellness'. This is because we have to fundamentally adapt when change is around, regardless of whether we view it is as positive or negative.

These new ways of organizing will have an impact on stress levels. When people have to adapt continuously they feel less able to cope with their job. They may experience instability in relationships at work which have previously been a source of support. The new patterns of work can even affect the amount of personal space available into which to retreat. They may find that they are overloaded with information, and the rate of change in all of this seems exponential.

The discomfort of feeling incompetent

The impact of these changes is that the pressure for high levels of performance is continuous. There are higher demands on people to adapt and learn new skills more frequently. They often have to rely on team members whose skills are very different from their own and which they are unable to assess. Professional wisdom may be challenged more often. People may be in situations for which they feel underprepared and where they are unsure whether they have enough skill to deal with unforeseen crises. It is more difficult to feel competent. At the same time, creativity and learning will be the competitive advantage that is sought.

Instability in work relationships

There is now less security of employment than we have been used to. Social patterns at work are frequently disrupted as reorganizations occur. Many teams form around temporary projects with previously unknown colleagues.

More pressure on working relationships will be experienced. This is because there will be a need to co-operate with others to get the task done, and at the same time fewer social 'safety devices' to manage and contain difficulties. These inevitably arise from working in groups and organizational systems and from trying to work co-operatively with people with whom one feels in competition for resources, position and recognition. This occurs regardless of how sensible the co-operative working is thought to be.

Home working may improve some aspects of efficiency and decrease the frustration of commuting, but simultaneously lower the possibility for social contact and support.

Less personal territory

People may have less personal space at the public place of work; as home working increases the sharing of desks and offices may increase so that our personal territory at work will disappear or be mobile. Yet walk round any open plan office and you can see the value people put on personal territory and personalizing their space. Territory is particularly important for non-routine activity requiring concentration. This may also put new strains on our relationships and has been associated with stress.

Information overload

A few days in a country retreat puts some space between us and the constant bombardment we get from TV, radio, billboards, background music, traffic roar, phones, faxes and email. We are shocked for a few hours on our return to this constant noise and interruption. The impact fades, but it tells us how important it is to recognize the energy we unthinkingly put in to scanning, screening and sorting this overload of information every day. We can no longer digest all the available information relating to our work and this fuels our anxieties about staying on top of our jobs.

The continuing presence of stress in the workplace

Although this overview covers only a fraction of the organizational pressures we have to learn to deal with, we can see that many of the pressures that are the precursor of stress will continue to be present in the workplace. The rate of change that we encounter today is increasing exponentially. Technological innovations come at a greater and greater pace, resulting in social change and the need to adapt. This change encompasses all areas of our lives, from our food, changing patterns of family life, our transport, our medical treatment, our leisure activities, to the products and services we are engaged in producing at work.

Whereas our grandparents could only imagine space travel, our children expect to experience it in virtual reality and in reality.

These are ways in which the changing world of organizations can take a toll on energy levels. A high level of energy is vital for top performance. Without a revitalized organizational life, performance will decline.

Key points in Chapter 2

■ Stress directly affects performance capability.
■ Stress costs money.
■ Taking organizational stress management seriously demonstrates care for staff.
■ Managing pressure levels is part of good leadership.
■ Current changes in organizational life lead to loss of energy and vitality.

Part II
Understanding the Undercurrents and Tides that Create Stress in the Workplace

Strategic Approach
for
Top Performance
and a
Revitalized Organization
depends on
Emotional Focus
with
Systemic Thinking
to develop a
Supportive Environment

In this part of the book we explain in depth the two elements, emotional focus and systemic thinking, which we introduced as key parts of successful organizational stress management. We need to understand these two factors in order to gain insight into how stress is created in organizations, how stress will be manifest and to explore the links between what individuals experience and the organizational system. This knowledge provides a solid basis for choosing appropriate stress management interventions in your organization.

In Chapter 3 we look at the stress response and how this is manifested in individuals. Understanding the psychology of stress enables us to make the link between the symptoms of stress and perceptions of threat and the feelings of anxiety that are present in the workplace.

In Chapter 4 we look in more detail at the nature of the anxiety which will be felt at work. We then outline the defenses which can be enacted to protect against the discomfort of anxiety. This emotional focus is needed to gain a thorough understanding of how stress is generated by our organizational experience.

In Chapter 5 we move to present a systemic view of organizations. Systemic thinking is needed to gain an overview of how stress is created within the organization and how it is experienced and transported within and around the whole organization.

In Chapter 6 we incorporate what the individual brings into the organization to complete the whole picture. Every person has his or her own history and experience, assumptions and beliefs. These will mesh with the organization to provide healthy productive working or unhealthy energy-sapping dynamics.

How individuals experience stress

What is individual stress?

Stress and pressure are not the same thing although we often use the two words as though they mean the same. In fact the whole history of stress research has been plagued with the problem of definition, because stress is seen in a variety of ways: some people notice tiredness or irritability, others notice a tendency to illness or allergy, others just can't get on with their work.

As there are these difficulties with the word 'stress', it is important to get some common understanding about the meaning of stress. It is also important to share the meaning of the word because people often dismiss stress as 'all in the mind' or 'just psychosomatic'.

Stress is not all in the mind, as we shall see in this chapter. In fact, psychosomatic is a much better description, although when we use that word we do not mean it as a critical judgement, as the term is often employed. Psychosomatic means that the body (soma) and mind and emotions (psyche) are linked. What happens in the mind affects the body and what happens with the body affects the mind. This is certainly the case with stress. How we perceive the world is a key factor in the experience of stress and the experience is physical as well as psychological.

The stress reaction gives us an important understanding of how seriously we should take the whole stress issue, both in terms of humanitarian concern, but also in organizational life, as a matter of central importance to the management of people to enable them to perform at their best.

The term 'stress': the role of inappropriate levels of pressure

The term 'stress' causes difficulties because we are unable to define it solely in terms of objective events that happen to people, since people react so differently to the same event. In the introduction we described stress as the result of an imbalance between our inner resources and our coping skills on the one hand, and pressures we encounter and the support we receive to deal with these, on the other. When there is an extended imbalance between the challenges we have to deal with and our capacity to deal with them, a range of physical, psychological and behavioural symptoms are demonstrated.

Thus the use of the word pressure is neutral. Pressure is all the demands made on us, from tackling last night's washing up to writing a difficult report. There is nothing problematic about pressure; some of it we enjoy, some of it may be a chore or even dreaded. The notion of something being disliked is not enough to equate it with stress and some things we actively seek may result in stress. The repetitive workload and the exciting new job may both be stressful to us.

For something, or some period in our lives, to be stressful there must be an imbalance. The imbalance is between what is demanded of us to deal with a situation, on the one hand, and our belief in our capacity to meet that demand on the other. What each of us regards as stressful therefore varies; you may enjoy giving lectures or you might break out in a cold sweat at the thought of it; you may enjoy managing crises or you might find that very stressful. It also varies depending on what is going on in our lives as a whole. Most of us can look back at some period in our lives and wonder at the amount we took on at work. How on earth did we cope? Well, perhaps we were younger, or fitter, or didn't have children or elderly relatives to worry about, or perhaps we shut out our friends and family. Although we are all different in terms of the amount of pressure we can manage happily, when we look at our lives in the round, we can realize that there is only so much that we can do, before something has to give.

Likewise, there is only so much boredom that we can cope with before that feels stressful, too. Some people have a much lower boredom threshold than others; they want to be learning new things and keeping busy to feel that the pressure is right for them. Spare time is to be filled with hobbies or trips, not by becoming a couch potato. Others need less busy lives, with perhaps more time for reflection and slowing down. Again, however, we all have our limit to lounging about!

Whilst we feel overwrought and tense when there is too much going on, we tend to feel stodgy and energy-less if there is too little to keep us occupied in an interesting way. Keeping this balance is the key to managing stress. Although we may not spend all our time at the level that is ideal for us, the more we manage to keep boredom at bay without over-stretching ourselves, the more likely we are to be able to avoid stress. Avoiding stress means keeping this pressure balance at an optimum level.

At the personal level, we can enhance our chances of keeping the balance by developing an understanding of what we experience as sources of high pressure, to know and use our skills for dealing with challenging situations, and get appropriate support. We can live a lifestyle that helps us cope resiliently with the daily pressures we need to meet. It also requires us to monitor the level of pressure we are under over a period of time. The odd off-day can be dealt with, but continuous high pressure takes its toll. What begins as an exciting project becomes a nightmare. Although, it is worth reminding oneself, as one manager reminded us, that you wake up from nightmares; long-term work pressure can be never ending.

Stress results from extended imbalance in the pressure people experience and their perception that they cannot deal effectively with this. At the same time as feeling that they cannot cope, they are held accountable for their actions and responsible for the outcomes. The feeling that you cannot effectively take charge of events is central to organizational stress. In the workplace it is often implied that you will be in charge and competent, whilst how you feel may be very different. Although some jobs appear to have a lot of latitude in how they can be done, and are staffed by competent people, the demands for novel solutions in unknown territory are sources of pressure. Other sources of pressure include those over which the jobholder perceives he or she has little control. In this type of situation the potential for stress across the organization is high.

The last part of our definition of stress has to do with our capacity to deal with it and the supports we receive in doing so. In understanding organizational stress, the way our work is managed is crucial. As we shall explain in Part III of the book this has an emotional as well as task focused dimension.

Organizational stress is a complex web comprising the emotional life of the organization, the way the organization as a whole impacts on individuals and their personal makeup.

The stress response

The physiology of the stress response is common to us all. What heightens this reaction differs from person to person.

The early studies of stress were a result of the perceived inadequacy of a simple cause–effect model of health and sickness. This model worked very well for many illnesses; for example, if you are infected with a particular virus you have the symptoms of the corresponding disease. This did not account, though, for the fact that in many illnesses not all infected people have the symptoms. Nor does it help explain everyday descriptions of being 'under par', 'not A1', 'feeling off-colour'. The early research on animals focused on the discovery of a generalized physical response to noxious stimulants to the body, rather than the particular response to a specific one.

The research did indeed show that there was a pattern of body responses that occurred whether the cause was loud noise, poison or other unpleasantness, and which was common to all. Later it was found that this applied to humans too.

This response was called the general adaptation syndrome. This means that, whatever unpleasant stimulus (or stressor) a body is subjected to, the same pattern of response is observed – a general adaption to the stimulus. This happened in addition to specific steps to deal with the particular stimulus. The notion of adaptation reflects the body's need to maintain its equilibrium, despite the fact it is having to cope with some unwelcome intrusion.

The general adaptation syndrome has three stages which occur successively over time. In the first stage, called the alarm reaction, the body responds to extra demands placed on it by mobilizing its energy resources to cope. The first stage is the one in which gearing up to deal with a challenge can feel exciting and challenging as well as threatening, or worrying. The key to this stage is the release of energy to deal with whatever is necessary.

The second stage is one in which the body is dealing with the problem in an ongoing fashion. By this stage the problem (or opportunity) has a longer-term feel to it and the body is not so much mobilizing resources as depleting its supply. The phase was described as the 'plateau of resistance', which seems to capture its essence very well. The body has reached a plateau and is plodding on with the problem in a dogged way, keeping going even though it feels increasingly like hard work rather than excitement. 'Just keep going' is the essence of this phase.

The third stage occurs when it is no longer possible to keep going. It is the phase of exhaustion. The body's resources have become depleted and there is nothing left to draw on. At this point the body has no way of maintaining its energy and so it breaks down at its weakest point. In humans this may be either emotionally or physically, and a range of factors including our genes and lifestyle may influence the particular type of health breakdown we have. For example, some people may have a family history of heart disease, a sedentary lifestyle and a smoking habit which might predispose them more to coronary problems than other people.

The general adaptation syndrome focused on the immune system's response to stressors and the early findings are still the basis for much of the subsequent work on stress.

Subsequent interest turned to the body's response to acute stress. This is described in the next section and explains what takes place when there is an immediate threat to well-being.

The fight or flight response

When we are faced with an immediate threat to our life or well-being, the well-known fight or flight response occurs. As its name suggests, the fight or flight response is designed to help us take quick action to deal with a threat. It is primitive and we react before we become aware of all the factors involved in the situation at a rational level. For example, if you are approached by a gang who look likely to mug you, it is possible to find yourself lashing out and demonstrating your kick boxing talent before your rational thought processes work out that the odds are not in your favour. However, whether you run or fight you will find that the energy and forcefulness with which you respond will exceed your normal capability.

This stone-age response was helpful to our ancestors when they were facing ferocious beasts and is still helpful today for dealing with many dangerous situations, even though most of us don't meet woolly mammoths at work!

The fight or flight response involves the sympathetic adrenal medullary system. Sympathetic in this context means 'before feeling', that is, we react very quickly. The sympathetic is part of the autonomic nervous system and medulla part of the adrenal glands. Adrenal glands are above the kidneys and produce the hormones involved, adrenalin and noradrenalin. This system is responsible for the wide range of reactions which mobilize our energy. When triggered, our heart rate rises, our breathing becomes quicker and more shallow, glycogen (a form of carbohydrate energy store) is released from the liver, blood pressure rises, capillaries constrict so that blood can be diverted to the major muscle groups for running and hitting, muscle tension increases, digestion slows down and, because we are preparing for vigorous exercise, the body's cooling mechanism switches on; we begin to sweat.

Of course at work, we do not meet woolly mammoths or muggers every day, which is what the system is designed to deal with. However, the trigger for this reaction is the perception of threat. Perception of threat leads to anxiety. Because we react so quickly, when the brain mobilizes the body for action on the basis of perceived threat, it does not wait long enough for our rational thoughts to tell us that the mess-up on the accounts or the computer failure or the person who has just told us that we have failed to meet a crucial deadline we didn't know about, will not be solved by getting up and running a mile or two or by hitting out in fury. We have learned, by and large, not to take such career limiting action at work, but by the time we stop ourselves acting in this way, the whole physiological reaction has been triggered. Because very little physical action is taken, the body takes time to rid itself of these unnecessary changes. If we had really had to run away or fight, it would have been the trigger for the parasympathetic side of the autonomic nervous system to click in. This is the relaxation response that curbs the action of the fight or flight reaction. Since physical action didn't follow the stress reaction, it takes a while for the body to unwind.

In experiments, the physiological response has been found just by being asked to do mental arithmetic, play a computer game or make a speech. So it is easy to see how it would be triggered many times a day in the workplace. This can take its toll; the response is helpful, but not in work. It has been said that at work 'we do battle sitting in a chair'; as a result we are triggering the response inappropriately and this can cause long-term negative effects. Many events which trigger the response may feel more like heightened arousal than stress, but the psychological effect is the same. In this, the perceived ability to cope with the event may prove to be a key variable. For example, most people expect to survive a theme park ride! Nor do they go to theme parks for the thrills 200 days or more a year!

The second stress system response

The other part of the stress response involves the hypothalamic pituitary adrenal system. This system, triggered by the brain's hypothalamus, involves the release of adrenocorticotropin (ACTH), which in turn triggers the release of steroid hormones from the cortex of the adrenal gland. Most prominent among these is cortisol. Corticosteroids are known to affect the immune system. Modern researchers use the terms up-regulation and down-regulation of the immune system because this reflects the notion that fluctuations are to be expected normally. However, when the immune system is down-regulated, a number of things happen. One is that the blood cells which attack invading viruses and bacteria are less effective. The cells which attack and destroy tumour cells may be affected. Levels of antibodies produced may also change.

Profound stressors such as bereavement and divorce have been shown to be associated with down-regulation of the immune system. More recent studies have been able to link this with a much broader range of stressors. This is the pattern for chronic or persistent stress.

If we look at some of the recent studies of acute stress, however, the pattern is different. Where some acute psychological challenge is to be met such as public speaking, there appears to be an immediate effect of up-regulating the immune system. The number of cells which target tumours, for example, go up. Over the period of a week, studies show that people appearing more stressed over the period had down-regulated immune systems on the measures taken. Yet, on the very worst days they had up-regulated immune functioning over the course of minutes after the unpleasant event had occurred.

The interpretation of this is that the acute up-regulation reflects the influence of the first stress system, the sympathetic adrenal medullary system.

These responses to stress are fundamental to the way we function. Initially our system gears us up for action and dealing with threat, but quickly another response lowers the immune system's capacity to deal with invasions of foreign bodies and mutations. There is a difference between acute and chronic stress but both have wide-ranging impact on our levels of functioning and health, and at work, on our performance.

How to spot when people are stressed

The early studies of stress set out to identify the definitive list of stress symptoms. This was an understandable quest but one which proved fruitless. There is no one definitive description of the way in which stress appears in everyone. Different people experience and manifest different symptoms. The common factor is that however someone responds to stress, there will be a difference, a change in how they function. This change can occur in any area of human functioning: physiological, behavioural, emotional or mental. It is the change from our normal pattern in any of these functions which gives the clue that stress may be present and is the key to the whole issue of stress recognition. We can observe changes in each function in ourselves and gain clues to changes in others.

Physiological responses to stress

As we have outlined, there is a physiological base to the stress response. Therefore it may be easier to understand how stress is experienced as illness or lack of physical well-being. Although there is a common physiological basis to the stress response, the way in which people actually respond varies. Some people get tension headaches, some develop ulcers or other digestive complaints, some will experience pain in the muscles or joints, while others will succumb to a virus or serious illness. There are as many possible ways of actually exhibiting the stress response physically as there are people, for the response is personal to each of us.

The physical response will depend on several factors. The most important will be family history, that is, if there is a tendency to weakness in one area of the body. In a family where there is a history of digestive problems, then 'tension tummy' would not be a surprising manifestation of stress. Alternatively, where there is a history of migraines, then a headache would not be unexpected as the response to high pressure.

The specific physical response to stress will vary from person to person, depending on that person's area of physical weakness. There will often be a pattern, a personal characteristic response. In whatever way the response is manifest personally, the person will not be at their peak of physical health and well-being. The level of the response can vary from succumbing to a cold, to developing cancer or heart disease. Energy will be depleted and vitality lowered.

Behaviour change as a response to stress

We use phrases such as 'a person is not themselves' or 'that is not like you' in everyday conversation when we observe changes in a person's behaviour. The experience may be described by the person concerned in words like 'I just don't feel myself today'. This is linked to the fact that behaviour can change whenever stress is around.

Again there is no definitive checklist of specific behaviour changes; each person will respond in their own way. There are common experiences. An increase in snapping at others, being short-tempered or withdrawing from contact with others are common. These can be seen to have direct links to the fight or flight response. Although we rarely take the swing our body demands, we often fight with words. Although we do not leap to our feet and run out of the door when a meeting becomes tense, we can withdraw our attention and mentally run away.

There are as many different ways of stress showing in behaviour as there are people. Some behaviours are linked to an attempt to find relief. The extra glass of alcohol, the unplanned stop at the pub, the chocolate bar bought when not really hungry, the increase in smoking; all these changes in behaviour may reflect a wish to find comfort or escape from a difficult and stressful situation.

Whenever stress is experienced it is possible that behaviour will change in some way. When the stress is acute this may only last for a short period of time, but when stress becomes chronic, then behaviour change may be long lasting. In this case sometimes self-defeating behaviours become habitual. Energy will be diverted into attempts to find comfort or relief, rather than dealing with the reality of the current situation.

Emotional response to stress

We can observe behaviour changes in others. What is not always apparent is that there are changes in feelings which accompany stress.

A very basic way in which feelings can be affected is in the area of self-confidence or self-esteem. Effective functioning depends on possession of a solid base of self-confidence. Often the experience of struggling to cope can deplete the stock of confidence, at the precise time when it is needed to deal with extra demands. A feeling of not being able to cope does not add to the ability either to deal with the situation or to feel good about yourself.

Again changes in feeling can be experienced in many different ways. Some people experience a decrease in feeling, as if they go numb in the presence of stress. Others experience a heightened level of emotion in a general sense. Others report feeling more aggressive, more sensitive or more vulnerable.

In whatever way we experience stress, there is the possibility that the emotions or feelings will change. Rarely does this happen in a way which enhances performance, usually the change in feeling inhibits effective performance and decreases the feeling of well-being.

Mental responses to stress

The final area of human functioning which can be affected by stress is the mental or cognitive functions. We rely on our brains and thinking capacity to enable us to deal well with the demands we face. However, when stress is present, the ability to assess information objectively, to make good judgements or construct a coherent argument can all disappear. Some people report feeling as if their heads are full of cotton wool, as if they just cannot think straight. Modern organizations need a high quality of mental facility, yet this too can be impaired by stress.

Stress and perception

Stress is triggered by our emotional response to events, although the body reacts as if the threat were to life and limb. The way we perceive or interpret events gives rise to the experience of being under threat. The root of the stress response is anxiety. Following this may be a range of reactions to deal with anxiety and threat.

The stress response was designed to enable our early ancestors to deal quickly and effectively with threats to their very physical survival. Nowadays threats to our physical well-being are not encountered so frequently. Instead the threats perceived in modern life and modern organizations are threats to our emotional or psychological well-being.

The boss may not approach us with long tusks or a sharp instrument, but how we interpret the harsh retort or put-down may have exactly the same effect. People do not often see the boss as about to kill them literally, but they can perceive the boss as about to kill their chances of promotion.

Although there are physical dangers in the modern world, our sense of survival and safety is less dependent on surviving physically. In the developed world there is less immediate concern about where the next meal is coming from. But there is concern about success and recognition, as well as money to provide food.

It is these issues which we need to understand if we are to gain insight into the nature of organizational stress. Using our knowledge of the stress reactions described in this chapter can help us to identify individuals who are stressed. How to identify what to do to prevent stress means unpicking the complex emotional life of organizations to see how the threats and anxieties are created and how they can be contained so that high stress is not prevalent.

From the stress reaction to organizational stress

In concerning ourselves with organizational stress we are concerned with more than spotting how many people exhibit signs of stress, locating them and helping them cope. We are interested in how stress is an expression of the difficulties people have as the result of being part of an organization in which these emotional difficulties and anxiety are not sufficiently dealt with. Some individuals may be carriers of stress for the whole system, as we shall see in Chapter 5, some may have unique

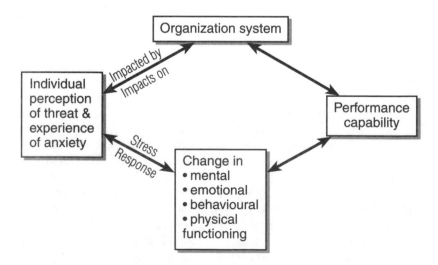

Figure 3.1 Organizational impact of the stress response

difficulties with their work and these people will need personalized support. However, as we have emphasized, it is not enough to look for the causes of stress as a simple 'bad experience = stress' equation. The roots of stress lie in the difficulties we often have to deal with in working with others, in keeping our self-esteem and sense of identity strong in the organization and in joining and belonging to groups of others who will be different from us.

The value in recognizing stress at an individual level is to see danger signs for those concerned and deal with them, and to spur us on to keep organizational stress firmly in our mind and on the organizational agenda.

Even if only one person is experiencing stress and therefore performing below par, that is sufficient to give rise to organizational concern. However, when the experience of stress is widespread, the need for concern increases. This is when it becomes important to view the organization as a whole system. If one department or section is not working well due to stress, that will have implications for the whole of the organization. No part of the organization works in isolation. In addition, stress can be passed around the organizational system.

As psychologists, we take the view that what is going on for people is a rather more complex process than simple 'cause–effect'; it is not the case that a bad experience automatically creates stress. We take the view that there are many experiences which people may call exciting, nerve racking, interesting, a 'stretch', challenging and so on, which can be managed in the organization. However, the fact that organizational life requires us to join with other people in our enterprises, so that we need to manage influence and power in the organization, get our self-identity validated in the organization, our feelings of self-worth and contribution acknowledged, gives rise to a whole range of emotions that are often overlooked or not discussed because they are tricky to deal with. There is plenty of scope for anxiety and the perception of psychological threats to our well-being.

Our experience of work can be satisfying and fulfilling. Equally it can be destructive and alienating. Although some of the factors that create this difference can operate from outside the firm (economic and political factors) or arise from our personal make-up (desire to be perfect, control the universe, please others), there is an important organizational dimension. Anxiety, as we describe in the next two chapters, is an integral part of work. When there are uncertain conditions, such as a merger, downsizing, expansion, reform or new leadership, anxiety levels throughout the organization rise. Some people will be more sensitive to this and feel it more than others, but careful people watchers will notice subtle and not so subtle changes in behaviour which indicate this.

Envy, competition, rivalry, powerlessness, feeling different, feelings of failure, dependency and so on are not on many meeting agendas. Yet this is all part of the experience which we have, however unconsciously, of our work. How these experiences are processed and managed is a key part of our experience of stress in the workplace.

What makes these difficult to deal with is that they are often out of immediate awareness and they are not easy to be in touch with. Whilst you may genuinely be glad that your colleague got that appointment and that your former member of staff is promoted, you may also be envious and feel less than successful yourself. Additionally, your feelings will be part of the tangle of feelings that form the emotional web of the organization. Some of your feelings may be passed to you from other parts of the organization. If you are a manager, for example, you may find yourself feeling as though you have to act like a super hero to save the day, because your staff need to feel that someone can 'save' them. You may find yourself feeling surprisingly critical of staff and punishing, or you may find yourself part of a group that feels smug and confident even though other parts of the organization are feeling dejected. These emotions can be understood when the whole system is taken into account. Feelings can be passed around the system and particular groups or individuals acquire them – like a kind of emotional velcro! This makes it particularly difficult for people to deal with, because without this perspective on the experience, people find it hard to say 'I'm feeling really critical and I don't know why' or 'I'm feeling picked on here'. How this operates is explored in Chapters 4 and 5.

When the emotions associated with the experience of work are running high and they cannot be contained or talked about because they seem too difficult, dangerous or illogical, they are carried around, and for many people they become expressed in the classical symptoms of stress, which we have described in this chapter.

We have explored the nature of stress and the link between personal experience and the implications for the organization. Now you have a clear picture of the nature of stress, we shall turn to a more in-depth understanding of the emotional dimensions of the organization as a system. This is the next step needed in the development of an organizational response to stress management.

Key points in Chapter 3

- Stress is inappropriate pressure and stress management is attaining an optimum level of pressure.
- Individuals have a stress reaction to inappropriate pressure.
- Stress can be either chronic or acute.
- Stress is manifest in a change in physical, mental, emotional or behavioural functioning.

- The stress response is triggered by anxiety or the perception of threat.
- Organizational stress is more than 'too many stressed people'; it is best understood as a whole system problem involving emotions and is expressed through individuals exhibiting classical symptoms of stress.

Developing an emotional focus for understanding organizational stress

Emotions at work

To understand how perceptions of threat, anxiety and a range of associated emotions operate at work, we need to explore how deep feelings can affect how we interact with others. Just by being part of an organization involving others raises many feelings and memories of previous experiences. We are not always aware of these, indeed we work hard to avoid any difficult feelings that arise. Thus to relate these to stress we must attempt to understand what is going on by looking at the emotional issues below the surface.

Let us illustrate why we think it is relevant to do this exploration. In one company we work with a lot of effort has gone into stress management initiatives. The company has excellent facilities for staff in terms of fitness, health and welfare. We have run many stress programmes there for managers and staff. The issue has been taken up in some departments as one of real concern. For example, one group has worked hard to reduce a long list of factors which have been identified as stressors in a survey and in focus groups: interruptions, too much customer contact time and too little back up time, unclear priorities and so on. However, stress is still high as monitored by their own system. As soon as one problem was addressed another cropped up. By the time that had been dealt with, the first problem was back again.

A clue was offered when one of the group said that 'everyone's putting so much effort into reducing stress, that it's becoming hard to talk about; it just feels like griping yet there's still a lot about'. As the culture of the organization was familiar to us through our work there, we were able to offer an observation that people seem to find it hard to express feelings that may be interpreted as negative. Everything always has to be so positive and upbeat. This unleashed quite a torrent; it was, according to the group member, really hard to find ways of expressing doubts or resentments or deeper and 'irrational' feelings. He used the example of someone getting promoted: 'we're so competitive here that you can be pleased for someone and envious at the same time. You're disappointed that it wasn't you, but we have such a strong congratulatory culture that you have to go out of your way to be nice. People have fixed grins for days; there's no way you can let your jealousy show, we have such a cult of niceness here.'

Some of us, more used to a blame culture, might like the idea of working somewhere where niceness prevails. But this example shows us the root of the problem in this particular instance; in this system many 'not nice' feelings are denied. This is partly a result of the culture of the larger organization of which this site is part. It is partly to do with the specific group that was represented here, and it is partly to do with the individual who spoke and his difficulties with coping with this aspect of the organization. But it is none of these alone. Therefore, tackling the most obvious things reported in a departmental survey did not have the desired effect. The emotional experiences of those people, working at their particular tasks, within their specific group and in the organizational context provided by that organization, were left unchanged. When asked 'what causes stress here' in the survey, people could not articulate these emotional experiences. This is because they often remain out of awareness. They remain unconscious because they are hard to acknowledge. Few people feel able to say to themselves, 'I feel stress because there is so much envy and jealousy here', let alone report it in a survey.

One explanation of this group's stress level can be understood by the clearly articulated company value statements about achieving excellence through respect for people, customer focus and teamwork. These values have become embedded like a hologram in every bit of the system. By recognizing these positive values we can also see how they may mask other emotional experiences. In fact, these were the undercurrents that were going on in this group and which were so hard to address. The shadow or down side of these values was part of the organization's experience, and was leading to an undercurrent of anxiety: Do we measure up? Am I good enough? Am I respected? Do I show enough concern for others? Does the fact that I'm not promoted mean that I have failed?

How do people manage their 'not nice' feelings in the group? From time to time in a competitive setting, difficulties in collaboration arise. From working with this group it is known that it is a highly competitive one. Some of the pay policies in the organization mean that some people will visibly and inevitably lose out to other members of the group in terms of perceived success. This gives rise to anxiety about 'surviving' in the organization, which is felt at a primitive level. This feeling can give rise to desires to spoil another's success and can be unconsciously acted out, for example by delaying work delivery or being unco-operative. When thinking about how this was dealt with in this group, it raised the possibility that perhaps this unacknowledged, shadow side of the organization was best expressed through the classical stress symptoms.

We tend to think of organizations as places of rational activity, where decisions are taken on the basis of objective analysis of information and best technical or professional know-how. This is only true for some of the organization's activities. For example, many decisions are taken when there are real dilemmas about the way forward, sometimes the size and shape of the problems are new, information is simply unavailable, or the way forward must depend on the values and beliefs of those involved because there is no known or obvious route to take. In such cases, though, the decision takers have to present their choices with a degree of certainty, if they are to get their preference adopted. One might describe much of what passes as rational and logical as, in reality, guesswork and persuasion. But there is also another dimension to non-rational behaviour at work. People have subtle ways of managing their work environment to keep it sufficiently familiar and comfortable to cope with. Some of their strategies for staying in their personal comfort zone may even be out of their awareness. There are individual and organizational ways of keeping discomfort at bay and some are more helpful than others.

Discomfort at work: keeping anxiety at bay

When we enter the workplace, we do not leave our emotions behind. Our feelings have a great influence on how we work. Sometimes we are aware of this; often emotions are an unnoticed undercurrent. For example, there are few managers who have made people redundant and who are unaware of their feelings about this. If they have to do it often, they will find ways of managing these feelings, even to the extent of becoming less aware of them. They need to defend against repeatedly experiencing the discomfort in order to get on with the task.

Deep emotions underpin much of our behaviour in organizations. They warrant descriptions such as love, rage and hatred. Most of us would say that we are unaware of such deep feelings, particularly at work. However these deep feelings are primitive and have much to do with basic human survival needs for security, acceptance and protection.

Anxiety is an emotion that is important to take account of in the workplace. Anxiety is a response to the unknown in oneself or the environment. There is a sense of threat or danger about the unknown. When people are asked about sources of their stress they cite concerns such as redundancy. Redundancy of course has concrete consequences. However, it is often the feeling of something looming or threatening that provokes the deepest feelings. Paradoxically people can even feel relief when the outcome of a reorganization or change actually becomes known. In times of change the most frequently heard plea is for 'them' to tell us what is happening. Finding positively constructive ways to manage these feelings and to feel in charge of our own destiny, is a hard route to take. Most of us harbour a hidden hope that 'they' will do this for us.

Because these deep emotions can be so powerful, we can feel as though we may be overwhelmed. Since this is perceived as undesirable, we devise ways to avoid the possibility of being swept away, so that we can get on with what we are doing. Some tactics for avoiding anxiety may become so rigidified that they eventually get in the way of doing the task anyway. However, by then we have lost track of their original purpose which was to stop us from feeling the primitive emotions that threaten our comfort. Examples of this are seen in jobs which require the holder to deal with life or death dramas. Anyone who has worked with uniformed services and does not understand the nature of defenses against anxiety, would be horrified at the gallows humour employed in grim situations. Yet this is one way of coping with difficult emotions. Sometimes less helpful methods are used; the doctor who has distanced herself from her feelings could end up treating a patient as the 'transplant on ward 4'.

However, few people deal with such horror on a daily basis; so are most staff 'exempt' from work anxiety? In fact, anxiety is present in work on a very regular basis. Anxiety comes from three sources: the tasks we undertake at work, our personal history and the deeper primitive level.

Anxiety and the tasks we do

The first level of anxiety is generated by the tasks we do; the engineer who designs a bridge has a job which if badly done could result in carnage. The fast food assistant who fails to follow hygiene regulations courts an epidemic of food poisoning. The human resource consultant who does not give appropriate consideration to a job applicant's references may create problems for the client. To a greater or lesser extent, there will be an element of anxiety associated with the job itself.

Anxiety and personal history

The second level of anxiety comes from our personal history. Each of us brings with us a specific history which relates to elements of the work situation. We have experience of authority, of success and failure, of competition and rivalry, of being valued/undervalued and so on. These will influence our expectations of today's work environment, even if some of those experiences are deep in our memories and not consciously accessible. We may 'see' some situations as though they are similar to the past, even when they are not. These past experiences are often unconsciously re-activated because they have some difficult aspects to them, which in the past we could not deal with or were painful. Any situation that reminds us of these may re-activate the feelings 'recorded' as associated with the past event. We may or may not actually remember the past, but as we deal with today's problem the feelings often flood back.

Primitive anxiety

The third level of anxiety we experience comes from a more primitive level which is not just dependent on our own particular past, but is universally experienced by human beings. This primary anxiety comes from the first few months and years of life when the psychological separation from the mother figure and discovery that we are individual beings occurs. The struggle for separation, on the one hand, and the desire to be at one with the mother on the other, causes great anxiety. Associated with this struggle are strong reactions such as rage, love and hate. Primitive anxiety is particularly important to the understanding of stress as an intrinsic part of organizational experience because these early struggles are evoked and re-created in our struggles with belonging, with identity, with being 'ourselves' within the organization which requires us to adapt to its purposes.

A variety of mechanisms is employed to cope with these strong feelings. In infancy the dilemma is partially resolved when the infant, realizing that the person it both loves and hates is one and the same, feels the need to make reparation for the past emotions projected at the mother. This human drama is re-enacted in many situations faced in the infant's subsequent life. In particular, membership of groups and organizations evokes this reaction. As an adult, we seek to belong and be accepted by the group or organization, and yet at the same time we fear that by being too close we may lose our individuality. In giving up something of ourselves, such as our time, our fixed opinion, our right to do as we please, we hope to meet those needs for inclusion. On the other hand, in struggling to control the group or maintain our personal viewpoint at all cost, we seek to remain a freethinking individual. But the struggle evokes deep anxieties.

Anxiety associated with tasks we do, our personal history and these primitive reactions often resonate, so they can create a high level of anxiety for a particular individual. Naturally not every situation at work activates the same level of anxiety, nor to the same extent for everyone.

However, what can be observed is that in various ways these anxieties are acted out in the organization and that most people are not conscious of this influence most of the time. Indeed if anxiety constantly broke through, no engineer would design a bridge, no one would ever get a fast food burger and no recruitment decisions would ever be taken.

What happens when difficult emotions remain unacknowledged?

Many things which shape our lives are difficult to talk about openly; we feel shame or embarrassment or feel that it is too painful. A group of employees chatting at the start of their departmental meeting about the cold and hostile climate in one of their supplier organizations, followed by a discussion about the importance of personalizing their workspaces may well be trying to get some message across to their own manager about their own group. This is in addition to the validity of these subjects taken at face value. Complaints about the quality of the Christmas lunch puzzled one manager; it had seemed fine to him. It only made sense if it symbolized some other complaint that was hard to talk about. Understanding the way emotions impact on work means that events can be understood both at consciously expressed levels and at the unconscious level.

Tuning in to the unconscious level is not some clairvoyant activity. It means putting information together carefully to form an idea of what might be happening but which is not being talked about. Ideas about how we deal with difficult feelings help us to know what to look for. Institutions, like people, find some feelings too painful or threatening to acknowledge. These may arise from the nature of the work itself, such as dealing with children at risk or building a bridge that is safe, or from the conflicts between groups and individuals, or from the nature of having to work in groups in close proximity to others. In organizational life there is great scope for anxiety; the job may go wrong and people may be hurt, the group to which we belong may reject us or we may lose our personal identity by belonging to the group, we find ourselves in a position within a hierarchy and we have to deal with feelings about authority, dependency or vulnerability.

None of these make for casual coffee break chat; furthermore, if we let any of these overwhelm us we would be unable to continue in the job. Therefore we need to erect defenses to prevent us from noticing and feeling these things too strongly, if at all. Some of these defenses are healthy and appropriate to the task; for example, the professional who refers back to codes of practice to help sort out a tricky problem, uses the defense of professional practice to enable them to take a tough decision. This stops them being immobilized at the appalling vision of what might happen if a bad choice were made. But sometimes unhealthy defenses are used which stop the painful feelings but don't deal with, or even actively interfere with, working on the problem. Understanding how defenses to painful feelings work and the form they take can help us gain extra insight into behaviour which occurs when stress is around.

There are many ways in which we can erect defenses against difficult feelings. Denial is one well-recognized example. The world needs new skills, but it is more comfortable to ignore what is happening and go on focusing on the old, familiar patterns. The ostrich who puts its head into the nearest sandpit is not such an uncommon feature in organizational life. It may provide a degree of comfort but it does not help deal with current reality.

The defenses we use echo our very early experience of life and can be found in every person and every organization. The very nature of organizational tasks and structure, the differentials in power in even the flattest structure, the interpersonal difficulties of working together inevitably give rise to anxiety and to the use of defenses to avoid feeling discomfort. These operate at a personal level. But they have an impact on our relations to others. This is the tangled web of emotions which binds the organization's members together. My defenses affect you and yours affect me. Let us look at how this operates.

Defenses at work

These defenses are part of normal early development and can be re-activated throughout life. 'Splitting' is a crucial example. In splitting, complex feelings about others and ourselves are split off from each other, because it is too difficult to acknowledge at an emotional level that contradictory feelings exist at one and the same time. Splitting makes sense of chaos by dividing the world into good and bad experience and keeping the two apart. The price of this, though, is that some part of the self, usually 'badness', is located outside the person with others in the real or imaginary world. The image children have of 'fairy godmother' and 'wicked witch' captures this. Their experience of mother is either all good or all bad; this of course does not correspond to the real life mother who is sometimes kind, sometimes angry. Adults can 'do' the same thing to people around them; this means some people end up as the equivalent of the fairy godmother or the wicked witch. When splitting is used as a defense, the person may expect the 'bad' others to direct their 'badness' at him or her. The person feels that persecution is possible and anxiety is experienced. For example, the bad feeling I have about myself is split off and I only acknowledge some feelings not others. I 'decide' I am caring. I treat myself as though only one aspect of myself can be true and deny that I am also vengeful. I may see others as having this characteristic of vengefulness which I find difficult to acknowledge in myself. In addition I may assume that 'their' vengefulness will be directed at my group or me. In failing to notice my own vengefulness I may also fail to notice their caring aspects. They are denied. I may start to behave as though they are being vengeful. This may become a self-fulfilling prophecy. All kinds of assumptions about others can be created this way and they have little to do with the real people involved – at least to start with!

The childhood game of 'goodies and baddies' at work

From this example we can see that the split off parts which I do not deal with in myself may be projected on to others. Like a cine projector beam, the projection falls on to them and looks as though it were part of them. In reality it is part of me located as though it were part of them. For example, my feelings of envy and vindictiveness may be difficult for me and I may project them on to my staff who I then see as vindictive and envious. This allows me to continue to see myself as not possessing these traits, just as nice and caring. These defenses are illustrated in Figure 4.1.

Sometimes the splitting process goes on between groups and some groups become the bad or feared group, whereas others are seen as good or ideal. Thus individuals or whole sections come to represent many different emotions which are not acknowledged within the group as belonging to themselves as well. This leads to familiar conflicts such as marketing versus production, or the anger directed towards 'the accountants'. To the extent that the other party accepts the aspects that are projected on to them, they may identify with them as though they 'were' them, and begin to behave accordingly. Sometimes a symbiotic relationship develops. If that is the case, I can be caring, with another person taking up a harder edged role. We 'like it' that way. But this doesn't work so well when I need to understand my powerful side and they need to be in touch with their sensitivity.

We can also engage in the process with organization leaders. An example might be if we have difficulty locating in ourselves our authority to do the task we have agreed to do. We feel helpless and dependent; the leader by contrast must be able and all knowing. We need this to be the case so badly that if she says that she is looking for our ideas, we 'know' she must be withholding her own. If the leader identifies with the notion that she has to know what is to be done, she may try to become the heroine who saves the day. Since real life super heroes do

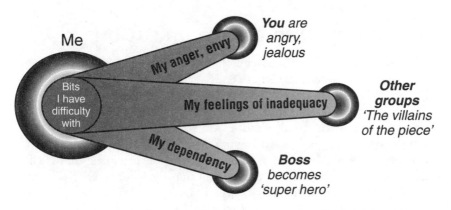

Figure 4.1 Emotional defenses and organizational stress

not exist – leaders need to work with the rest of the team to succeed – the heroine inevitably fails to live up to expectation, leading to disappointment, feelings of being let down, despair and even bitterness.

Defenses operate at an institutional level

The processes we have described explain how these dynamics are carried out at an institutional level. It is not just the individual who carries the anxiety and the defenses within their mind. Through these types of mechanisms, the recipient whether it is a group or an individual, may act as though the feelings projected on to them were their own. The true source of those feelings may remain obscure until there is a realization that people are trapped in this process. Through this mechanism, one group can come to serve as a sponge for all the anger or guilt or depression, for example, felt by others, on behalf of another group. In this instance it is false to locate the problem as belonging to one group alone. One person or group can appear to be the problem, whilst other groups or individuals are trouble free. This is when we see scapegoating occurring, which is painful for the recipients and does not reduce stress in the organization as a whole. Some individuals or groups may experience temporary relief at the expense of others but their anxiety does not entirely go away. The issue that needs addressing is that because it is difficult to face our feelings we have placed them elsewhere and made someone else carry more than their fair share of the burden.

Identifying with the organization

This process is also involved with the development of commitment to an organization or leader. Cohesiveness arises from common identification with the organization's ideals, represented by the leader, or the mythology of the organization left by a previous leadership. Projection of some of our own 'good' qualities on to these enables us to identify with the organization. Thus it is important to work for a world/brand leader, or a household name or a socially desirable organization that fits our values. Through this process we feel ourselves linked to broad cultural ideals and hopes and this helps to ward off anxieties and feelings of stress. Thus those particularly close to the sources of power may experience less stress than those who are excluded from the power bases that make up the organization's unevenly distributed power system. Responsibility and stress do not always go hand in hand. When institutions are linked to universalistic values such as truth, patriotism and faith they express values that belong to all of society and everyone can feel enveloped. To the extent that the leadership of the organization links into only those issues around success, the values become associated with ambition, conquest and status. These are by their very nature exclusive and many employees cannot be associated with them and feel, and may be, more vulnerable.

Emotional focus and organizational stress

Emotion and stress are often linked; people are more 'emotional' when they are stressed. However, we are using the term 'emotional focus' in a less obvious way. We are joining the term 'stress' to the perception of threat and to anxiety. Anxiety does not just arise because of situations in which obvious attack is present. It is all pervasive, a consequence of actual events happening here and now and also because of evoked memories from our past and because of the relationships we need to enter into in order to be part of an organization. Anxiety is always around, mostly below our level of awareness but in uncertain times, anxiety levels rise dramatically. There will be the actual work to deal with, but also more primitive fears which feel overwhelming.

This in itself leads people to experience stress. However, we did not, as the human race, wait for twentieth-century psychologists to evolve to tell us how to overcome many of the disquieting feelings we carry around inside us. We have developed our own psychological methods for keeping parts of ourselves, feelings and thoughts out of our consciousness. These defenses come into operation when we need them and when stress is around we use them to help us manage the situations we are in. We fall back on old mechanisms that have worked in our past. Because the use of these methods to keep discomfort at bay uses a lot of energy we often experience tiredness and feel less able to access our creative potential, along with feelings that 'leak through' our defenses. To the extent that these feelings cannot be acknowledged and openly dealt with, they continue to influence our reactions to events. As we have seen in this chapter, these feelings do not 'stay' with the person who has them. Our defenses have an interpersonal dimension; what I cannot abide in me, I may see in you. What I can't deal with myself, I may want my manager to do for me. Because of the primitive nature of these defenses, which primarily hark back to our early experience as a vulnerable infant, these emotions often centre on fantasies about authority figures, being dependent, power, envy, hate and rage. If I am the recipient of these powerful fantasies I may become confused by your behaviour towards me. But to the extent that I take them on board, I may begin to behave according to these 'ideas' that I have acquired. This may apply to individuals and groups in the organization and these 'extra' feelings often fill up the recipients in a way that is confusing and too much to deal with.

Thus, the way stress gets passed around the organization is very complex. It is not just that my bad temper is a nuisance for you. At a much deeper level feelings influence how we behave. Sharing and collusion can enable these feelings to spread out and touch a wide range of people.

As we explore in Part III, we can take steps to help people address these emotional undercurrents.

Before we can complete the picture of stress that we are creating here, we need to explore the way in which stress is passed around the organization and how whole groups can become involved in stress. This is the focus of the next chapter.

Key points in Chapter 4

■ Emotions play a key role in stress creation.
■ Emotional experience can occur at work in both a conscious and an unconscious way.
■ Anxiety is an important component of stress. Anxiety associated with work can be linked to the tasks undertaken, personal history or to more primitive and deep-seated issues.
■ Primitive anxiety is linked to issues of separation and inclusion and exclusion, and this can be experienced in the workplace.
■ Whenever uncomfortable feelings cannot be acknowledged or openly dealt with, defenses will come into play.

■ A defense against anxiety can involve the splitting off of certain feelings from personal experience, the projection of those feelings on to another person or group and the identification with the feelings projected on the part of the other person or group.

■ Individuals or groups, other than the originator, experience the impact of these processes and can carry these emotional burdens and experience stress.

The need for systemic thinking when exploring stress in the organization

Seeing the big picture

The description of emotional processes that are the undercurrents of organizational life begins to illustrate how feelings get passed around the organization. They stick to some people and groups who may be overwhelmed by the emotions they are filled up with as they go about their daily work. To complete this understanding, we need to look at how organizations operate as whole systems. That is to say, to understand what is happening we need to keep the whole organization in mind and to recognize how things that start in one place, have a knock-on effect elsewhere. How a pebble in the pond of one group can feel like a tidal wave elsewhere and how the experiences of a group or individual are a microcosm of the struggles and unresolved issues of the organization as a whole. As an organization comes to terms with the changes it is undergoing or the unresolved conflicts within it, every part of the organization experiences this and is part of the whole drama being enacted.

Let us see what we mean by this. A senior manager spoke about one of his managers who had started losing her temper quite dramatically at work, with a variety of people. He recognized this as a common stress symptom. His immediate thought was to reduce her stress levels. He was tempted to help her with the offer of counselling or relaxation training.

As he contemplated this, however, he realized that her predecessor in the job had left due to serious stress-related physical ill health. Perhaps he had appointed two particularly vulnerable people to the job in succession? But that didn't seem very likely. The current manager was very experienced in similar environments. The predecessor had been an RAF pilot who had flown aircraft designated for retaliation in the event of nuclear attack warnings. It seemed unlikely that he was particularly stress-prone. Reflection on these two people led the manager to look at the whole system which provided the job context. He widened his attention to look at the system that operated at his level, and took his attention away from focusing purely on the jobholder. Even though he could

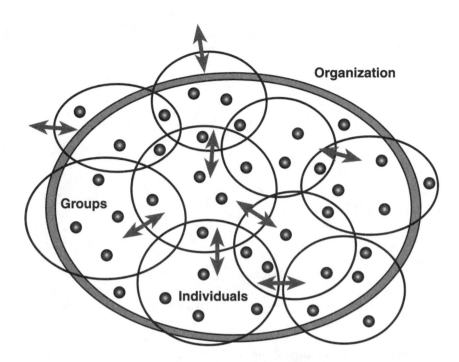

Figure 5.1 Systemic thinking and organizational stress: the whole is the part and the part is the whole

not alter the part of the organization that he felt was the origin of the problem, or be in charge of policy on stress management, he realized that he could still have a significant impact. His new thinking eventually resulted in the redefinition of her department's role rather than stress management training.

This is shown diagrammatically in Figure 5.1. All of the parts interact with each other such that movement in any place would impact everywhere else. A bit like frog spawn.

By gaining a systemic understanding of what is happening in the organization we can begin to change it. Understanding it and changing it are both sides of the same coin if we look at the organization processes involved. To look at an organization from a systemic point of view is to understand how all of the parts of the organization interact and affect each other in a complex way. None of the parts can be understood sufficiently without reference to the others; it is the whole, the big picture, that needs to be grasped.

This is not to say that we cannot look at small parts of the organization and make sense of them. However, the part we look at is also in contact with other parts of the system and will be affected by the organization as a whole. If we remember to look at the effects of these on each other, at what goes on across these boundaries, then we will have a much better picture than if we only look inside the part that initially concerns us most.

There can be some confusion between the word systemic and the word systematic. We are suggesting a systemic look at organizations, viewing the organization as a whole system. This is not the same as looking systematically, in a thorough and painstaking manner. We are not discouraging approaching stress management in a thorough manner, but that is not the point we are emphasizing here. To take a systemic approach we need to explore the process of what is happening in the organization at both conscious and unconscious levels.

To understand organizations from a systemic perspective it is helpful to be aware of the contribution made by general systems theory. In this approach a distinction is made between an 'open' system which is in contact with its environment and a 'closed' system. An open system has imports of energy, some means of converting that energy and then exporting that energy back into the environment in a new form. This is unlike a 'closed' system, such as an electric battery left to run down. In an 'open' system, work is done that maintains the system. In an 'open' system there must be some way of maintaining import and export across a boundary for it to remain functioning and balanced. How this is managed is of importance. Examples would be living cells, a human being or an organization.

An organization is an 'open' system. It has a boundary, although what constitutes a boundary in a modern organization is a good question to ask. Across the boundary the organization imports raw materials and exports a service or product with added value. Within is some process of conversion. The organization survives if it continually adapts to the forces from outside, and the amount of adaptation required is related to the stability of the environment. It has to manage across this boundary, changing and maintaining what is going on inside so that it is not cut off from the environment nor swamped by it. Within the organization are smaller systems, each with a boundary across which resources cross. These resources may be people and ideas, materials and technology. They are converted into something with added value, which is then delivered elsewhere in the organization or externally.

The essential task of management therefore is to manage all these exchanges across the different parts of the system; being in touch with the environment, managing the boundaries of the subsystems or departments such that they get the resources they need to convert to outcomes needed for the organization as a whole. It is much like a living organism; whilst the function of the heart can be understood as a pump, the point of its existence is related to the circulation of the blood and in turn to respiration in the cells. Each subsystem is part of the import/export process going on in another part of the organism. So it is in the organization; within each group the task is not only to manage whatever conversion process is appropriate, but also to manage the boundary between the group and the organization, with some groups sitting at the boundary with the external world. Thus the organization is actually a complex set of interrelationships and there is the possibility of transport of issues and events around the whole system, and of breakdown in these interrelationships.

Stress and boundaries

Stress can occur when there is a retreat from managing across the boundaries; subsystems are swamped or cut off from essential supplies and authority to do the tasks within the system is not taken up.

We see this when a disaster occurs and it is ascribed to bad management. A world famous example of this is the Challenger disaster, when a technical failure in the 'O' rings of a rocket booster led to one of NASA's space shuttles blowing up and killing seven astronauts. The failure was the management of the system to recognize technological demands, the failure to manage across different sites and suppliers, the failure to listen to expertise in the organization but in particular to manage across the organizational/political boundary and secure the funds that the organization needed to meet the conflicting expectations of politics, commerce and technology. The 'O' rings caused the accident, but they were not the source of the problem.

We are seeing this problem with a client with whom we work. Brought in to help them with stress, we found an organization in dire straits. The organization, whose task is to help and protect clients, has had several enormous failures. The death of a child in their protection, evidence of abuse by an employee of children in their care, evidence of bullying of staff and other such issues has led to a public report of lack of confidence in the ability of the organization to avoid a reoccurrence of such problems. The root of this is suggested as 'management'. Another way of describing this is to say that there has been insufficient attention paid to managing across the boundaries between the various sections of this large organization. Evidence suggests that the management group have become separated from the field workers in a dangerous way. Policies and ideas from the top are routinely ignored by field staff; non-compliance is the norm. Field workers feel they are struggling on in a vacuum and middle managers find themselves sandwiched between the two, feeling impotent. Stress is palpable and is being passed around the system; everyone feels both responsible and unable to impact on it, because the roots lie in the management of the boundaries between various aspects of the organization and not at any one person's door.

Therefore management both at and of the boundaries of the organization is a very important aspect of looking at the maintenance of the organization as a system. This begins to clarify the ideas of the organization as a system and that there is impact between the various subsystems.

Let's explore this using the example of this organization which is caught up in massive failures in protecting the clients it was set up to serve. We can see some of these dynamics at work.

In this situation, and with the knowledge of hindsight, we can discover an organization that previously had a charismatic leader. Times became very difficult, with financial restraints, restructuring and delayering. Problems arose which gave rise to much anxiety, and feelings of powerlessness in the face of such massive change abounded. The charismatic leader was the obvious target for some of the projection that was going on in the organization. Here was the 'all powerful' leader who could solve all the difficulties. His identification with the hero role meant that he and his team had to come up with solutions to the problems across the board. They worked very hard, but of course as human beings they could not have the answer to every dilemma. Their solutions were less than perfect. As perfection was required from the hero the solutions soon came to be routinely dismissed. The field workers' anger at the leader's 'failure', and also perhaps their anger with their difficult clients with whom it was 'impossible' to feel angry, was redirected at the management team. The management team had turned out not to be infallible when they were supposed to save the day. They became the targets of people's resentments. The anger was demonstrated by the simple passive–aggressive method of non-compliance with policies issued by the management team.

The leader resigned and a new, more *laissez-faire* leader was appointed; but the real source of the feelings was not located and the management team continued as the target of passive resistance. The new leader has moved on too and they await a new appointment. Some groups within the organization seemed to be more immune to stress than others, but the problem has escalated with an increase in reports of bullying at work, which may well be combinations of displaced anger and paranoia. The 'bad' management, particularly the top team, is 'cut off' from the field workers, with communications becoming ever more difficult. This maintains the possibility of splitting, in a vicious cycle. In this situation it is probably true that at the moment the management cannot be sure of preventing another tragedy, despite the fact that they are competent and committed professionals doing their very best.

We will return to the issue of what can be done to begin to alleviate such a situation in Chapters 7 and 8. Let us just note here that the irony is that they will need to address the pain which these defenses have been set up to alleviate, but which have instead led to, amongst other consequences, stress. The stress reduction will not be pain free.

In this example we have explored how this unconscious emotional activity has affected and been transported round the whole system; we can also see how these get played out within a group.

How emotions are played out within subsystems or groups: recognizing stress in a group

Groups can be understood as systems operating within a wider organizational system. Understanding group stress by looking at the group as a system, gives us a different perspective from the one formed by considering each individual separately.

As psychologists involved in management development, we used to tutor on personal development in outdoor events. One such programme illustrated how anxiety and task achievement are intertwined. The participants also demonstrated vividly what could happen in groups when primitive emotions are unaddressed and the whole group is swept along by group emotion.

This particular programme involved participants in a 'gorge crossing'. At 9 am the managers were presented with ropes, pulleys and so on with which they could design a 'Tyrolean traverse'. They would use this construction, once safety checked by the experts in the tutor team, to cross a gorge. The group would divide into two and the aim was for everyone, starting from whichever side of the gorge they had been allocated, to swap sides by 5 pm. People looked interestedly (nervously) at the equipment. Then a diagram of the gorge went up. It was 45 metres across and 30 metres deep, rather a daunting prospect. Interest in the equipment and the diagrams of how to tie knots and so on intensified!

Anxiety in the comfortable hotel room was almost tangible. There were some white faces, some people stood silently by and someone shredded a paper tissue. No one said anything about the emotional aspect of the task ahead, but several people began to dive into the ropes and began drawing sketches. This sort of activity persisted for more than an hour and then someone said 'has anyone any experience of doing this?' One person said quietly that he had abseiled. He was immediately 'volunteered' for a leadership role. He protested that he did not know how to do this task, but the group was determined to have him lead. He had not led much on the course up until then. As the next hour passed his status as the 'expert', the 'boss' seemed to rise dramatically. It was clear to everyone that he was the only one who could design, direct and organize them to do this task. Compliance was the order of the day and the group made its plans in accordance with his directions.

Our role was to help the participants with a thorough debrief at the end of the day, but it was hard to sit by as the group grew more infantile and dependent on this man's ideas. At the same time as the busyness of the group increased in order to get the gorge crossing set up, we became aware that the likelihood of anyone getting across was diminishing by the minute. It seemed as though they were busy appearing to do the task, whilst undermining their efforts. For example, a full half-hour discussion was held on the order in which people should cross, and it took 45 minutes to sort out the already prepared and packed lunches. Needless to say the group failed to achieve the gorge crossing. They didn't even come close.

In the debrief, the full impact of their failure was felt. As this was a personal development programme, the 'leader' was particularly under the spotlight. He was the subject of some very acrimonious feedback from members of the group and tutors needed to intervene. What we wanted people to reflect on was the way the *whole* group had been party to the day's experiences. The whole group, with different individuals having different levels of anxiety, had been highly charged. Some were just plain scared of heights, some of the fear of failure. Whilst the task was safe in reality, it was perceived as unsafe and threatening in many different ways by group members. At no point was this ever explored. In their anxiety, the group disempowered themselves. Competent and experienced engineers claimed they could not design a rope and pulley system. Leaders of industry could not divide up the lunches and the eventual distribution of equipment to either side of the gorge was not done according to their own plan.

The whole group, whilst believing themselves to be hard at work at the task, was actually turning itself into a dependent, infantilised system 'as if' they had no relevant expertise or skill. Fortunately for them, however, rescue was to hand. The 'expert' was made leader and now everyone could relax. He would save the day and tell them how to do the task which was, at least unconsciously, redefined to ensure that no one had to hang out at a great height above a raging stream from a few ropes. The discomfort of the whole group and their unhappiness at the end of the day was rapidly in danger of turning on the hapless 'leader'. He had failed as 'super-hero', could be blamed and scapegoated for their failure.

As tutors we encouraged them to focus on the complex situation they had created around this task and to learn from what the whole group had created together; this gives a different level of insight than the somewhat dubious 'feedback' the 'leader' could otherwise have been subject to. We have offered this example at length, because it pulls together the ideas about emotional focus and systemic thinking that we introduced in Chapter 4 and this chapter.

Emotion can sweep across a group and to cope with this the group can begin to behave 'as if' something is going on that they have to manage. That something is not the real task that people outside the group, tutors in the above example, managers and directors in other organizational settings, would recognize as the group's purpose. The assumptions the group adopts to manage their stress, take them away from the real task.

Instead of managing the feelings and relationships that surround the achievement of the real task, most groups in high pressure circumstances find ways of avoiding tackling them appropriately. In the group on the outdoor programme there were all sorts of rivalries, power plays, jealousies and so on that made the selection of a less than obvious leader 'ideal'. In addition to anxiety about the gorge, this 'solution' avoided any real clashes over bids for leadership which were creating ripples of concern for many in the group and had been so far unacknowledged. The leader chosen could be sacrificed.

Dependency is not the only assumption that groups appear to operate. Sometimes they appear to behave as if they have to deal with a hostile enemy. Since there is always some element of this in the world it is often difficult to spot the depth of paranoia and suspicion that sweeps the group. The leader's role is to deal with the 'enemy'. The group engages in behaviour associated with fight or flight, but this is not directed at the real task and managing the group boundaries effectively, but in dealing with the paranoia of the group.

By contrast groups are sometimes swept by a different feeling: optimism and hope. This may be unrelated to the real effectiveness of the group in getting on with its task. The group comes to believe that 'something is about to be produced': a strategy, a project plan, a new leader, a new beginning in which all will be well. Two members often have this hope invested in them 'as if' they will give birth to this new start.

All groups are prone to such activities as these. The difficulties of belonging and at the same time being one's self echo primitive and early infantile struggles. Feelings are deep and often out of awareness as the group struggles with the same kind of issues as children do with parents and siblings; except that as more sophisticated adults it looks a little different.

As observers of the gorge crossing exercise we were able to witness the drama of group life. In organizations where we are group members, it is harder to spot. This is particularly true because groups oscillate between these two states where 'group emotions' take a hold or they work effectively as a group at their task. The more difficult the conditions are for the group, the more uncertainty, the more dangerous the environment is, the more threats to survival that are around, the more likely these kinds of scenes are.

Thus one clue to stress in a group is that changes in the way the group works can be seen. The group is *collectively* engaging in behaviours which seem to make them incapable, vulnerable, dependent, in need of direction. Instead of working with the leader of the group, they wait for the leader to decide. Or the group engages in fight/flight as though it is dealing with enemies. It is paranoid and suspicious. Alternatively it may appear overly optimistic and be unrealistic about what everyone needs to get on with to meet the group aims. It is not that these things are observed that causes concern, all groups experience these kinds of states. It is of concern, though, when these seem to dominate group life and the group becomes less able to do its real job even though those involved believe they are working hard at it.

The group which fails to pay attention to all of the supports it needs to do its work, to the relationships and to the difficulties its members experience in doing the work will find itself stressed when there is higher pressure. It will lose its way, put its energy into dealing with emotions inappropriately and fail to work with its leader in a way that makes for high performance. Like the gorge crossing group it will find scapegoats to blame and will be puzzled by the fact that its hard work did not lead to success.

Additionally, as we look at the whole organization we can see these dynamics being exported around the system as a whole. Splits and division in one part of the organization are re-enacted elsewhere. A top team behaving like our gorge crossing group should not be surprised to find that no one in the organization feels empowered to deal with the situation they are in; stress will be spread like wild fire.

The practical answer to many organizational problems of adaptation and change has been to create teams working across traditional functional boundaries. The membership of such groups gives rise to many issues to do with working closely together. There is a need for mechanisms to maintain one's own identity and separateness within the group, and to deal with rivalry and competition in a Western society that still values individual contribution over group effort. In autonomous working groups there are issues about how leadership will be exercised and authorized in the group and how followership and dependency will be dealt with. People will take different stances about these issues and will come to take up different roles in the group such as scapegoat, worker, critic, nurturer and leader in addition to the professional roles they bring to the task such as accountant, engineer, trainer and so on. There is tremendous room for individuals to become stressed in a group.

How group needs shape individual behaviour

There are unconscious needs which arise within a group. These come to the fore when the group is faced with feelings which are hard to cope with and an experience of differences in the group which is not acknowledged. These can result in a need for someone to play a particular role. Individuals will take up roles to deal with these group needs.

The individual taking up a particular role is meeting the need of the whole group rather than just acting on their own behalf. However, that is not necessarily how the person would report their experience if questioned. The person might have their own 'reasons' for their behaviour which are rooted in their own values or reactions to the task. The individual taking up a role such as clown, flight leader, dumb, spoiler, scapegoat, hero, clever, and so on, meets the group's needs and may collude with roles other members take up. This deals with worries about authority, status, power, dependency and so on, without the issues being knowingly addressed. Thus the roles are socially constructed and not just an individual's own idea. Clearly, however, individuals have their own propensity to take up some roles and avoid others. This personal dimension is explored in Chapter 6.

Group dynamics cannot therefore be managed by getting rid of 'difficult people'. When we understand the group as a system rather than only as the individual personalities that compose it, we can see how people play their part in the group drama.

In a group brought together to develop and learn as managers, such occurrences were apparent. One member missed a deadline for some work and began to become the focus of the group's anxiety about its success. Despite the fact that he then made an enormous contribution he was continually questioned as to his commitment and work. The others felt quite smug about their own efforts and overconfident about their individual success. He was the problem member. After an assessed piece of work was returned, he had done particularly well, compared with the others. The group came to believe that the system of assessment was faulty and voiced their thoughts about it to the assessor. They continued to pick on the individual who was 'uncommitted' and he eventually felt the strain of his position and left. The group now knew that they could get on well together and succeed. Three months down the line they were falling apart as another member of the group whose contribution was deemed insufficient had become the next casualty of their denied anxiety about success, competition and rivalry. This member fell ill and had to miss a significant part of the programme.

Whilst it may well be the case that some interpersonal conflict is based on simple dislike of one person for another, much can be explained by these complex interdependencies in organizations and the feelings they give rise to.

The anxiety of change in a system

It has long been accepted that change is a time when there is likely to be stress about in the organization, yet it is not always understood how this happens. This is particularly important in a time when change is an ongoing fact of life in most organizations. The need is for innovation and change to keep up to date and at the forefront of the field. Yet how does this necessary business driver lead to such stress for so many people? There are two main ways in which this happens. Firstly, it happens because change disturbs the processes set up to contain anxiety. Secondly, it happens because the process each of us goes through when change occurs requires the organization to engage once again in the world of emotion.

Containing anxiety and change

It is important for people to contain their feelings of anxiety at work in order to get on with their job, so ways of doing this evolve during the lifetime of the organization. Some of these are very useful and healthy processes, whereas some may come to pose problems in actually getting the job done. For example, rituals and strict procedures may help people avoid the anxiety of making mistakes. On the other hand the rituals or procedures may become an end in themselves. The original task may become submerged. Often when change is introduced getting rid of these time-wasting procedures or structures is part of the impetus for change. To become more efficient and effective, the organization strips away many of these activities, not realizing how important they really were.

We use organizations to defend against and manage our anxieties. In this way defenses become externalized and institutionalized in the system. So there are two kinds of defenses at work, those we each use personally and those which have become part of the organization. Therefore there is a part we all have to play, but there is also the part which organizational cultures play.

Procedures, structures and systems may evolve which have more to do with keeping anxiety at bay than addressing the task. It is important to recognize this; if you dismantle them to become more efficient and effective without paying attention to their psychological worth you may find that the anxieties break through. Thus it can appear that there is an outbreak of anxiety, which in fact had been present all along but managed by the previous way of doing things. We will look again at the importance of containing anxiety in the organization in Chapters 7 and 8.

Transition and change

Whenever we face a change in work life, there will be a process of letting go and re-engaging with the new. Most organizational change is based on a sound rationale and most managers hope that this rationale will be a firm enough grounding for people to make the transition. It rarely is. Dealing with change is an emotional process, with its own tasks and stages. When change is unwelcome, the first response is often one of shock. A friend of ours has recently been told that he is to take early retirement. While that may be the dream of many, for this person it was an unwelcome announcement. No amount of reassurance could counter the deep shock he felt on being told. Shock was the primary state of this person for some weeks. Shock is often followed by a period of denial. In this case that was not possible as the timescale was short and the event about to happen only too soon. But in other cases, we have observed examples of people continuing as if nothing was about to happen at all. In a reorganization which involved people taking up different roles, we noticed that the way most of them responded was to cling even more strongly to the old way of doing things. The letting go process was gradual. Letting go of a past part of work life involves feeling the sadness of the parting. Sadness does not often feature on the agenda of management teams.

Too often the management of change does not allow either the time or the space to express feelings. This will simply delay the process of adaptation or drive it underground. Where the process is not allowed, there will often be groups of staff getting together to grumble or moan. The process each of us experiences is often dismaying enough, without being told that you are not supposed to be feeling it in the first place.

Where does stress come from?

People will give lots of reasons for their stress. Some may be the real reasons! Some of these may require obvious and immediate attention: the chairs that cause backache, the poor ventilation, the lack of fat-free food in the canteen, having to cover for someone on maternity leave. But in looking at their reasons you will find a lot of things that are far less easy to deal with: culture, long hours, not enough influence, too many priorities, not enough control, too many managers, too few managers, change, not enough risk taking, too much instability, not enough computers, too much emphasis on computers, no flexible working, too much home working, boss always away, boss too interfering, open plan office, geographical separation. We have seen lists as long as your arm that are difficult to make sense of. We can only suggest that you look to see not just what is on the list, but also what they represent and what else may be going on in the organization. It is tempting, borne out by the wish to remedy problems, to look at it in a static way.

But look below the surface; what makes the culture difficult to be in, what is the downside of the positive features, what is the problem that cannot be spoken about, why do people think that long hours beyond the possibility of productivity are vital, why is the car park such an issue? There is a well-known phrase in managing change: it is not the change (external imposed event) that does you in, it's the transition (the psychological adjustment required). This is the essence of this chapter; it's not the event out there that causes stress, it is the psychological impact that it has on the system and the part we play in it. Unhealthy systems do us in; this is the threat that in the modern world impacts on our immune system. To find out how stress in your organization occurs you need to understand this process.

When beginning to explore the systemic and emotional perspectives of organizations with one group, a member offered the thought that 'you mean we have to understand the mess here'. That is exactly what we meant.

As we began this chapter, we went back to some material prepared some time ago on sources of organizational stress. There was a neat table in which the risk and preventive factors for stress at the individual and organizational levels were listed. Looking at it, the table looked quite inadequate. How could these factors explain the depth of feelings about their organizations that people have when they are stressed? The factors listed included things like relationships with boss, organizational culture, home/work boundary, relationships with co-workers. It seemed to us that a lot lies below the surface of these words. The neat list of dull and dry words did not even begin to explain the depth of what it can feel like to be in a subordinate relationship with a boss who does not value you, or to be part of a culture that thinks it espouses empowerment for staff but in fact just means that those in charge don't take up their authority to change things, or how it feels to find yourself in a role that doesn't suit you or to be seen as a troublemaker when your intention was to shake out complacency. It firstly drew our attention to the sheer intensity of emotion that can be present when stress is experienced. Words like culture, structure, relationships with co-workers sound detached. Yet it is clear that those who feel stress from work, feel intensely involved in the pressures and demands they face.

When people feel stressed, they often feel locked in or trapped by the situation. The situation does not feel as though it is entirely of their own making or within their scope to resolve. This feeling arises because the experience is constructed from the presence of the person in a social setting. Very few people work in isolation. Other people are involved in getting work done. This involves relating to and dealing with others in a series of encounters and movements, a social dance. When working, people are involved in a social dance in which each person is, metaphorically, being grasped by other dancers. Therefore one can certainly take the step of wrenching oneself free, but it is hard to do. From the organization's point of view, it is important to recognize both that a dance is taking place and the nature of the moves and sequences. If the organization doesn't recognize the nature of the dance, one person leaving exhausted will not stop the dance carrying on. It may simply mean that the next one to go may be more than just tired. Seeking the causes of stress in the organization does not just mean looking for the weak dancer and helping them, it means understanding the nature of the dance itself and how it can be differently choreographed, to be more exciting and creative and less repetitive and tiring.

To understand the depth of the stress experience and how it is created, we need to go beyond simple cause and effect models. It is too simplistic to say that to have a critical boss will lead to stress. It will simply not suffice. We need to move from identifying what is happening to understanding how it happens. Only when we get a full understanding of how stress occurs can we make informed choices as to how to stop repetition in the future.

In this chapter we have emphasized the need for a systemic view of the organization as a whole. We have emphasized some of the dynamics that can occur as deep-seated emotion is played out at work. We looked at the way people are cast into roles, which suit the group or organization. We have placed the focus on understanding how stress comes about from an organizational viewpoint. In the next chapter we shall place the individual within the picture. Whenever stress occurs it is a complex meshing of the person in the organizational setting; both play their part.

Key points in Chapter 5

- An organization is a system in which the parts interact.
- An organization is an open system in which energy and resources are managed across the boundary with the outside world and across the groups that make up the organization.
- Effective management at and across the boundaries of the organization is crucial to keep pressure manageable.
- Stressful experiences can be imported and exported around the organization as a whole.
- Within the group anxiety linked to issues of separation and inclusion and exclusion is evoked.
- Groups can be swept by 'group emotion'; some people will feel the emotion more acutely than others, but the whole system behaves 'as if' it is dealing with the feeling.
- Groups behave 'as if' they cannot access their capability and become dependent on a leader they want to be all knowing, or they may become paranoid, treating the world as a hostile jungle, or overly and unrealistically optimistic.

- This detracts from their ability to work and deal with real difficulties; the group then feels the consequences, which may be stressful, and so the stress levels rise: this is a reinforcing cycle.
- The issue that is not acknowledged is the difficulty of relating to each member and to the task.
- These processes can be played out in the organization as a whole system or within groups within the organization, or by individuals.
- Change in an organization can dismantle some of the protective structures which normally operate to minimize and contain anxiety.
- Change forces people to make personal transitions which results in a range of emotions which need to be understood and respected.

How individual characteristics influence the experience of stress at work

The individual characteristics which influence the experience of stress in the workplace are shown in Figure 6.1. We explore each of these areas in this chapter.

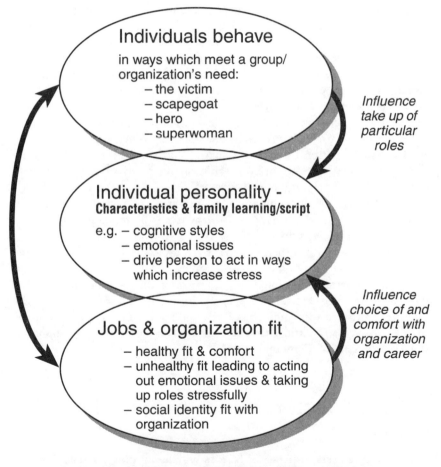

Individuals behave

in ways which meet a group/organization's need:
- the victim
- scapegoat
- hero
- superwoman

Influence take up of particular roles

Individual personality -
Characteristics & family learning/script

e.g. – cognitive styles
– emotional issues
– drive person to act in ways which increase stress

Influence choice of and comfort with organization and career

Jobs & organization fit

– healthy fit & comfort
– unhealthy fit leading to acting out emotional issues & taking up roles stressfully
– social identity fit with organization

Figure 6.1 How individuals' characteristics influence the experience of stress in the workplace

We identified some of the ways in which organizational processes lead to stress in the last chapter. However, there is also the part that each of us plays in colluding with what is going on. This may involve projecting aspects of ourselves on to others which we then disown, or see as part of the organization's expectations. In this case we may see the problem as belonging to the workplace and thus avoid having to deal with the aspects of ourselves which encourage stress. The other side of the coin is that, unless you look at the organizational context, your attempts to help individuals outgrow unhelpful attitudes through stress training and personal development will not alter stress levels enough. It may help me to identify that I am a perfectionist, but unless I also see how I play this out at work, it will still leave me overstretched. It is not a case of seeing stress as caused by either the organization or by the people themselves, rather it is a case of seeing the person in the organizational system and recognizing the interplay between the two.

Much effort goes into managing stress by attempting to get individuals to change their attitudes. Through personal development programmes and stress training some fundamental attitudes can be made conscious and reviewed for their efficacy in the person's current life. Usually on such programmes participants explore a case example of how it is affecting them in their work. One outcome of these events is that many participants subsequently leave their job or their employer.

People come to such programmes because something is not going right for them at that time. It is amazing that some ever make it to the event itself. We have sat in consternation on many courses as stories unfold of horrendous hours of work, of covering two or more jobs for months on end, of discrimination, of bullying, of lack of simple care and courtesy, of downright hostility from a manager, of being someone's political pawn and many horror stories of pain and misery, causing mental and health problems. Even allowing for the fact that we may see a biased cross-section of people, and that people may even 'produce' something for our benefit, we see enough application forms with a reason for attendance filled out by human resources or the manager, and see the same organizations represented on programmes over many years, to know that it is not all figments of vivid imaginations on the part of a few managers!

Personal factors which may lead to stress

There are three sets of personal factors which can play a particular part in the creation of stress. One is the set of beliefs and expectations each of us has learned and which we will bring into the world of work. The second is our personality and the third is the characteristics we bring with us, be it a certain professional label, or membership of a certain age group, lifestyle, gender or racial background.

We all bring our beliefs, personality and history to work with us as well as the skills and knowledge we possess. The organization ostensibly selects people on the basis of their ability to do the job and fulfil the job specification. There may also be a person specification attached to the requirements of the post. These usually cover such attributes as ability to manage pressure, leadership, the ability to communicate and manage a team. These are all vital managerial skills which are without doubt necessary for doing the job well. What is often not spelt out on a person specification is the need to subjugate the rest of one's life to work, the need to be a workaholic, to discount the importance of areas outside work, for example. Nor is the requirement to be deferential to the boss in a suitably subordinate way often listed. Yet it is often a fact of organizational life that such behaviours are required.

We know of a young engineer who has just taken up a new post and is encountering the reality of the organization's culture and expectations, as well as the task demands of the job. This particular organization demands very long hours from its employees. There is a history within the company of financial difficulties and this is used as the reason for demanding a great deal from employees now. The threat permanently looms, if you do not all work 12 hours a day we will go bust again. There may be some reality to that. Of course hard work is needed to keep a competitive edge and to keep abreast of the marketplace. Yet the reality is not challenged, it is accepted and the pervading climate is one of fear rather than healthy hard work and competition.

The expectation of hard work is reasonable and may well be needed to achieve targets. However, the message that in this company it is not acceptable to have a life outside work is subtly reinforced in other ways. The expectation is that every engineer is available to do overtime whenever requested, even late into the night and at the weekends. Pleading a prior engagement is not an acceptable reason for refusing. In addition it is a serious offence to make or accept personal phone calls, and as for personal emails, this is totally unacceptable. This causes our young engineer a slight problem. If asked late in the afternoon to work late that night, he is not allowed to ring his fiancée to let her know. At the same time as starting this new job, the engineer is also about to embark on matrimony. The extra money from the overtime is very useful at the moment, but the company culture is not enhancing the relationship between the young couple. The message is clear, work is work and it takes over your life, there is no place for a life outside work or for fun.

There are other elements to this particular scenario but the main point the young engineer is discovering is the balance in his own life. When people accept a job they have to take up a role which will enable them to accomplish the tasks that make up that job. They have to manage the boundary between the different elements of their life. This means managing the boundary between their inner world and the job demands. A mature ego, for example, helps the person maintain a balance between their own needs and the demands of others, but the situation is complex. In this case the young engineer is being brought face to face with this struggle to maintain a balance. The company is bringing to the fore all the expectations of work developed over years, the experience of authority figures and the balance between home and work and the need for love as well as productivity. It is too simplistic for this young person to say, this is what the company demands and therefore I have to do it. He does not feel good about the effect the new job is having on his relationship and is dealing with this by expecting his girlfriend to be more understanding. She feels excluded and discounted and the situation looks certain to continue to decline.

It would be tempting in this example to suggest that this young engineer go on a stress management programme to develop strategies to deal with the organizational pressure. It could even be argued that he needs an assertiveness programme to enable him to develop the skills of standing up for himself. While both or either of these may be of great benefit to this person, this is only focusing on a partial view of the situation. On the other hand it could be argued that a piece of organization development work is needed, to examine the organizational culture and change the expectations. Again this may be very helpful, but again is only recognizing a part of the picture. It is where the individual's personal history encounters the organization that stress is created. It is at that interface that work needs to be done.

This example highlights the way that what the individual brings to work can mesh or fail to mesh with the organization. Aspects of the organization's culture both attract people with certain dispositions and once there, activate those characteristics. This is part of the selection process; looking for the face that fits which, like falling in love, is the finding of an unconscious fit between people. Some people and some organizations have healthier attitudes to life than others do, but at some level we choose the organization which feels familiar. Even the word familiar demonstrates the link to what we have learned before, as the word has the same roots as family. Although the young engineer was having a difficult time he may well have chosen an organization that endorsed his propensity to be a workaholic; he will be able to point to the reality of having to work 12-hour days in the face of his partner's criticism. He may have chosen a boss who is overly critical and hostile; this will enable him to feel familiar feelings of resentment to his heart's content. Much of the resolution to these dilemmas does lie with the individual to change. But the wider context of the organizational setting and complex organizational relationships have to be considered too.

How our beliefs can lead to stress

Each person carries with them a belief system they have learnt, probably early in their life. Some of these beliefs can remain relatively unsophisticated and unconscious, such as the belief that all authority figures are cruel, or that it is impossible to get what you want in life. Most of the time these belief systems go unnoticed and unacknowledged. They become so much a part of us that we fail to even notice when they are at work in our lives and how they influence our behaviour.

Some of the most pervasive beliefs we learn are to do with our personal sense of worth. For some people the early learning within the family leads to the belief that they are a valuable and worthwhile person. This will then be taken into the workplace and they will look for and expect to be treated as a valuable and worthwhile person at work. On the other hand early learning may lead to the conclusion for some people that they are of no or little value or worth. This negative sense of self-worth will also be carried into the world of work and unconsciously an organization will be sought which reinforces this belief, in this case, an organization that does not treat staff well, where the customary exchanges between people are hostile. More commonly the early learning leads to a belief in conditional self-worth, along the lines of 'I will be an OK person, if . . .' and there are many phrases which complete the sentence. Common conditional beliefs we have seen operating in the way people work are the belief that as long as I please everybody else, or as long as I get everything perfect, or as long as I work really hard, or do everything very quickly or do it all by myself without any help, then and only then will I be a useful, worthwhile human being. It is hardly surprising therefore that if these beliefs are present either in the person or the organization, the requisite behaviour will be manifest.

There will be the person who goes around the office meeting everyone else's requests and needs and denying their own, all with a feeling of satisfaction. After all is this not the way to be useful and valuable? Alternatively there will be the person who needs no encouragement to sweat and slave away over a report, putting in way too many hours and never taking a break, all because putting a lot of effort in is the way to be a good person. There will be the manager who is always in such a hurry that staff never can get an audience, let alone a full conversation, merely a glimpse of a puff of dust as the manager races off to yet another meeting elsewhere. All this because doing things really fast is the only known way to feel worth while. Or the person who struggles on with the work, never bothering anyone else and never asking for help until the day comes when the major system collapses in the computer, or the heart collapses in the person. Or the person who is mortified at making one small typing mistake in an important document and goes into an emotional nose-dive to the bewilderment of colleagues. They do not understand that making a mistake is the worst possible thing that can happen and it just proves what a useless person he really is. All of these are patterns that the person has learnt early on and will bring to work with them.

The differences explain how people's perceptions of threat differ so greatly. What causes one person anxiety may not trigger any response from another. How they are dealt with in the organization impacts on stress levels. We know of a case in a university where the unfortunate meshing of the person's belief system and the expectations of the organization led to tragic consequences. In this case the person was a firm believer in the value of hard work, to the extent that it could even be described as having religious overtones. Hard work, long hours and a high output were the means to salvation for this person. He worked incredibly hard, achieving a great deal and becoming well known and respected in the process. The organization rewarded this person, heaping academic honours on them and watching the star rise in the academic firmament with pride.

Yet at the annual departmental meeting it was noted that this person regularly exceeded the required workload targets. Initially this was felt to be a slur on the laziness of everyone else. But over time as the effects of this overworking began to tell on the person, some concern was expressed. This took the form of comments that it really was not a good thing to so consistently exceed the organization's expectations. But nothing was seriously done about it. No one took this person on one side and seriously addressed the overworking. Yes, concern was expressed to the person but at no point was it said that this was unacceptable to the organization. The organization colluded with the person's behaviour, equally the person colluded with the organization's implicit expectations that hard work was required, and brushed aside the expressions of concern. The result was tragic. The person died of a heart attack at a young age, leaving a bereft group of colleagues as well as a young family.

For those people who have a managerial role, these outmoded beliefs which can drive the way we work cause additional difficulties. They may exert influence over the manager's self-expectations in their job and also on those around the manager, particularly reporting staff. Even when the manager explicitly states that they do not have the same exacting standards for others that they impose on themselves, staff will feel the pressure to conform to the manager's implicit style. The manager who operates to a rule of perfectionism, for example, may have unconscious expectations that staff will also operate in this way. Even if he or she really does not have these assumptions, staff may find it hard to believe.

This can lead to two kinds of difficulty: staff with similar self-expectations may find this pattern so familiar that they do not question its usefulness and it can be a self-reinforcing vicious circle between them, such that they may even make each other 'worse'. Alternatively, the member of staff who does not have a similar set of beliefs to drive them on, may feel that however much they reach the stated and explicit targets, they cannot please their boss. This leads to a great deal of tension. An example of this arose at a team workshop we were running. An argument broke out between a manager and a member of his team. The manager claimed that his subordinate was uncommitted to his job. The subordinate claimed that he had succeeded every performance target that year and the manager had to agree to the truth of that. For the manager, who was driven to work excessively hard and for long hours, the issue centred on the subordinate's stated intent to leave on time four nights a week in order to be involved in sports coaching for a local team. The manager found it difficult to separate long hours from commitment and achievement. For him, they were intimately connected. For the subordinate they were not, and the result was a lot of extra tension and pressure in the group.

How personality can influence stress

There have been many attempts to classify personality types. The personality of the individual sheds light on how certain traits can lead to stress arising in the workplace. For example, people differ in the predisposition to experience tension. Some people are able to maintain their perspective and keep a relaxed approach throughout, whatever the world puts in their way. Others are less able to stay calm and are more prone to tension which is then shown in their behaviour. This is exacerbated when the person comes to thrive on tension and even to get addicted to the adrenalin rush that can accompany it. This leads them to seek out and create tension to fuel a liking for it.

At a deeper level people differ in the way they relate to the world. There are some people for whom contact with others is their life force. Deprived of contact with people such a person would feel discomfort at the very least. Equally there are people for whom dealings with others are a drain on their emotional energy. Coming away after a long day at work where about 90 per cent of the time was taken up with contact of one kind or another, this person would feel very emotionally depleted. Some organizations value independent individual work, others insist on a team approach. These different ways of working will suit people differently, it is important to recognize that and not to impose a uniform requirement on all people. This is in addition to the different requirements of different types of work.

People differ in the way in which they prefer to make decisions. For some people the brain is the sole organ involved in problem solving. The cognitive function in such people is well developed and they will enjoy grappling with intense abstract issues. On the other hand there are people for whom the heart takes precedence and a cold and arid intellectual climate is not one in which they will thrive.

Just as different roles require different behaviours, so do different people have different preferences. Some people have a good eye for detail, whereas others have more of a feel for the big picture approach. Asking a person who likes to get to grips with nitty-gritty detail to take a strategic overview is about as appealing as asking the big picture person to enjoy proofreading. There will not be a fit between the requirements and the preferences of each person.

Planning is often held to be a key managerial skill. It is assumed that planning is essential to successful completion of a task or project. While this may be the case, there are some people for whom planning and bringing a project to completion is a nightmare. This does not relate to lack of skill or knowledge, it relates to personality. For some people, having a plan with well-worked out steps and timescales is what is needed for comfort. If they do not know what is happening on Wednesday week, there will be a level of unease. For others knowing what is happening tomorrow may feel too constricting and having a plan is just an alien notion.

These reflect differences in the way people relate to the world. There is nothing inherently good or bad in these traits, the difficulties can arise when the fit between the person's personality and the organization is wrong. The implications are twofold. There is a responsibility for each of us to work with knowledge and acceptance of ourselves and our personality characteristics. However, there is also a responsibility for the organization to know and accept the different approaches and traits of people. Working with differences between people is one area where a great deal of stress can be caused in the workplace. We will look at this in the next section.

How different characteristics can play a role in stress

Whenever you take up a role in an organization you bring with you your whole person. This means that your age, lifestyle, gender and ethnic background join the organization as well as your qualifications and work experience. Dealing with these factors within an organization highlights how the ability of an organization to manage difference is crucial to stress management.

There has been much attention paid in the last few decades to equal opportunities. The values of equal opportunities are enshrined in legislation in many countries and certainly are stated clearly in policy statements in many organizations. Yet the ability to manage differences between people is often still problematic. Some differences do not even appear in diversity programmes.

When considering differences, there are two dynamics at work. The first is simply the differences between different social identities. The second is what happens when one group is in a majority, with the consequence that the other is in a minority.

As with personal beliefs, it is not very easy for organizations and their members to be consciously aware of the assumptions that are made. Very often the beliefs which underpin an organization's way of working are so familiar that they are taken for granted. This has been seen in the gender area where traditionally the senior posts were held by men and the support roles taken by women. As this was the common pattern for a long time in most organizations it is hardly surprising that it came to be believed that this was they way the world was and even had to be. Equally when the faces around the board table are not only male, but also all white and middle-aged, the introduction of a woman, a younger person or someone who is black may cause problems.

The problems that can be caused are rarely to do with the person's ability to undertake the role or do the job. However, the feelings of discomfort may be loaded on to that ability because that is the official language of organizations. On the one hand the majority group members may feel uncomfortable and may not be able to explain their discomfort easily. It may be easy to explain it as doubts about the incomer's ability, rather than discomfort with the colour of their skin. On the other hand the person who is ostensibly different may also experience tension. This tension arises because assumptions about them are projected on to their social identity – 'women managers do this', 'black managers will do that' – which they may not experience as part of their own personal identity, who they perceive themselves to be. In addition they are often expected to speak on behalf of the social group they are seen to represent, the women's perspective or the black viewpoint which, of course, they cannot do.

Many attempts have been made over the years to grapple with this issue. There have been positive action programmes designed to equip people from minority groups to progress within organizations. There have been programmes of childcare provision to enable people with childcare responsibilities to undertake their work more easily. But again it is not as simple as saying that either the individual has to get their act together or the organization has to provide facilities.

Where there is a majority group and a minority group, along whatever lines the distinction is made, the relative size of the groupings will have an effect. In the last two chapters we examined emotional dynamics and defenses against difficult feelings. One arena in which these are played out is where there is only a small minority of one group. The smaller the proportion of the whole taken by the minority, the more likely it is that the members of the majority group will focus on the group characteristics of the minority and the less focus will be placed on the uniqueness of the minority group's humanity. For example, in a management team we worked with there was one woman on the team. In the interactions between team members we came to notice the particular quality of interaction between the male members of the team and the woman. They seemed to take little notice of what she actually said and how she behaved. Instead they responded as if she had said or done something quite different. This was taking on a bizarre quality until we realized that the men were responding to her as a woman, rather than the unique person she was. The men were not noticing her behaviour, they were responding to their expectations of how a woman behaves, whether or not it corresponded to the reality. This dynamic can be seen whenever there is a small minority, be it with different ethnic background, sexual orientation, even professional labels. The situation changes when the proportion varies between different groups. The more even the proportions become, the more the members of the majority group are able to see the human being and not just the group characteristic.

The assumptions held by the organization of the nature of the world are demonstrated very vividly when attention is turned to physical disability. The area of dealing with differences in physical ability is structured into the physical environment of the organization. A person who uses a wheelchair will have difficulty working in an organization where the five floors only have stairs between them and split level floors were built for aesthetic appeal with little thought given to wheelchair users. An organization where important communication happens verbally will be an unwelcoming place for a person who is deaf. Equally a person who uses a guide dog for help with sight will not be welcome in an organization which strictly allows no animals.

The dynamic which can occur, however much effort goes into denial, is discrimination against members of a minority group. It has long been recognized that this is stressful for those on the receiving end of the discrimination and prejudice. What has not long been recognized is that wherever discrimination occurs, the members of the majority group suffer as well. This highlights the systemic nature of events within the organization. When members of the minority group experience stress, the majority group are still within the same system of the organization and they experience stress too. This emphasizes the interdependence of groups within an organization.

We have looked at the personal factors which can contribute to the creation of stress within an organization and the importance of the fit between what the person brings and the expectations and assumptions of the culture. There are two other areas where the meshing of individual needs and the needs of the organization can bring about stress. We will now turn our attention to the roles people play in groups and the nature of change as a stress factor.

The roles people play

There has been much work in recent years on the roles that people play at work, particularly when thinking about the roles people play in teams. There have been several classifications of roles, aimed at clarifying what roles are needed for successful completion of the work tasks. There is also the work role itself with its own set of demands and requirements. However, what we want to look at here is the process by which an individual has learnt to play a particular role and adopts this role on behalf of the work group.

Recently when starting a stress management programme, one participant introduced herself as 'I am the one who gets stressed'. As other participants went on to outline their interest in the programme and their awareness of stress and how they experienced it, we were struck by how different a ring that phrase had. It was not a description of how she experienced stress, but rather a declaration of a role that she played. The words 'I am the one who' seemed a clear claim on the role of the person in the work group who got stressed.

None of her colleagues contradicted her, but equally none of them reinforced her claim. It seemed to us that somewhere along the line, this particular person had found some benefit in being seen as the one who was stressed. Maybe the pattern went back to her early family life, maybe it elicited sympathy from others. For whatever reason, it seemed that it was a part she was prepared to play. Being prepared to play this part may have had some benefits for her personally, but she was not taking up the role of stressed person in isolation. She was claiming to be the person in this work group who got the stress. If there is benefit or at least familiarity for the person, equally there is a benefit or familiarity for the group.

We saw an example of this in the last chapter, when a group needed someone to blame or criticize for lack of achievement in a learning group. This is akin to the old tradition of loading troubles on to a goat and sending it off into the desert, to take away the troubles of the tribe. Nowadays organizations do not have goats for this purpose, but the process of scapegoating still continues. We are referring here to more than the process of scapegoating whereby one person is picked to become the depository of the group's woes. We are referring to a process by which a group has an emotional need for a particular role to be played and there is a person for whom this role is familiar.

In a management team we have worked with, one male member of the team surprised us with the comment, 'I am the honorary woman around here'. As this was an all male team, we asked what he meant by this. The way he saw the picture was that the all male group still had needs to be cared for and nurtured. This was not a role any of the men were prepared to take on readily as it conflicted with their perceptions of the male role. It was not seen as manly to be caring, that was woman's work. The team did not have a woman on it, and looked around for one of the men to take this role. The emotional focus alighted on the man who took the nearest to a caring role in his profession, the Director of Personnel. It became clear to the man concerned that he was expected to do the caring for the team. He was not only invited to do so, but was castigated when he failed to do so. The way he saw it was that he was expected to do the work traditionally ascribed to a woman on the team.

Another very common role which meets both the organizational needs, particularly in a crisis, and can tap into deep individual needs, is the requirement to play out the role of hero or saviour. One organization which was in deep trouble felt that the only way out of their dire straits was to find a superman, someone blessed with extraordinary powers who would come in and rescue them. The morale in the place was so low that there was no belief that anyone already on the staff could do anything to help. In fact there was such a dispirited feeling that it was doubtful whether anyone believed they even had any skills left. In this powerless place, the cry went up for a saviour, a hero, a knight in shining armour to transform their world. Needless to say this was not spelt out in the job specification, nor in the person specification. At interview the candidates picked up the situation quickly and one by one withdrew from the process, feeling that the demands for salvation were unreasonable, until one person entered the interview room for whom the role of super hero was only too familiar. After a deep breath and a mental squaring of the shoulders, the person got and accepted the job. The ensuing months in this organization were fraught. No one could live up to the emotional expectations of the staff and the resentment was rife when this person failed. For the person himself it was a very stressful time and ended with a parting of the ways soon after. The last we heard was that the hunt for the super hero was being repeated.

The taking up of roles in this way is not a conscious process. It is a part of personal history which is played out at a deeper level. The person who took the job to rescue the company talked simply of liking a challenge, of believing he had the skills for the job and of seeing it as a good career move.

The fit between the person and their work

Throughout this chapter we have been emphasizing how it is the fit between what we bring and experience and our workplace, which provides the fertile ground for stress to grow. The nature of the fit can take three forms: where the fit meshes and is healthy, where the fit meshes and is unhealthy and where the fit does not mesh. It is in the last two cases that stress will be experienced.

The fit between us and our work can be between us and the particular organization in which we work. The fit can also be between us and the nature of the work we choose to undertake. Choice of occupation can provide a good healthy fit for us, or it can be a cause of stress. There has been much work focused on people who choose to enter the caring professions, for example. Sometimes people choose a particular profession in part because it gives them an opportunity to work through some experiences or personal concerns. For some people becoming a 'carer' for others is a way of ignoring or managing a lack of care that they have experienced in their own lives. For some, providing care for others can help them to come to terms with their own experience. For others, the need to care becomes disconnected from what is feasible in reality. They never stop work. They never look after themselves. The world of work, be it occupation or place of work, provides opportunities to positively experience and reflect yourself. Alternatively it can be a soul-destroying experience and an arena for playing out one's neuroses.

Where there is no fit

When there is no fit between the individual and the organization in terms of emotional processes, discomfort will be felt. This is irrespective of the nature of the misfit. An individual with an unhealthy work pattern will feel ill at ease in an organization with a sound and healthy set of expectations. In the example given earlier of the person prone to overworking, it would have been interesting to see what the response would have been if the message had been given that overworking was not acceptable. At the least we would hazard a guess that the individual would have paused to consider the dilemma. It may have led to energy being put into work outside the job or it may have caused the individual to rethink their working patterns.

Equally a person who has a healthy notion of the role of work and its demands will feel ill at ease in an organization which makes unreasonable demands and expects total devotion to the exclusion of all else.

The example we gave earlier of the young engineer could develop into that situation. If that is the case the person is left with two choices, attempt to change the organization or leave.

Where there is an unhealthy fit

It may appear at first sight that an unhealthy fit is a stress-free situation: you require an obsession with detail, I am obsessive about detail, we fit fine! At least there is a fit between the personal factors and the organization. But because the fit is between unhealthy patterns, as in the example of the overworking academic described in this chapter, the outcome is rarely happy. You encourage me to be obsessive and I can 'over achieve' to meet your expectations.

Where there is a healthy fit

This is the desired outcome, where a person with a healthy way of working is in an organization with a healthy culture and demands. There may need to be changes made either at the individual or at the organizational level to achieve this, but this is the situation needed to ensure top performance.

In the next two parts of the book we map the steps needed to move to a healthy organization and describe the options for good organizational practice which will help you achieve this.

Key points in Chapter 6

- Individuals can be caught up in things going on in the organization as a system but they can also carry their own personal characteristics which when played out in the organization lead to stress being created.
- Personal history leads people to form a view about how to survive and 'be OK' in the world and which may be played out even when it is inappropriate for the situation and this leads to added pressure.
- Personality preferences lead people to feel comfortable with some work and some types of organizations and less so with others.
- Membership of a particular minority group within the power structure of an organization can lead people to be seen as though they only have characteristics which are perceived as stereotypical of that group and not as unique individuals.
- People are themselves in organizations but their behaviour is modi-

fied by membership of groups; they can take up roles within a group which meets a group's emotional needs rather than their own.
- The individual may have a healthy or unhealthy fit with the nature of their work and their organization.

Part III
Providing a Supportive Environment

Strategic Approach
for
Top Performance
and a
Revitalized Organization
depends on
Emotional Focus
with
Systemic Thinking
to develop a
Supportive Environment

In this part of the book we look at the support element of our STRESS model. This builds on the exploration of how stress is created at an organizational level and how our deep-seated emotions are an integral part of our experience of stress. Without this understanding a more creative approach to reducing stress cannot be developed. Providing a supportive environment is the crucial factor in reducing stress levels.

The support processes outlined in Part III entail the movement of effort away from the management of individual symptoms of stress towards the management of organizational causes of stress. We pay particular attention to the processing of experience. It is necessary as well to process the relationships and structures that are necessary for doing the work we are employed to do. Producing a plan for stress management includes the provision of well-constructed spaces for people to do this work. Out of this their own solutions to many issues will emerge. It is important that the organization provides the structures, budgets, places, experts and time for this work to be done. This is a rather different role than finding prescriptions or answers for the whole organization to follow and can be very challenging to get to grips with.

In Chapter 7 we look at the options for providing support for managing stress at the organizational level. In Chapter 8 we look at the options for the management and personal levels. In fact there are overlaps in some respects, but it is helpful to keep these three levels as a 'map' of where it is possible to develop inventions.

Options for providing support to the organization to manage stress

In this chapter we explore what can be done at the organizational level. At the organizational level the options range from putting into place a specific structure to provide support, such as an Employee Assistance Programme, to putting into place processes which provide support, such as support groups and organizational pauses. Providing support is not simply a matter of putting a specific structure into place, providing support also means looking at the processes and interactions which go on throughout the organization.

As we go through the various options, in this chapter and the next, do not see them just as a shopping list of things to choose from. It can be tempting to devise a checklist of possible options and to tick them off as they are introduced. This can give a sense of satisfaction and movement on the issue. However, it may not always be the most effective way to move forward.

One organization that contacted us had done a whole range of things to address stress. They had done a survey, provided a counselling scheme and some stress management training seminars. They had sent a leaflet to all staff stating how seriously they were taking the issue of stress and had also provided a checklist of things to look out for in self and others. They were planning to extend the stress management training programme and were contacting external trainers to run a stress management course for all staff, over the next few months. When they approached us we asked about the role of the senior management team. The reply was 'oh, this is the responsibility of the training group'. Yes, we countered, but what would our role be in supporting the senior managers in looking at stress in them and in the organization. 'They don't see themselves as involved at that level' they replied. What was being done to explore and understand the sources of stress in the organization? Well, nothing, they were too understaffed to even contemplate that. Would the understaffing be a source of difficulty and should that be explored? 'No, it is not to be discussed or acknowledged because there is nothing the organization can do about it.' How was the proposal to run these seminars being received? 'People are rather cynical, but we're sure that will change when they are actually underway'.

Needless to say we were not so convinced of that. It seemed to us that this particular organization was planning to extend the training programme without seeing the situation as a whole. Doing something about stress seemed to have fallen to the training group rather than being a concern of the whole organization, or at least the senior managers. This was not a co-ordinated, strategic approach owned by the senior managers of this organization.

All the actions planned need to be seen as part of an overall strategic approach. Each action needs to be seen as part of the whole rather than another item on a list to tick. That is not to say that you can't start small and move on from there, but it is important for people to know and feel that there is serious commitment to change the situation. This means curbing an understandable impatience to get on and do something about stress by pausing to consider all available options to tackle sources of stress. It also means resisting the urge to rush to rapid solutions. Between identifying that there is an issue which needs to be addressed and deciding on the final actions to be taken, there is a stage of reviewing what is available. This is needed before considering whether it would be appropriate in your particular organization.

Unfortunately there is no one single answer to the issue of the problems caused by stress at work. In this chapter we emphasize the need to get an overview in order to really tackle stress seriously, remembering stress is a dynamic process. If all the parts of the strategy link up, then there will be a real impact. If you don't really want to change it, there is little point in pretending that you do by providing sops to current fashion. Stress is too serious an issue to be at the whim of fashion and 'flavour of the month' thinking. While new things are being tried all the time, they need to be considered on the basis of how appropriate they are to this particular organization, rather than that they are the latest thing.

It is important to keep in mind the purpose of the stress management strategy. It is not to remove all pressure, but to keep it as much as possible at a level which keeps people working at their best. Keeping pressure at an optimum level involves focusing both on the pressures which bear down within the organization and the factors which keep people afloat, which we refer to as buoyancy aids. Reaching the right level of pressure and thereby managing stress can be achieved by providing buoyancy aids, reducing pressure or by a combination of both, tailored to the need. This is what we mean by providing support.

There are two options for providing support as a way of managing stress at the organizational level. The first is to take account of the organizational processes which need to be in place as well as the processes which need to be guarded against. The second option is to identify structures which can be put into place in the organization to manage stress. We use the image of buoyancy aids for these supports.

When pressures are so great that they 'push you under' or leave you furiously treading water to keep going, aids to comfortable and relaxed floating are needed for survival.

Providing support by paying attention to organizational processes: what to pay attention to

In this chapter we focus on the importance of providing support by enabling people to process what is happening. In this section we explore three processes that need attention. Encouraging people in the organization to process their experience and gain an understanding is a key factor in managing stress.

By processing, we mean acknowledging reactions and feelings to events, paying attention to the quality of relationships, understanding the meaning of events and how they are interpreted. This applies to both individuals and groups. It also involves exploring how all of these elements are impacting on people and the way the organization deals with situations. The key issue is that the organization acknowledges the importance of this and provides an appropriate space and resource for this to happen. It is different from casual chat; the depth of the conversation and its relevance for the workplace need to be understood. We need to be careful of the way the word 'process' is used; in some organizations it is synonymous with the word 'procedure'. Clearly, we are using it differently.

The processes are: making the distinction between different types of pressure, providing containment for anxiety within the organization and providing the necessary context for autonomy. We will consider each of these and then consider how the processing of these issues can best take place.

Sorting out the necessary from the unnecessary pressure

Working with organization process can usefully start with sorting out different types of pressure. This focuses on gaining a shared understanding of where the pressure is coming from. It is the process of making the distinctions in your particular organization which is the key.

To understand the pressure producers which push people down, it is useful to sort out the difference between necessary, unnecessary and inevitable pressure. This was developed as an idea in a company we worked with. People frequently said that stress was uncontrollable because of pressures they could not get rid of. The training manager helped them to make the distinctions between necessary, unnecessary and inevitable pressures.

There were necessary business pressures from the market, from regulators and the nature of the business. Nothing could be done about these. They were essential for organizational success and therefore were necessary. There were also pressures which were seen as inevitable, though not necessary for business success. These included the management style of the current chief executive who was described as a workaholic. He said he was always open to meetings with staff. He was available from 6 am when he could be found on the treadmill in the gym. He would talk with anyone on the treadmill next to his. However he was not prepared to look at his style of working and its impact on the whole organization culture; this is what made it an inevitable pressure. Then there were the unnecessary pressures which could be changed. These included factors such as the self-imposed deadlines and outdated paperwork systems. It is in tackling these unnecessary pressures and tackling them collectively that a real difference to overall pressure levels can be made.

This is the sort of discussion that needs to take place, with people sorting out for themselves what they can be responsible for changing. However, your organizational strategy does not have to assume that because nothing can be done about certain pressures, that they can be ignored. Just because these pressure are perceived to be necessary or inevitable does not mean that people simply have to be weighed down by them. These may be the things that need more buoyancy aids attached to them.

An example of where a necessary pressure was made easier to bear is in one company which was faced time and time again with the information that business travel was a source of pressure. As a multinational company with global markets there was little they could change about this necessity. However, they decided they could ease the burden. Firstly they began to put staff in touch with other staff travelling or working in the same location. There is a sad sight in many hotels on weekday nights of people sitting at individual dining room tables eating as quickly as possible. No one wants to be forced to eat with strangers. However, this company found that quite often people would discover on return that there were people they knew who had been out on the same site at the same time. It was a simple matter to put people in touch with each other so that they could choose whether to spend the evenings alone or not. Secondly, they changed their policies on partners accompanying staff on longer trips to make travel easier. They also changed their policy on payment for personal phone calls from hotels staff were staying in.

Another company decided to tap directly into the stress of travel by booking staff into hotels which had excellent health and fitness clubs and which provided health conscious menus in the dining room for those that wanted it. Information on these would be routinely given to travelling staff so that they could pack the appropriate swim wear or gym kit and not miss out on the facilities on offer.

In the discussion of different types of pressure people often focus on concrete or tangible things which can be changed. However, if an appropriate space is provided in which pressures are identified and discussed, the areas that are less easy to talk about can also be explored. Some of the emotional pressures we explored in Part II can be brought into awareness, once time is set aside and permission given to discuss pressures. This highlights the need to pay attention to containing the anxiety present within the organization.

The need to contain anxiety: allocating time and resource to an intangible problem

As we saw in Part II, anxiety can be created by different factors within the organization. Often this is seen as inevitable. Yet if the organization understands the need to contain anxiety, much can be done to alleviate unnecessary anxiety and stress.

Each individual employs personal strategies to manage their own feelings. This process may be largely unconscious. What is of interest here, however, is the role played by the organization, the manager and by external influences such as professional bodies, in helping to keep these anxieties to a creative or manageable level. This is known as containment. It is vital that there is a healthy functional containment of anxiety within the organization. It is a crucial process in the management of stress. Even though most of us do not 'know' about it, or give it a label, it goes on all the time. When containment is of the rigid, unhelpful variety it can constrain the organization's potential. When containment is appropriate, it is a vital contribution. When we change old working methods, however, we can inadvertently disrupt the process of containment. If that happens we will observe both resistance to change and less risk taking and creativity, as well as a higher level of anxiety.

There are many ways of containing anxiety and other 'unacceptable' feelings. For example, professional training and apprenticeship play an important and positive role. They can provide frameworks, supervised experience and codes of conduct to follow. In so doing we reduce personal risk of misconduct and this helps us to do tasks that might give rise to a great deal of anxiety.

Organizations as a whole system can contain anxiety. The 'container' functions by receiving the parts of themselves that people do not like or want to acknowledge. These are the parts that are difficult to deal with and are split off and projected on to and into others. In the workplace, these can be projected into 'the organization', or 'the management' or another repository. The 'container' acts as a focus for blame, for frustrations and for locating conflict. It is not we who are lazy/incompetent/lack imagination/break the rules and so on, but those 'over there'. 'Over there', we can locate those disliked or feared aspects of ourselves and thus the 'management', or the institution, can be something to hate, to love, to depend on, to idealize, to rebel against. 'They' insist we do it a certain way and this reduces some of the anxiety we experience. It is safe to project our feelings on to a distant group. These processes were explored in more depth in Chapters 4 and 5. We looked at how this results in stress for some people because they are landed with emotional issues that don't originate with them.

What we also need to see is the other side of the coin. By some people acquiring these disturbing feelings others may be 'saved' from them. In fact whole edifices can be erected to prevent particular groups from experiencing primitive and disturbing feelings or their own personal unresolved issues.

We need to have organizations that are capable of protecting staff from being overwhelmed by layers of anxiety. However, what evolves through the unconscious desire to create an organization that provides this containment may be at odds with the well-being of everyone engaged in the enterprise or, frequently, with the task which the organization set out to do in the first place. Defensive routines may be set in place. These will have more to do with people having a sense of belonging, of being saved from feeling lost and alone, anxious, hateful and so on, than they have to with the task. They may even be anti-task. Any attempts to change such routines will be met with resistance, even though the changes may be logical and efficiency/effectiveness oriented. The loss of these defenses leaves people exposed to emotions they wish to avoid. Change, in structure, groupings or tasks, automatically challenges these defenses and re-evokes primary separation anxiety.

Similarly, many practices evolve which protect people from anxiety rather than further the work on the task. Routines can stop people from getting too close to difficult situations and getting too involved. In a famous study of nurses it was observed that rotation of wards and other practices stopped nurses from getting too personally involved with patients who may die. Similarly, paperwork and red tape may stop those who are dealing with people, whose needs they cannot sufficiently meet, from feeling too bad about saying 'no'. They can immerse themselves in the detail and routine of the procedures they have to follow.

Frequently our attitudes or ways of doing things become not only unspoken and unexplored but unexplorable. This stops organizations from learning about their systems and practices and from being creative in finding new ways of doing things. They may even set up processes for improvement and think that they are looking at themselves. However, their thinking and assumptions are, in reality, about keeping these bad feelings of failure or anxiety at bay, rather than exploring the way things have been done. In this way the defenses become built into the organization, rather than just being an individual experience.

In some ways one can argue that the bureaucratic, many layered hierarchical organizations which were common until recently, with their power bases clearly and top-down defined, were ideal 'containers'. Everyone 'knew' who could be safely hated and where to locate bad feeling. Since real contact across vertical and horizontal divides was rare, no one was confronted much with the real people on to whom feelings were targeted. Those on the 'top floor', or in a distant town, or down the corridor could remain shadowy figures. Divisions of responsibility, carefully parcelled out, prevented anyone from feeling too exposed. Impersonal personnel systems took care of welfare and feeling issues, and removed the anxiety that one's self would not be acceptable; one's skills and merits in a specific job only were employed. Dealing with conflict was not a personal issue. The unions and management contained and managed the deep feelings of anger, resentment and hatred that existed. They did this through ritual and impersonal action.

Of course there were personality clashes and petty feuds with consequences for individuals, but as an organizational system it worked pretty well, and to some extent this situation persists. But we have had the 1980s and 1990s. In that decade or so, the edifices which had been so successful at containing the feelings generated by becoming involved with others in an enterprise, were disrupted and much was swept away.

Whilst the change from the industrial to the information society may throw up quite different needs for work management, these particular needs for managing emotions still have to be addressed. At the moment people are far more exposed in their work; responsibility is not divided and parcelled out; less division into minute aspects of the whole task leaves groups and individuals carrying much more responsibility in their jobs. Delayering and downsizing has left people dealing with the realities of other people's needs and managing interpersonal conflict themselves in a way that is much more challenging than before these changes began to occur. Dealing with our aggressive energy to fulfil ambitions is much harder in flatter structures where portfolio careers are expected and rivalry, competition and envy are submerged under the call for team achievement.

It is important that the organization makes the opportunity for people to explore their experience. It is also important that people are encouraged to recognize their experience as part of the organization, rather than simply taking it on board personally. Where there are personal issues raised then it is helpful to have somewhere within the organization to work those through. We look at this in the next chapter when we explore what to do to support managers and other individuals.

Successful containment of anxiety by the organization needs to be an area of focus and decisions made with this very much in mind. We recognize that it is an intangible notion. It is not as simple as putting another layer of management in place, or providing counselling for when anxiety gets too much. It is a tricky area to grapple with. However, without recognizing the vital importance of containing anxiety and being clear about how this is done, stress will continue to grow in the changing world of organizations. It is important for the organization to acknowledge the importance of this, and to help managers to consider what may be needed.

In addition to recognizing the need to provide containment of anxiety it is also helpful for the organization to consider what needs to be done to create an environment where empowerment can take place and members of staff grow in personal autonomy.

Developing autonomy in the organization

There has been much talk recently about the importance of empowerment in organizations. Empowerment is the process by which people are enabled to feel their personal power and can therefore take up the authority and responsibility that goes with their job. Enabling empowerment has been heralded as a key part of the leadership needed for today's organizations. It is also been put forward as fitting with the ethos of respect for staff. Empowerment, whereby staff gain an increased sense of their own personal power and autonomy is also a key way in which the organization can provide support. It is often introduced as the way forward and yet it is not easy for staff to increase their sense of their autonomy and feel their personal power. It is important to focus on what needs to be done at the organizational level to develop autonomy and thereby provide a more healthy and resilient environment.

Organizations talk about empowerment and bring about structural changes or different reward systems. But making structural changes and introducing new reward systems are not the way to develop a sense of being one's own person in difficult situations. There is more to it than that. It takes a mature ego in a well-defined and non-punitive context to really function autonomously. The organization needs to focus on creating such a context.

It is helpful to understand personal autonomy and how it works. People can only function autonomously if they are able to emotionally separate from authority figures and can access their personal, internal authority. Attachment to an authority figure can give us a sense of security that we are protected from blame and are not on our own in the organization.

When people are pressured into acting autonomously, there is an increase in anxiety, resentment and depression. To move from dependency, which is a feature of organizational life, to autonomy requires considerable adjustment. These include dealing with reactions against the authority for demanding it. Here we refer to the authority *role* not an individual manager's style of taking up that role. However, if the style of the organization is authoritarian, the possibility of coming out of the protection of authority figures is even more difficult.

Autonomous staff are not an undivided blessing for leaders either. It is not unknown for leaders to set up a system whereby the trappings of autonomous functioning appear to be in place, but in reality there is a much more symbiotic relationship between the leader and his or her staff. The nature of these relationships is partly dependent on the overall organization culture but is also a function of the individuals concerned. How do they relate to the exercise of authority and the demands of functioning in a less dependency-based relationship? Vicious circles can be set up in which fear and anxiety are managed by the junior in the relationship seeking the protection of the senior person. The senior person has their authoritarian aspects 'confirmed', and then acts this style out, which creates more fear and dependency which again activates authoritarian behaviour. This can continue indefinitely and does not further the development of autonomy.

Thus, in new organizations in which empowerment is embraced and people's autonomy is called for, managers need to create boundaries within which individuals can be autonomous. We have already emphasized the way in which pressures can be generated around organizational boundaries and how pressure increases when the boundaries are not clear. If a well-defined context is needed for healthy functioning, it highlights the importance of discussing and setting clear boundaries. Only then can people engage in the tasks productively and creatively.

A non-punitive context is also needed for autonomous functioning. This means that the culture of the organization may need attention. The phrase 'blame culture' has been used much recently and there is growing awareness within the world of organizations that such a thing can exist and may not be the most productive. That awareness needs to be encouraged and worked on within the organization to move the context from punitive to non-punitive, if autonomy is to grow.

Providing support by paying attention to organizational processes: how to pay attention to them

We have identified three areas of organizational life which warrant attention as a way of providing support. If the distinctions are made between different types of pressure it will provide a clearer focus as to where interventions need to be focused. If the need to contain anxiety is recognized, then the level of anxiety will not reach such intense proportions. If the context for empowerment can be provided, then autonomy will increase. However, there is still the question of how and where in the organization these issues get addressed.

In our experience the most effective way an organization can provide support is to provide the time and space for groups of people to process their own experience. This may be unfamiliar, but encouraging processing within work groups and teams is a vital contribution to providing support.

Encouraging team processing

Earlier we looked at two organizations dealing with stress. In the case of the organization with child protection responsibilities described in Chapter 5, there needed to be a forum for staff to express their distress and grief about some of the things which had happened in the organization. Staff needed to be encouraged to take up their professional and managerial authority to address the splits that had been created in the organization. This had to take place in a safe enough environment for feelings to be talked about. Such an environment is not personal counselling for everyone involved, although that may be appropriate in a few cases. The setting had to enable people to share their feelings and for these to be publicly acknowledged. The process had to develop a collective vision for the future. The senior managers needed to develop a sense that they could all create the future they wanted for the organization together. Such work is not a gripe session but of the nature that makes real the possibility of joint action to shape the future.

This work began with a change of routine in the regular management conference. Instead of the usual presentations on initiatives and feedback on progress, several dozen top managers met to begin a quite different journey. A day spent with us processing their collective experience and hopes for the future was the start point. During this conference people talked for the first time with their colleagues and management team members about what the experience of the last few years had been like. There were some extremely hard things said. A few people in particular felt able to speak out in the large forum and this paved the way for smaller group work. A wide range of emotions was revealed, the things people said were listened to with respect and often what one person spoke of moved another to share their reactions and experiences. People shared different perceptions and feelings. This shared understanding was sufficient, not to forget what had happened, but to begin the process of moving forward without needing to hang on to these feelings that were now part of the openly acknowledged collective history of the organization. This happened because a forum was provided for the processing to take place.

Providing a forum to allow and encourage groups to process their experience needs to take place at all levels in the organization. However, there is a particular role played by the top team which is far more than simply adding all the individual responsibilities held by the different people. The top team in particular needs to have a forum and develop familiarity and the skills needed to process pressures. Issues which are left unattended in the top team can have a far-reaching impact on the whole organization. Thus a crucial part of the work done at the organizational level is helping the top team to review their roles and the way their values and dynamics affect the organization. The availability of the top team for discussion on these issues varies enormously from organization to organization. Our experience is that the more the top group is willing to look at the psychological aspects of its working on the organization, the more the rest of the organization can perceive that the espoused policies on stress are taken seriously and are being addressed at all levels. People do not need to have any knowledge of the discussions behind closed doors; the impact will still be apparent.

When we work with organizations on their stress initiatives, we suggest that they seek the commitment of the top team in principle to having an organizational push on stress. Getting the whole team on board rather than just the general manager, chief executive or MD makes it easier to come back later to work with the team. In addition, the top team may well benefit from looking at the pressures they are themselves under, in terms of reducing their own stress. They may also begin to see the role they play in shaping the culture of the organization and how they may be passing the pressures they experience around the system. This can be achieved in a number of ways, from being part of a regular meeting to specific time off site to address organizational stress. The key issue is that this does not turn into a 'blame the managers' day. The point is to explore the pressure in the whole system of which they are a key part, in terms of their own experiences, of what is put on to them internally and externally and how this affects them and the broader system.

It is also important to work with other senior groups who have an impact on the culture and practices of the bit of the organization which is addressing stress. That depends on the organization; it may be the departmental directorate or divisional management team or the main board. It is not enough that the most senior team engages in processing their experience and recognizing the role they play in the stress system, this needs to happen with management teams throughout the organization.

The key for providing support at the organizational level is that the management groups who carry a large responsibility for the working of the organization come to recognize their role in setting the culture and providing pressures, as well as monitoring targets.

We have looked at areas where the process within organizations needs to be looked at in order to provide support. We have emphasized the importance of providing time and space for the processing of experience to enable movement forward. This processing needs to take account of the distinction between different types of pressure, the working of the top team and other senior groupings, what is needed to develop autonomy and how anxiety is contained. We are aware that these are unusual items for a management agenda, but they are needed to move forward to manage stress.

Now we will go on and look at what might be more familiar territory, how support can be provided by putting structures into place in the organization.

Putting in place structures in the organization to provide support

Many organizations feel that to be credible in encouraging well-being at work and reducing stress, they need to put in place some structural changes to provide some benefits which are tangible and practical expressions of this strategy. There are many worthwhile things that can be done here. Some options involve rethinking existing provision, others will require expenditure. The benefit is both the actual assistance with a healthier lifestyle and the psychological benefit of working in an organization that takes well-being seriously.

Such options have included healthier menu choices in canteens, wellness checks with a health centre paid for by the organization and often done in working hours, fitness centres or membership of fitness centres. Although larger organizations may have their own centres for these, smaller organizations can still take action. A small enterprise, for example, discovered that the nearby university gave preferential and very cheap corporate membership to local companies for its fitness centre and swimming pool.

One organization found that as it put its stress plan into action the key issue was not what was provided (it actually did quite a lot already) but how this was packaged, advertised and put together with the stress plan was what mattered. It is important to plan how facilities are 'sold' to staff. It is not enough simply to inform people of their existence. In this case, previously provided services to staff became used much more after the re-packaging and selling. A leaflet outlining the nature of stress and how it could be tackled was sent to all staff. In this leaflet all of the existing provision was highlighted, for example training courses, such as report writing and time management, not usually 'sold' as stress reduction, were included alongside the occupational health facilities.

Out of the variety of options available, we would like to focus on three: changes in working arrangements, providing pauses for the organization and setting up support groups.

Changes in working arrangements

The possibility of working in quite different patterns will arise in most organizations for a variety of reasons, not solely in relation to stress management. However, they do give an opportunity for reducing some of the pressures people experience, such as commuting and problems with dropping children off at school and so on. The more these kinds of life issues are picked up and supported by the way organizations structure the working day, the more energy staff have for their work.

It is important to see another side to this as well as the certain benefits. Homeworking has many advantages and is enjoyed by those who can do it. It also means that the organization can save on resources with 'hot-desking' and so on. Where these savings are made, however, they may have a detrimental impact on the employee's commitment to the organization and positive sense of belonging and identification. This, despite all the difficulties in working with others, is a key benefit of having a job. The social contact and sense of belonging is not entirely met with email contact.

It is possible to tackle this in different ways, depending on resources. Some organizations enable staff to keep a permanent desk in the office even though it is used less. Some set people up in teams with a recognized social dimension, with regular meetings on joint tasks. Others are paying more attention to social gatherings, and not disguising them confusingly as 'team builds' or 'strategy away days', acknowledging their purpose and content. One organization has thought of having 'local offices'. These would be joint ventures with other organizations who were also widely scattered and had many homeworkers. Office facilities would be provided and staff could go into these offices, which would have a full-time administrator, to use facilities and meet other 'regulars', who work in other organizations but also live locally. This may sound futuristic, but highlights the need to be creative in meeting people's needs as the nature of working life changes.

Organizational pauses

The idea of organizational pauses arose with one client organization as we were talking about the pressure people were under. It came from the metaphor of physical training to take part in a sport. In doing physical training people have been found to benefit from a particular regime; you train hard for a certain period, say three weeks, allowing what you do to get progressively tougher. Then the next week, instead of pushing yourself even harder, you actually ease off, without stopping altogether. Then you go back to the progressively tougher regime, then ease off again and so on. People's fitness levels are higher than if they had just kept pushing and pushing. We felt this was a really good analogy for the fitness needed for running the 'organizational marathons' people find themselves in. What we then reflected on was that many of the 'ticking over' periods have gone from organizational life: the slack time, the three-week training programme, the long business lunch.

What is needed in an organizational pause is not the annual holiday entitlement, but time which is work-focused but not so pressured as the rest of the time. Again this may reflect a need for creative new responses to discovering what appropriate 'organizational pause' could be incorporated into the organization's practice.

Setting up support groups

Setting up support groups for different groups within the organization provides a good mechanism for embedding support in the system. Such groups when run well can provide a safe place for people to explore and make sense of their experience, but you do need to structure them to be effective. The time taken up with these also needs to be acknowledged as part of the workload, rather than just another thing to slot in.

By setting up support groups people can discover that experiences are shared. This lessens isolation. Support groups can also be a forum where action planning takes place to deal with the pressures of being in the organization. Support groups have been found to be particularly helpful for groups who are less used to being in the organizational lime-light, such as minority ethnic groups of staff, women and more junior staff. Some organizations provide financial support for these or for associated network structures.

The integrating factor

There is a range of things that can be done at the organizational level to provide support. These can have a big impact on the well-being of people at work. However, you really only make a big impact when you keep in mind what is going on in the organization as a whole. This involves thinking how the subsystems relate to each other and how individuals and the organization interrelate as part of the bigger picture.

But remember that the aim of all this activity is to keep pressure at an optimum level so that people are ready and energized and capable of their best work and creative effort; if the vision is lost sight of, then it will seem like another load of pressure to exacerbate that already present! This is really crucial if those championing this work are to find ongoing enthusiasm for it, rather than it becoming a tick-done list.

When considering what can be done at the organizational level, it is tempting to focus on what can be put in place in the organization structure. This is more familiar territory. However, putting in place structures you still need to pay attention to processes. A really good initiative will not work as well unless there is time and space given to allow people to process their experience. A healthy menu, good sports facilities, working from home, for example, do not help the process of understanding what is happening and being able to move forward.

Providing support to the organization

To keep in mind the scope of what we are suggesting in this chapter, it may be helpful to draw an analogy with investigating accidents. If an accident at work occurs in which serious damage is done, it is usual to hold an inquiry. There are two ways of approaching this. The first is to follow every event leading up to the accident to pinpoint the moment when something went wrong and then to put right whatever procedure or mechanism that failed. In this process the person or persons who caused the accident can be traced and so they can be punished or re-trained as appropriate. The alternative view is that an accident occurs because many small things come together at one point to create the conditions for the accident to occur. There is no one single cause but a series of events that means that at that moment disaster strikes. With this perspective it is more appropriate to take a complete audit of what these are, to try to change the whole system to make it safer and prevent the accumulation of problems. Everyone has a part to play in evaluating what they can do in their role to make the system safer. Many things may get put right in this case. The 'problem', though, is that no 'culprit' will be found. Some people will find this disturbing because eliminating a culprit may give one the sense that nothing will now go wrong. People feel safer after firing the person to 'blame'. However, they may actually be safer if everyone takes part in changing the system. This is really what we mean by support to the organization; looking at the whole will enable people to look at the accumulation of events that may lead to a percentage of people getting stressed. Processing experience together enables people to manage their anxieties well enough to figure out how things can be seen from new perspectives and tackled differently.

Key points in Chapter 7

■ Providing support is the main way to manage stress.
■ Providing support means reducing pressure or putting buoyancy aids in place.
■ There are three levels at which support can be given: organizational, managerial and individual.
■ Support in organizational processes as well as structures is important.
■ Providing time and space for people, individuals and teams to process their experience is vital.
■ It is helpful to make distinctions between different types of pressure.
■ The context needs to be set for developing autonomy.
■ Understanding the nature of containing anxiety is crucial.
■ The system as a whole needs to be borne in mind.
■ Putting in new facilities or structures without providing means for processing experience will lessen their impact and value.

Options for providing support at the managerial and personal levels

Providing support to managers

As we now move the focus to the managerial and personal levels, it is important to make one thing clear. We are aware that managers are people and therefore have as much need for support at the individual level as any other member of staff. However as a manager within an organization, there is a clear role and part of the role is acting on behalf of the organization. When a senior manager does something, it is taken as an action of the organization. Therefore we will be focusing in this chapter on the support that can be given to managers in their role as managers in dealing with stress, although they may also benefit from the options available for individuals.

Managers at all levels need to get to grips with the subject. They need to know what it is and what can be done about it and what to look out for in their staff. They need a briefing on this information fast, because staff will be raising issues with them, particularly once stress is well and truly on the organization's agenda.

Managing stress levels in the part of the organization for which they are accountable and in staff who report to them, is a central facet of the manager's role, as we see it. This is because pressure level is so connected with performance level and, above all else, a manager has responsibility for ensuring maximum performance. There is an additional responsibility as legal rulings require managers to manage the well-being of their staff. Failure to deal effectively with stress can now be grounds for grievance against a line manager. Ignorance of stress is no longer a defence against grievance procedures and can even be grounds for harrassment charges.

This means that no longer can managers plead ignorance about stress in the workplace and its management. However, managers do need to be supported in getting to grips with the topic. As we have been emphasizing, stress management is a potentially sensitive subject and one which can be perceived as threatening to managers in their role. So there is a clear need to support managers in dealing with stress as it arises.

In addition, attention needs to be paid to the managers' role in managing stress by preventing it. They need to be supported to take on board the impact of their own behaviour on the working of their section. This can be done through training and awareness initiatives and through work with their teams on collective measures to deal with stress. These will also help in looking at the fit between individuals and their jobs.

We will give two examples of the critical role that a manager's actions can have on the individual's experience of stress. One is given as an example of how a manager alleviated a very stressful time for a member of staff. The other shows how it is possible for a manager uncomfortable with dealing with stress to actually make the situation worse.

The case of the supportive manager

This case took place in a further education college. The college was facing severe financial difficulties and a new principal had been appointed to get things in order. The number of students applying for certain courses was dropping and the college was faced with possible drastic action in order to balance the books. This is not at all an unusual scenario. Eventually and with a heavy heart the new principal realized that redundancies were going to have to be made. She did not like having to do this but, having considered at length all other options, came to the conclusion that redundancies it would have to be.

Staff first heard of this when the rumour started circulating like wildfire that redundancies were going to be made. This was before any formal announcement from the college management. Partial information was being passed round and there was agreement as to which departments were likely to be affected, based on declining student numbers.

One particular teacher, who had not long been at the college, realized that she was likely to be in the firing line of any redundancies. The possibility hit her hard. This person was a single parent and also loved her job. On hearing the rumour, she became ill and was off work for two days. On her return to work, the Assistant Principal sought her out for a talk. The content and quality of this talk was what made all the difference to the teacher's feelings.

First, the manager sought the teacher out. There was no summons from on high. The topic was addressed straight, with no beating around the bush. The manager spoke as a human being who was concerned at the impact of the rumour on this person. He also made it quite clear that this teacher's work was highly valued and that it was not personal. As a result of a half-hour talk, the teacher felt quite differently. The situation had not changed. The manager had made no vague promises and was not reassuring her that all would be well. But the experience of knowing that she was recognized and deemed important enough for a visit from a senior manager, and the open and straightforward quality of the discussion swung the balance. As a result of the meeting the teacher viewed it as a potentially difficult problem, not an overwhelming catastrophe. This was all due to the intervention and skill of one manager.

The next step was that her worst nightmares did come true and she received a redundancy notice. However, she felt so empowered by the discussion with the senior manager and so convinced that she would be heard by management, that when the Principal offered to see all the people concerned, the teacher asked for a meeting. At the meeting with the Principal, the teacher was clear as to why she wanted the meeting. She wanted to discuss the chances of moving into other areas of work within the college. She did not go in to moan or blame and found again a human, open reception. As a result of both these meetings, what could have been an intensely stressful experience was turned into merely an intensely difficult one. It was not the fact that the meetings were held, it was how the managers conducted themselves and treated the member of staff that made the difference.

The case of the unsupportive manager

This case took place within a university department. It involved the head of the department and the administrative staff. There were two administrative staff in post and over the years difficulties arose between them. The Assistant Administrator came to feel increasingly bullied and harassed by his line manager, the Senior Administrator. Eventually things reached such a peak of discomfort that he sought out the Head of Department who was the line manager of his boss. Initially the Head of Department was sympathetic and said that these difficulties would have to be resolved. A series of meetings was held as well as personal discussions with the distressed person. However, these conversations did nothing to help the Assistant Administrator, who had found it difficult enough to talk of his problem in the first place. Gradually he began to sense impatience in the Head of Department and began to suspect that the Head of Department was taking sides – with the Senior Administrator. At that point the Assistant began to feel very unsafe. In a quandary as to where to turn to resolve what had become an untenable position, he went to the personnel department. Again they listened but did not propose any solution or route to solution. The Assistant struggled on to do his job, feeling unsupported.

Finally the Head of Department also came to the realization that this could not continue. This realization dawned after the situation had been steadily deteriorating for nearly three years. The solution was to move both people, one to a higher job, the other to early retirement. There was no personal discussion with the Assistant, it was all done through formal channels. The Assistant felt by then that he had little choice but to take the early retirement and left, to an outcry from the rest of the department who had not known what was happening.

In this case the financial deal was generous and it could be argued that the Assistant should be pleased at such an offer. However, the way the matter had been handled left the Assistant with a generous payoff and a mountain of bitter and difficult feelings to deal with. Any stress that was inherent in the original situation was magnified by the manner in which the manager took action.

These two cases demonstrate a very key skill needed by managers in any organization, providing a holding environment. We will look at what this means before we go on to suggest some specific ways in which managers can be supported.

Providing a holding environment

The concept of a 'holding environment' comes originally from the notion of what good enough parenting does for the infant. The environment needs to be sufficiently supportive for the child to experiment and for it to do so without feeling the full force of its dependency and vulnerability. At first the child needs the presence of the parent or caregiver; eventually the holding environment is internalized and in the mind.

In the adult version of this, the holding environment enables the person to work through their anxieties and to face reality, without losing track of the difficulty of the task. It holds the projections, hence the term holding environment, and remains clear both about the task and what is projected. It is thus an extension of the notion of 'container'. By not 'buying into' all the fantasies around it enables people to explore their world in a different way.

As pressure mounts and anxiety increases as organizations change, rather than resorting to old practices or developing new defensive routines and structures, something different needs to be provided. To enable this, the environment needs to provide a sufficiently safe place for people to explore and understand their experience so that alternative structures for handling anxiety can be generated. Instead of the staff getting out of touch with the realities of the task in order to manage feelings, which can happen, other more appropriate ways can be discovered. These need to be more in tune with the tasks to be done, and be less rigidified or codified into the organization. This is only possible if the managers in the organization recognize the importance of this and provide the appropriate mechanisms, such as processing work with their groups, as we discussed in Chapter 7, or with individuals.

Firstly, there needs to be discussion of the nature of the task. What is it that people are actually coming together to do? This needs to be clarified and discussed. It needs to be clear what the authority structures are in relation to the task and who decides what it is. There need to be multiple forms of debate about this so that people are able to explore their understanding, their feelings and their ideas. The discussion can then go on to the roles people take up in the group and how they manage their boundaries with other groups and what they have put into them, what the expectations are of other groups and what they take on board from other groups that may not be appropriate. For example, in working with a human resources group it was apparent that the members felt that the organization at large had a view that this was the group who took care of people. The group members were running themselves ragged trying to meet this expectation, whereas their business role was quite differently and specifically defined.

Managers need to give time and create space which enables people to share the anxieties and difficulties that arise from the work they do. People on management development programmes often remark that one benefit is being able to share experiences of stress or unhappiness with some aspects of work and find that they are not alone. However, it is important to have that opportunity closer to home with people who share the organizational aspects of the experience or the professional connection and understanding.

This places demands on managers to deal with difficult and sensitive issues well and be clear about the nature of the environment they create. It is possible that some managers have an instinctive grasp of what is needed. However, the organization cannot leave that to chance and therefore needs to plan a way of giving support to develop the awareness, understanding and skill of managers.

Developing managerial skill in managing stress

A good start for you would be a seminar to give managers basic information about stress and what is expected of them in their managerial role. This would cover the fact that they are not expected to turn overnight into expert counsellors. They also need to know what the policies of the organization are and, very importantly, where they can go for more information and support as managers. Back up this seminar with a supporting leaflet, which can also be kept handy and given to managers who could not attend the dates offered. This starts the process of providing support to managers.

The next step is follow-up training for managers who are interested after the initial seminar on stress and their staff. This enables them to explore more fully their role in helping staff and can cover issues such as what to do with staff with severe problems such as drink and drugs, how to use basic helping/counselling skills to understand what is going on with staff, and how to provide an appropriate environment for staff to develop tactics for dealing with the issues arising at work which lead to stress.

Many successful training courses have been run for managers and have indeed increased understanding and awareness. However, managers need help to engage actively in their role of containing anxiety and helping their staff work with these issues. Managers need to have support systems which enable them to cope and at the same time maintain their management and leadership roles in the organization.

Executive coaching for managers

A form of support for managers which is growing in demand, is that of one-to-one executive coaching or consulting. This should be distinguished from counselling although on the surface it may sound the same. Executive coaching sessions focus on the managers in their role: how they manage the expectations of others, how they work with and negotiate with other parts of the organization and all other facets of their work as managers. The focus is on the kinds of systemic issues which were explored in Part II, helping managers to understand the part they are playing in these dynamics.

This type of work often accompanies other work that looks at the processes of the organization described here. We are experiencing more interest in this type of work as managers struggle to define and develop their role in managing new forms of organization and the demands of stress management.

The focus of this work is to help managers explore their experience and understand the feelings arising from their work and work relationships and to understand what function these have in the context of the organization culture and in terms of the tasks they do. This work is best undertaken with a consultant who takes the perspective of the managers' experience of the system as a whole. Whilst people may talk about their personal experience or relationship with a particular person, it is not intended to use such a session as individual counselling/therapy but as data for understanding what is happening to the manager and what part he or she is playing in the greater scheme of the wider organization. This includes the immediate work group, so it is a useful addition to the work done with the team.

This kind of work is appropriate for managers with teams who are trying to carve out new roles in the organization, where teams are put together to work on whole tasks which used to be done by separate groups, perhaps putting together diverse skills and perspectives, as well as groups who are under obvious strain because of their particular position in the organization. The training or coaching work outlined above may lead on to working with managers in their groups which they manage.

Assisting managers to work on stress collectively in their teams

This work encompasses the sorting out of unnecessary, inevitable and necessary pressures outlined in Chapter 7, but can also lead to discussion of the more hidden aspects of group life. For this work it can be useful to use a consultant to create an appropriate environment for this exploration. This enables the manager to take a full part in the discussions. The consultant can enable a space to be created which is recognizably separate from the usual meetings and away days and which is safe enough for people to process their experience of their work together.

In an organization we work with, this approach has begun. Alongside the stress awareness and stress management training and other wellness initiatives, the organization is using consultants to work with managers and their groups on their experience of stress. One feature of this is to explore the 'shadow' side of the positive values and culture which inform conduct in the organization. The intention is not to undermine these people-oriented values but to explore the impact of them on people and groups. Since real people are not simplistically positive and energetic but complex, these less 'acceptable' (in this context) aspects of people need to be respected too, and integrated into the creativity of the workplace. There are no formulaic answers on offer, but this work helps managers work with their groups to find their own means of expression.

We have looked at providing support at the managerial level. The final level at which to consider intervention is the personal level, providing support to individuals within the organization.

Providing support to individuals

Support can be provided to individual members of staff in three main ways which are familiar in many organizations and have been found to be very helpful. They are: providing employee counselling schemes, providing guides to stress management and stress management training. As these are widely understood and used a great deal already, we devote less space to these than the newer activities outlined above.

Employee counselling schemes

These are important organizational systems for supporting individuals. Many organizations employ outside trained counsellors, who are available for confidential consultation. Similarly some occupational health centres offer such assistance. We have also been involved with setting up 'peer counselling'. This was the method adopted by a police force which felt that officers would relate better to other officers, who would understand the nature of the work. They believed that external counsellors would not be taken seriously because they did not share the values and experiences of the officers. Selected officers were given a year-long training programme and support from the organization to develop appropriate counselling skills.

This highlights an important aspect of any counselling scheme. It does not offer long-term therapy for the person seeking help, although it may well address some deeply held attitudes and beliefs that stop the person from dealing differently with their situation. The importance of the circumstances and context of the organization need to be understood. In particular the fact that the organization has stress on its agenda should enable the person who has sought help confidentially, to have the confidence to go back to their manager and raise issues, if it is appropriate to do so, or go elsewhere in the organization. They should not feel that the benefits gained in counselling cannot be implemented or raised outside. For example, if they decide that their workload needs to be addressed, they need to feel that their concern will be taken seriously. This is not to say that the organization is committed to actions requested, but that consideration of what action is needed, will be given.

Many people have found enormous benefit from support from these sources.

Propagation of stress awareness material and guides for staff

The circulation of stress awareness material and guides is aimed at putting general knowledge about stress around the organization. Many organizations have designed and circulated a guideline booklet. These can be aimed at managers who need to become aware of stress and watch out for stress in others, or at managers and staff who want to take care of themselves. These may overlap with each other and with more in-depth training outlined below, but have different aims.

What can be offered to staff at the launch of a new stress policy is a booklet which focuses on the individual and gives basic information on stress, and where to go if you need further information and assistance in the organization. This is backed up with a leaflet which highlights new resources, but may also include facilities which have been provided before but encourage further take up.

Both of these offerings need to be backed up by the organizational tactics and group work, and by training available for managers and staff.

Stress management training programmes

Stress management programmes aimed at improving personal skills of managing stress have been part of the repertoire of organizational stress management techniques for many years. These programmes are usually designed to give staff an awareness of stress, and some guidelines for managing it more effectively. Such training has been found to be very useful in equipping staff with further skills to manage the pressure and do their job well. However, they do need to be part of an overall strategy and not be seen as the single solution to stress management in the organization. Although staff may well have personal issues which contribute to their experience of stress in the organization, that is not the whole of the picture, as we have been emphasizing.

Therefore well run training programmes for increasing personal stress management skills are very helpful to include in the package of measures proposed, in addition to a focus on the other two levels of support at the organizational and managerial level.

A comprehensive package of material or a training programme on stress for individuals will need to cover a number of areas. People need to take from these some understanding of what pressure and stress are, an ability to sort out for themselves what they experience when pressure is wrong for them, an understanding of the sources of pressure they are under and some personal strategies for becoming more resilient in the face of high pressure. We do not favour symptom checklists but encourage people to understand their own healthy and less healthy ways of functioning. Sources of pressure include the internal drivers that can get in the way of managing pressure and increase the pressure we put ourselves under. For this reason we regard many personal development programmes that explore these as very helpful in avoiding stress. Some of these issues were introduced in Chapter 6.

Strategies for dealing with stress at the personal level include healthy physical lifestyles, but also focus on balance of activities, personal support and finding calm and tranquil spaces, as well as fun and excitement, and work and a workplace that suit one's personal style. It is a range of preventive strategies which people need to be encouraged to use, despite a busy existence.

Keeping the context in mind when providing support to individuals

Even when exploring quite personal issues we need to keep the context in mind. People need to feel identified positively with their leaders and with the organization because this is one aspect of their social identity. Joining an organization means that people have to adapt. Adaptation may require us to give up or disregard certain aspects of ourselves in order to belong. There may be limits to the extent to which we can do that without distress. For most people it is a question of adapting whilst retaining important qualities they identify with. We select organizations sufficiently in tune with our self so that appropriate modification is possible for us.

However, in the process of joining, people may find a fit with the organization which is not good for them in all respects. They may be quite prone to take on too much or fall into an overly supportive role, for example, which may suit the organization in some way. They may have a propensity to 'overdo' such aspects of themselves. If it is not held in check they may find themselves stressed. In another setting which does not 'pull' this behaviour for them so strongly, they may be able to modify their potentially self-destructive side.

To deal with these issues people need access to personal support systems; in particular with someone who can combine working with the personal dimension with an understanding of how this can resonate with the system/organization a whole. This can help the individual understand how they operate in relation to the psychological system/context they are in. This can be provided through coaching or the kind of group work outlined above and is different from the employee counselling scheme.

To the extent that people can hang on to the fact that their experience is a result of the role that they have in the organization, and that many things are not simply a personal issue, they may be able to cope more effectively. To the extent that what is happening touches on something they find hard to deal with, they may be pulled out of their role and find themselves reacting in a personal and often unsophisticated way. This is because it taps into an unresolved or undeveloped

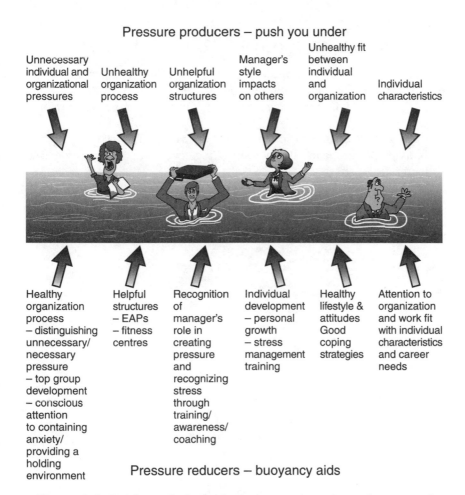

Pressure producers – push you under

| Unnecessary individual and organizational pressures | Unhealthy organization process | Unhelpful organization structures | Manager's style impacts on others | Unhealthy fit between individual and organization | Individual characteristics |

Pressure reducers – buoyancy aids

| Healthy organization process – distinguishing unnecessary/ necessary pressure – top group development – conscious attention to containing anxiety/ providing a holding environment | Helpful structures – EAPs – fitness centres | Recognition of manager's role in creating pressure and recognizing stress through training/ awareness/ coaching | Individual development – personal growth – stress management training | Healthy lifestyle & attitudes Good coping strategies | Attention to organization and work fit with individual characteristics and career needs |

Figure 8.1 Getting a balance between pressure producers and pressure reducers

aspect of themselves. This is where one-to-one work can help to clarify the position.

We have considered the two further levels of providing support at the managerial and personal level in this chapter. When added to the awareness of options possible at the organizational level for providing support, you can now be equipped with the necessary information in order to develop the content of your organizational stress management plan. As we have explored in Chapters 7 and 8 (Part III of this book), providing support involves paying attention to the pressure producers and dealing with these in the organization. It also involves providing the buoyancy aids needed to keep people afloat – increasing the pressure reducers. Both structures and processes are involved in this work. This is illustrated in Figure 8.1.

Key points in Chapter 8

- Managers need to be supported in their role in managing stress.
- Support for managers could include awareness and training.
- Managers may find executive coaching supports them in their managerial role.
- Managers need support to work with their teams in managing stress.
- Individuals can benefit from counselling schemes, stress training and materials on stress.

Part IV
Putting Stress Management in Place Effectively in Your Organization

S trategic Approach
for
T op Performance
and a
R evitalized Organization
depends on
E motional Focus
with
S ystemic Thinking
to develop a
S upportive Environment

In this part of the book we move on to cover the final component of the STRESS model: the strategic aspect.

We have looked at the key elements of emotional focus, systemic thinking and understanding what the concept of supportive options entails. These form the basis of the work that needs to be done for effective stress management. All that is left now is to put together a strategy and develop an appropriate plan for implementing it for your organization. No two organizations are the same, what works well in one may not work so well in another. What is needed is a strategic approach, information on the situation in your organization and political skill to see it through a successful course.

In Chapter 9 we look at what is needed to get a strategy off the ground. In Chapter 10 we focus on collecting data on stress in your organization. In Chapter 11 we look at how to pull it all together in a way which will work well in your organization. In the Endnote we provide a summary of how to put our new approach into action.

What you need to do to get your stress management strategy off the ground

However you have become involved in looking at stress management in your organization, it is crucial that you do not find yourself carrying the burden of progressing this topic alone. Stress management is a sensitive and potentially emotive topic within organizations. Whatever the current situation you face, in order to design a suitable strategy which will lead to successful organizational change, you will need support. The most successful strategies which we have encountered have been led by a group of people. We have worked with many which have all been drawn up differently, but they have all had one thing in common. They have all developed cohesion around a sense of shared purpose.

Whatever the origin of interest in the area, there will be benefit from the support of others who are equally interested in the topic, albeit from a different perspective. One stress management group which proceeded to bring about quite spectacular change was initiated by the trades unions. They were the first people to take an interest in this topic and put pressure on the personnel department to get involved. Eventually the personnel officer did become involved and a group which was composed of union officials, personnel officers and senior managers became the driving force for tackling stress. The personnel director who then involved the unions, the occupational health professionals and someone from the legal department to cover the legal aspects initiated another stress management group. The director of personnel and involved representatives of each department set up a third group. Another organization used an existing employee group who were interested in a variety of aspects of employee well-being and who turned their attention to stress.

There is no one format which guarantees success, but there is a formula which may help you to draw up a supportive and productive group.

Each person should have some relationship to the topic of stress and its management. We have argued in this book that stress is, or rather should be, of concern to each and every manager. However, at this early stage of building an interest group the useful formula is to firstly identify people who know about the topic. This may involve personnel people, occupational health professionals or lawyers. The basis for their involvement is that they have some knowledge or expertise to bring to bear.

But knowledge alone is not enough. It is also helpful to involve people who care about the topic. Knowledge and caring about the topic is a very powerful combination but the final ingredient is to involve people who are in a position to do something about it, people who can influence the organization and people who have a position of authority and power. Considering people who can influence the organization raises the role of the senior managers. You may find on reflecting on the current situation that the senior management team have shown neither a great deal of knowledge nor has there been much evidence of caring about stress management. However, they are very definitely in a position to do something about it and therefore cannot be ignored. Even if they do not join the group their backing for the group is essential.

It is useful at this early stage to involve those people who have time to give to taking stress management further rather than aiming for the ideal group. It is better to have a group of committed energetic people than those who feel they have been coerced or who attend meetings under duress. Once the people have been identified and have expressed at the very least willingness if not overt enthusiasm for the task ahead, the first step is to convene a meeting. Again it is worth bearing in mind the fact that stress management is a sensitive topic and therefore patience is a suitable frame of mind in which to approach this task. Successful strategies take a considerable amount of time and energy to design and it cannot happen immediately.

The aim in bringing together an interest group for tackling stress management is to ensure that no one person holds the whole responsibility, that the process of sharing the task throughout the organization starts at the outset and no one person feels isolated in taking this topic forward. The isolation of the person who champions this area can be a real possibility. If the organizational culture is one that is ambivalent, if not openly hostile, to having this topic raised and openly discussed, then the organizational system may take steps to reject the individual who is causing discomfort. It may do this by marginalizing the person, ignoring them or being hostile. None of these are comfortable options and at the very least to try and ensure the success of the strategy and avoid personal isolation, the building of an interest group bound together by a shared interest or concern with stress management is a necessary step.

Once the group has started working, it will need political skill to progress towards a successful stress management initiative. We will now look at what we mean by political skill.

Political skill: essential for designing an organizational stress management strategy

Every organization is a political environment. We do not mean that organizations are driven by party politics, nor are they political with a big P. Rather we recognize that in any organization there are a variety of different interests, points of view, access to power and influence and that wherever there is such a variety of standpoints, there is the need for skill to navigate through the cross currents. This is particularly necessary when considering the new approach to organizational stress management.

Engaging political skill enables you to avoid some of the pitfalls in organizational life in which your considered and objective arguments may be insufficient to win the day. For your arguments to be taken on board the key elements need to be positioned in such a way that people's sensitivities are not trodden on and that they can understand how your proposal fits with their perspective on the world. To achieve this you need to be able to read what is going on around you from other people's perspectives and put together different pieces of information to get the whole picture. So attention needs to be paid to connecting to the particular environment in which this initiative is to progress. Attention needs to be on reading the world around you.

Equally there needs to be attention paid to the internal world of the people who are taking the initiative forward. This is the second dimension of political skill in organizations, the awareness of what you are carrying with you through the exercise. You need an awareness of the roots of your position as well as the experience others bring, both of which may influence how you handle the difficulties in persuading power brokers in the organization to put stress management centrally on the agenda.

The dimensions of reading and carrying form the basis of the political skill which is going to be needed to begin working in the sensitive area of stress management. The topic is potentially emotive, therefore there is always the possibility that a stress management strategy itself will give rise to emotions. So not only is stress itself emotional in origin but any intervention to alleviate it may give rise to another layer of emotion. People may be actively for or against bringing stress on to centre stage in the organization. Thus one of the aspects of political skill that is needed is the ability to recognize and read attitudes and excuses for and against stress management.

Part of the analysis that needs to be undertaken at this stage is an awareness of what people's hopes and expectations are for any stress management initiative and how they compare with your own agenda. Bringing together your aspirations and the organization's will behind an initiative that will work in your culture is the outcome that this new approach can realize.

You may find that there are attempts to marginalize your work, your arguments may be met with indifference, even hostility. You may experience impatience, have feelings of exasperation or even anger. These will require managing. That is part of being aware of what you are carrying. Skilful awareness of the carrying dimension means constantly acknowledging and checking out what you are carrying and maintaining contact with present thoughts and feelings. Difficulties can occur if you are going into this exercise only in order to increase your own status, gain kudos and improve your curriculum vitae. That will lead to your focus being on your own advancement alone and may take your focus away from the advancement of the desired organizational outcomes. You will have your own reasons for being involved in the area but it is helpful if you can maintain awareness of those at the same time as focusing on the organizational outcomes you are striving towards. Unskillful political actions involve focusing on your own ends to the exclusion of the organization.

You may also find yourself tempted into a defensive position by the reaction of others to your initiatives. This can occur when you experience lack of interest from others. It can be tempting at that point to be only too aware of your own response, be it frustration or annoyance or however you experience it. One senior manager we worked with spent many weeks conducting interviews to ascertain the level of stress experienced within the organization. She worked hard on a report which was scheduled to be presented to the management team. The report was allowed half an hour. The manager recognized that the management team were busy people and had many items to consider. However, it did strike her that if there was willingness to put resources into the gathering of data, by allowing her to spend six weeks on the project, then maybe half an hour was a short time to devote to considering the results. She carried these feelings into the meeting. At the end of the debate, which she viewed as rather superficial and inconclusive, she was left with feelings of disappointment and resentment. At that stage she was tempted to get angry and hostile towards the team or withdraw from any further involvement in trying to take stress management forward. She was drawn into the familiar pattern of wanting to take issue with or withdraw from a situation where the reaction of others to her efforts appeared to belittle her work. This is the familiar fight or flight pattern being triggered. This is a particularly vulnerable moment for whoever is putting effort into tackling stress management strategically. It is the moment when it is tempting to focus on your own responses and take the eye off the organizational objectives.

This example shows that the two dimensions of reading and carrying in the political situation interact. What you are carrying in terms of feelings at any moment will be influenced by what you are reading in the situation. The seeds for this manager's resentment were sown when she did not act on her views that half an hour was too short a time to give to considering the results of the stress data gathering exercise. The information available to her was that half an hour was scheduled for the item. She read this as providing evidence of lack of interest on the part of the management team. She found this confusing as they had given considerable resources to the gathering of the data, by allowing six weeks of a senior manager's time, and she felt belittled. What she carried into the meeting was influenced by how she read the situation.

The interaction between the two dimensions can also work in the other direction. The ability to read a situation clearly is influenced by what is being carried. Again using the same example, we would hazard a guess that this particular manager's ability to read the meeting accurately was hindered by the growing feelings of resentment with which she presented her report. She may not have expected a high level of interest and therefore could have simply seen what she expected to see.

There are plenty of potential pitfalls on the route to a successful strategic stress management approach. We know from experience that it will not necessarily be either simple or easy to move the organization forwards. In order to deal with the barriers and difficulties which may be faced when introducing an organizational stress management initiative using the new approach, the political skills of reading and carrying are essential.

We will move on to consider how the two dimensions can be used to inform the analysis of the current situation and set the groundwork for your success. The outline for this analysis showing the political dimensions is shown in Figure 9.1. The first step is to understand what you carry into this work.

Carrying: what you bring to this work

The fact that you are reading this book hopefully indicates that you have an interest in this topic already and may well have some concerns about the situation in your organization. Understanding what you are carrying means that you are clear about your particular interest in this area. What has prompted it? Have you been delegated the task? Or has a particular event triggered your interest? Different starting points may lead you to have quite different feelings about your involvement, your commitment and your vision of what might happen as a result of this work.

At a recent seminar we ran we became aware of the variety of reasons

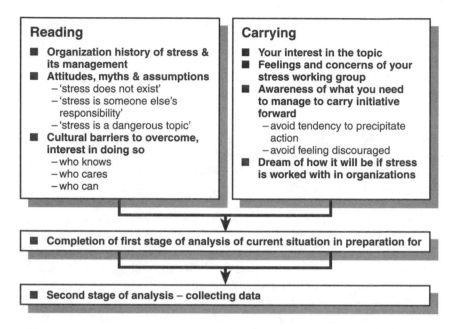

Figure 9.1 Analysing the current situation: political dimensions of the analysis

for interest in this topic. One person stated quite clearly and somewhat dourly that he was there for the simple reason that his organization was interested and he had been sent to look for answers for how to deal with stress. His personal level of interest was not well developed, it was simply part of his job. On the other hand, another participant talked movingly of some of the distress she had observed in the organization and the hours she had given listening to people unburdening themselves to her. She had been doing this, even though it was not part of her job. Her starting point was indignation at the level of stress that was present and the fact that this seemed to be viewed as acceptable by the organization. She had started a one-person crusade to do something about what she regarded as a dire situation.

These are two extremes and there are many other reasons for interest in the topic. At this point we invite you to reflect on your interest and its origins. What impact do you imagine your starting point will have on the work you do in this field?

If you have been able to bring together a group of people interested in stress management and have the beginnings of a stress management strategy group, explaining what each person 'carries' in relation to the topic is a good early exercise. There may well be differences in background and stance regarding stress and its management. It is good to bring these into the open and expose them. Whatever each person carries with them about the prospect of a stress management initiative, you do need at an early stage to bring about a shared sense of purpose amongst the group. This will unite the group, but it will do more. Having a clear and shared vision of the point of undertaking a stress management initiative can act to pull you through difficult times. Carrying a dream of what you are working for is a useful part of the baggage to take with you.

Identifying desired outcomes: allowing the dream to emerge

The next stage is to gain a clear picture of the desired outcome of the strategy in this organization as you see it at this point. Looking ahead is an absolutely key part of designing an appropriate strategy. The two markers for successful strategy making are that it is rooted in the current position with a clear eye on what is wanted for the future. Now and then are the two time boundaries which encapsulate the thinking and discussion which needs to take place about how to get from here to there. It is difficult to move forward on a strategic basis without a strong sense of what you are moving towards.

Therefore an early task in the life of the stress management group is to undertake an exercise which allows each person to focus on a vision for the organization in the future. Much has been made in recent years of the need for a vision within organizations, but the full reason is not always clearly understood. A shared vision acts as a uniting integrating force within the organization, which counteracts the forces constantly at work to fragment and divide the organization. It does much more, though. A vision can also release energy. That is why we suggest changing the language and talking about sharing dreams for the organization.

Early on in life, in childhood, each person has the capacity to have dreams about life and the way they want it to be. In childhood dreams can act as a bridge to move towards adult life. As children grow older they are discouraged from dreaming and encouraged to use rationality more. People are taught to deal with life as it is, and many phrases are used such as getting our heads out of the clouds, getting our feet back on the earth and other images are conjured up which discourage dreams. Unfortunately we often lose the ability or habit of incorporating dreams into our adult life. We forget that we are allowed to have dreams about how we really want things to be for our organizations and us. Rationality is much revered in the world of organizations; a strong intellect is a prized attribute. Yet recent work on leadership has rediscovered the importance of visioning, of inspiring and of releasing energy through visions. Rationality provides clarity; it does not release energy. Dreaming releases energy and can provide the clearest picture of all for driving forward a tricky and sensitive organizational initiative. Organizations do not just exist on the rational plane. Stress itself is not necessarily a rational phenomenon and the responses to stress are rarely rational. Therefore it is important to release the energy within the stress management group to allow the dream to emerge. How do you really want it to be round here, leave reality and rationality aside and allow your mind to conjure up the image of how it would be in this organization if stress were managed well. What is it that you want to see here, how would people deal with each other, what would it feel like to be working for an organization which had successfully faced the issue of organizational stress? These are the sorts of questions that can start the mind working towards generating a clear picture of the endpoint of the stress strategy. It is neither a sheet of paper nor a set of figures, but a dream of how you want it to be.

A dream is not the same as a performance measure or even a desired outcome. Attention to performance is vital for any organization and there need to be in place clear, focused performance indicators and measures. But they are based in rationality and are not the stuff of dreams. After all, who would recall the famous 'I have a dream' speech of Martin Luther King if he had started with the words, 'I have a desired outcome'. It just does not have the same ring to it, or the same ability to draw people together.

Our experience is that there is a lot of common ground when people start sharing their dreams of how the organization would be when stress was managed well. It is not appropriate to import a vision from elsewhere. One of the strengths of undertaking this exercise in a group which has been brought together to work jointly towards designing and implementing a successful stress management strategy is the realization that you are all working towards the same end. And the power of doing it together is a strong uniting force. One stress management working group we worked with found this a very powerful exercise. The group had been drawn together from very differing backgrounds, there were trade union officials, lawyers, occupational health people and senior managers. The early meetings of the group had focused on these differences and they were finding it difficult to find common ground. There seemed to be an assumption that the different interest groups represented would all want very different things from a stress management initiative. However, when they took the time to share their dreams they were amazed to find how much common ground there was. The vision of the future held by the trade union officials matched that held by senior managers. The dream of the lawyers and the dream of the occupational health professionals looked alike. Therefore, there may be differences in background, in the reason for being involved, but we have found that regardless of position, age or experience, most people have a very clear idea of what the organization would be like if stress were managed well, and that picture is often shared.

Now it is time to consider the other dimension of political skill, understanding the reality of the current situation in your organization as it affects stress management.

Reading the situation to see the current picture

To gain an accurate analysis of the current situation, you need to be aware of what has happened in your organization in the past relating to stress. You then need to understand the current culture and attitudes towards stress.

Understanding past stress initiatives

This aspect of analysing the current situation means being very clear as to what initiatives have been introduced previously and the story of each one. This will give important information to fill out the picture of where you are starting from now. Has there been training in stress management? Has this been part of a corporate training programme? Has participation been voluntary or not? What counselling initiatives have been set up? What information is available on how they have been used? Is this information fed back at a corporate level and how is it used? Has stress management been on the agenda of any senior management team meeting? Have the management team addressed this issue and how?

These are some of the questions which can be useful in guiding your understanding of the state of play regarding current stress management initiatives. Some of the key things to pay attention to when gathering this information are the reactions of people to the initiatives and how they have been followed through. If they are ongoing, you need to find out who is currently running these, as they will be important figures either for inclusion or exclusion in anything you propose.

Understanding the culture

Now it would be useful to assess what the culture is with regard to stress. We are not talking about the structure of the organization, but the intangible factors which influence the way things are in the organization. These are factors such as attitudes and assumptions that underpin everyday behaviour in the organization, as well as symbols which convey complex messages about the way the organization works and stories which circulate long after an event and which perpetuate myths.

One way to start to get a perspective on the culture is to focus on what people talk about within the organization. Do people talk openly about stress? Is it used as a topic of humour and jest? Is it a topic which is rarely mentioned? Do people talk about their own stress or only refer to it in an abstract way? One senior manager told us that in her organization there was a lot of talk about stress, but somehow it was always talked about in the abstract, as if somehow it existed out there. She had never heard anyone talk about their own stress. Her conclusion was that there was an awareness of stress as an organizational issue in a general sense, but reluctance to take it on board personally. Another person told us about how the conversation frequently focused on the stress that people were feeling but somehow it never got on to the organizational agenda.

The position is made even more complex by the fact that there are a number of different voices within one organization. One part of the organization may talk about this topic quite differently from another part. To help clarify the different things being said it can be useful to do some analysis of the constituent parts. Do senior managers talk about it one way, middle managers another, with front-line staff taking yet another stance? Is there a difference between departments, or between sites? Here is where your local and intimate knowledge of the organization will prove invaluable.

Analysing the current situation is not only about what is actually being talked about, but also about the subtle signals which give the message as to what is acceptable or not acceptable around here. What is your understanding of the messages prevalent within the organization which act as imperatives regarding stress? Again we are reminded of two managers from different organizations talking at a seminar. One identified that in his organization it was perfectly permissible to talk about how stressed you were feeling, but you must never take time off. The other talked about the silence which prevailed on stress, no one ever mentioned it, yet there was frequent stress-related sickness and absence. These represent two very different cultures.

Much has been written on organizational culture in recent years and it is a complex topic. Yet this complexity needs to be addressed. Gaining an understanding of the current culture is the starting point, the foundation on which the building of a strategy takes place.

One of the things that is most useful to discuss in the stress management group, if you are going to change the current situation, is the attitudes and assumptions about stress that may act as barriers to changing behaviour. You need to understand people's willingness to consider and take up new opportunities which you might propose. These need to be openly discussed, once you have identified them, as part of the whole initiative.

Common cultural barriers to addressing stress

There are many reasons why organizations have been reluctant to address this topic. It is important to understand the basis for these barriers. There are three main sets of attitudes which can lead to resistance to even addressing stress management within the organization. These are: a view that to discuss stress is dangerous, it is for someone else to deal with, and after all stress does not really exist.

Stress is dangerous

One primary inhibition to getting too involved in looking at stress and its management within the organization is that it raises much sensitivity.

One reason for not dealing with this topic is a view that it does not erupt until it is put on the organization's agenda. When we turn attention to it and discuss it then we cannot foresee what might happen. This reflects a rather head in the sand approach. If we do not discuss stress in the organization then it is possible to act as if it does not exist. Often this will lead to great resistance to openly discussing the topic. One personnel director relayed to us a very bizarre experience she had. Whenever she attempted to raise the topic of stress management with the senior team, they gave polite but uninterested attention then moved quickly on to the next item. At no point did anyone take issue with her or state openly that this was definitely not a suitable topic for discussion. She described it as if the senior managers were embarrassed by the topic. They displayed a reluctance to discuss stress, because who knew what can of worms might be opened?

Taking on board the organization's role and responsibility for creating stress and looking strategically at prevention involves taking a long hard look at the organization as a whole. This involves assessing policies, practices and behaviours and can be very threatening. One common way organizations deal with threat is to attempt to allocate blame. The phrase 'a blame culture' is one that we hear frequently and we examined this in Part II. It describes an organization which deals with problems by identifying a culprit and promptly heaping blame on them. It leads to a lack of ownership of problems, people trying to cover their backs and a lack of co-operation and trust between colleagues. This in itself can be a source of stress and it is certainly not an ideal climate in which to take an objective, constructive look at the issues of stress. To begin looking at the organization differently can feel quite threatening. Behind a blame culture is the assumption that the fear of being blamed will drive people to perform above expectation. Although we do not believe this is true, it can be an inhibiting factor as people fear that changing it will lead to staff becoming lazy or slack.

We have encountered several varieties on the blame theme when it comes to stress. A very common one is that it is all down to the person affected. If we can blame the person who is stressed for being too weak or incompetent to cope then it saves the organization having to explore these dangerous issues. The view that stress is purely a matter for the individual who is suffering is very strongly held and persists in many organizations. There is an understandable basis for this view. As we outlined in Chapter 3 stress is manifest at the individual level. The early work in this area detailed the stress response, particularly the physiological mechanisms which come into play when stress is experienced. As understanding grew of the nature of the stress response it placed the focus on the individual as the unit of analysis or concern. This formed the basis of the view that stress is a matter for personal concern. Many books on personal stress management reinforced the fact that stress is a matter of personal concern.

Stress is indeed a matter of personal concern. The variety of ways in which stress is manifested and experienced at the individual level does give rise to the need for personal attention to managing stress levels. There is without doubt need for people to take responsibility for managing their own levels of pressure. However, this is used as an argument to let organizations off the hook and place the blame for stress on the individual affected. After all, if stress is experienced at the personal level, then it must be the person's fault if they are stressed. Blame is often directed towards senior managers and the senior management group. If only they did their job properly then none of this would have happened, is the argument. There may be an element of truth in that, but blaming does not help to bring about change.

One organization we were working with discovered this in an interesting way. A working party had been set up to look at stress and it was not long before they reached the conclusion that prevention was needed as well as cure. Their attention then turned to the senior management team. Realization grew that in order for anything to change the senior team was central to making things happen. So the person chairing the working party, who was also a director and a member of the senior team, approached the Chief Executive to ask for a meeting between the Chief Executive and the working party. She was surprised to encounter a high level of resistance and defensiveness in the Chief Executive's response. Somewhat reluctantly he did agree to attend a meeting of the working party. At the end of the meeting, he admitted that it had gone a lot better than he had expected. He had been expecting a barrage of blame from the group. Instead he found a wish to discuss the matter, look at options and take it forward in a constructive way. Blaming senior managers does not encourage an open dialogue. In this case the Chief Executive was prepared to enter the discussion, notwithstanding his own feelings. It worked out well. However, in many cases the expectation of the blame being laid at their door discourages senior managers from even entering, let alone initiating the debate.

Stress is somebody else's responsibility

There is a view that because stress has a physiological base it is outside the remit of the organization. It is true that whenever stress is experienced there will be corresponding physiological changes, as we showed in Chapter 3. However, that does not then exonerate management from any responsibility or concern for the topic.

At times, the boundary between what is within the appropriate remit of the organization's concern and what is not can be unclear. If, for example, a member of staff tripped downstairs owing to a painter's ladder being in the way and broke a leg, that would be within the organization's concern. If working on word processors leads to eye strain, that again is within the remit of the manager. So the fact that stress is connected to physiological changes is not a reason for dismissing it as out of bounds.

Even if organizational responsibility is accepted there is another reason why attempts to raise stress management as an issue can be met with lack of enthusiasm. This is because it is often supposed to be somebody else's responsibility within the organization to do something about stress. There can often be a marked reluctance to take responsibility, even to discuss it. The two places in an organization where responsibility for stress management is commonly assumed to lie are with the top management team or with the human resources people.

The view that it is all down to the top team is a commonly held misconception. The top team in any organization is a very key part of the system. The top team has a particular role in creating and maintaining the culture of an organization. Whilst their backing and support are essential to the success of any organizational stress initiative, the causes and solutions do not lie entirely in their court. To the extent that you can gain their commitment to examine their role in the whole process of stress, you will have an important part of the system included in your initiative. But it is not solely their responsibility.

The other group which often finds itself in the firing line for blame is the human resources or personnel division. Some commonly held views we have heard expressed include: 'if they were doing their job properly, none of this would happen. And if stress is around then it is up to them to sort it out.' The personnel function varies greatly in the status and voice it has in different organizations. But because stress affects people and people are the business of human resources, then surely it is up to them to sort it out, runs this argument. Our response is to point out that obviously the human resource specialists have a very important part to play in the discussion of stress but that it is an issue of such central importance to the organization that it needs to be discussed widely throughout the organization.

Looking at stress in an organization is a sensitive matter. The more it is possible to move to a matter-of-fact, open spirit of enquiry into the topic, the more helpful it will be. Taking a view of the organization as a whole system and gaining an understanding of how the dynamics of pressure operate can provide an alternative to allocating blame. The more stress is seen as a function of the system, the less need there will be to find a particular person or area within the organization to shoulder all the responsibility.

Stress does not exist

There are several misconceptions that are held about the concept of stress, particularly when applied to organizations. A number of these question whether stress is an identifiable condition.

Stress is sometimes dismissed as a catch-all word. If anyone is feeling under the weather or fed up then they say that they are stressed. We are well aware that such different levels of understanding of the word stress, let alone different ways in which people use it to describe themselves or others, can exist, that there is plenty of room for confusion. However, that does not detract from the fact that stress does exist and that it is possible to identify it. To overcome this attempt to dismiss stress because of the confusion in the way the term is used, there needs to be a widely shared understanding of the term stress.

Another common cultural barrier to tackling stress strategically is the belief that members of staff will use the word as an excuse for malingering or trying to get out of work. This often reflects a belief on the part of managers that staff are really lazy people who have to be chivvied and kept an eye on otherwise they do not work. This attitude towards staff will then lead managers to view any complaint, not just about stress, as an excuse for poor performance or absenteeism. If the mention of stress is dismissed as just a convenient excuse, that will in all likelihood reflect a deeper, negative view of members of staff and their motivation and competence. This will be reflected in the organizational culture and will need to be addressed at that deeper level before it will be possible to look at stress management strategically. By tackling the problems openly the practice of hiding behind labels can be avoided. Conversely staff who claim stress can discuss the causes.

A further argument we have heard is that there is no such thing as stress. It is not the same as arguing that the term is misunderstood or misused, but rather that no such thing as stress even exists. Stress is merely a concept that has been invented in the latter part of the twentieth century, runs this argument. Reference is sometimes made to the lack of discussion of stress in the last century, and the fact that interest in the topic has only recently emerged. We would simply point out that many advances in knowledge and understanding have happened in this century. In fact the growth in knowledge has been incredibly rapid in recent years. Just because something was not known about in earlier times, does not mean it did not exist.

However, there is a possibility that stress in the broad sense that we talk about it today at work, did not exist. Of course people's physiology was the same and of course people endured suffering in previous centuries. Organizational stress, though, may have been built into organizations as we moved into the industrial society. People's home and work became divorced, ownership lay in different hands from management, tasks and jobs employed narrow routines and skills, rather than the 'whole person', and organizations became large and impersonal. All of these conditions gave rise to the experience of stress in the workplace. In the new information age, we see many of these factors continuing. So in fact, critics of the term stress do have a point, but we maintain that it is still a label which usefully describes people's experience. Indeed moving stress initiatives to an organizational level encompasses the notion that stress is 'man-made'.

Part of the 'stress does not exist' attitude is to treat it as a 'flavour of the month' issue. Without doubt there are patterns and trends in management thinking at any time. Both practising managers and management academics will focus on different concerns at different times. These areas of interest may be long-lasting or they may be short-lived. As we have shown earlier, concern with the area of stress has been steadily growing for many years. It has been viewed in different ways over the last 30 years. There certainly have been times when it has been at the forefront of concern for organizations and times when it has receded into the background. We believe stress management is not simply a flavour of the month issue. In the current climate it both is and should be a matter of lasting concern which warrants focused, strategic and continued attention.

Stress is complex

For all the reasons we have just explored, doing the groundwork is essential and complex. Without an accurate reading of the attitudes of the organization to stress it will be difficult if not impossible to develop a case for organizational stress management that will be adopted and taken seriously. If people think at heart that stress does not exist, that it is someone else's responsibility, or that it is dangerous to address stress as a topic then, at most, lip-service will be paid. This is vital information as part of the strategic analysis. Reading accurately is an essential part of the political skill you need to be effective.

You may experience a range of emotions as you scan the organization and read it for messages regarding the culture, attitudes, assumptions and myths around stress. You may feel dispirited about the uphill struggle you foresee, you may feel energized by the challenge or you may feel daunted by the complexity of the task. Organizations are large and complex entities. Having to take on a topic which is full of questions and very few clear-cut answers can be frustrating. It is important to pay attention to managing what you are carrying and how the group you are building around you to address stress is feeling as well. This is the other aspect of political skill. Acknowledging these feelings is important for you all because you may be tempted to dash into simple solutions to persuade other people that action is being taken or to give up or to become defensive about the group and its remit if what you are carrying is not discussed.

Lack of understanding of what you are reading and carrying can lead you to act naively or crossly when in fact you need to act with creativity and awareness.

The analysis of the current situation will probably leave you with more questions than answers. That is appropriate at this stage. Indeed, there are many questions in the stress field to which there are few ready-made answers. We now move on to considering how to obtain information in your organization by collecting data on stress.

Key points in Chapter 9

- Political skill is needed for developing and steering a stress management strategy.
- The ability to read the situation accurately is one component of political skill.
- The ability to be aware of what you are carrying into the situation is the other component of political skill.
- It is helpful to widen the base and establish a group around stress management.

- Reading the situation involves looking at past initiatives on stress management.
- Reading the situation involves understanding the attitudes, messages and myths around stress and its management.
- Reading the situation involves recognizing possible cultural barriers to addressing stress.
- Common cultural barriers exist around the notion that stress is a dangerous topic, it is somebody else's responsibility and stress does not exist.
- Stress is a complex topic and addressing it is not straightforward.
- It is vitally important to focus on and share the desired outcomes of a stress management initiative, the dream of 'how you want it to be around here'.

Collecting data on stress in the organization

An overview of the issues that need to be thought through for data collection is shown in Figure 10.1. The decisions on whether to collect data at all, how to collect it if it is to be collected and how to use the data once collected, are all important strategic choices. Sometimes the collection of data is seen as an exercise in assessing whether there is a need to address stress or whether it can be ignored. As we shall see below, it does not work like that in practice. Some organizations decide not to do an extensive formal data collection, with the stress steering group relying on anecdotal data or a tacit assumption that stress needs to be addressed and an expensive survey of some kind is not needed. Again, as we see below, the decision not to collect data is still a decision and needs to be

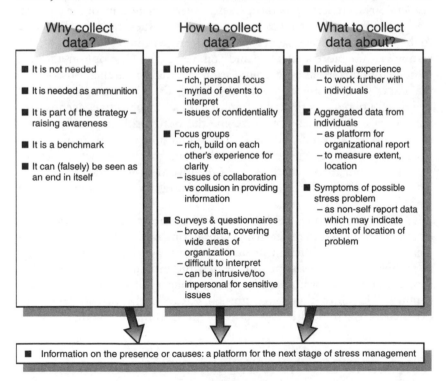

Why collect data?

- It is not needed
- It is needed as ammunition
- It is part of the strategy – raising awareness
- It is a benchmark
- It can (falsely) be seen as an end in itself

How to collect data?

- Interviews
  - rich, personal focus
  - myriad of events to interpret
  - issues of confidentiality
- Focus groups
  - rich, build on each other's experience for clarity
  - issues of collaboration vs collusion in providing information
- Surveys & questionnaires
  - broad data, covering wide areas of organization
  - difficult to interpret
  - can be intrusive/too impersonal for sensitive issues

What to collect data about?

- Individual experience
  - to work further with individuals
- Aggregated data from individuals
  - as platform for organizational report
  - to measure extent, location
- Symptoms of possible stress problem
  - as non-self report data which may indicate extent of location of problem

- Information on the presence or causes: a platform for the next stage of stress management

Figure 10.1 Issues in data collection for organizational stress management

made consciously rather than by default. Alternatively some organizations see the collection of data as an end in itself, as if that were a way of managing stress. We shall explore the pitfalls of this assumption in one of the cases described.

The first thing to emphasize on collecting data on stress in the organization is that it is not essential before designing the stress management strategy. The decision about data collection on stress is an integral part of the strategy itself. As soon as the topic of stress is raised, expectations will be raised, assumptions made about the management's view of stress and attention will be drawn to the topic. Thus a decision on the collection of data, or not, will be giving messages to the staff at large. So this decision is an intervention. This needs to be borne in mind. If data is collected there will be an expectation that it will lead to action. If data is not collected it raises questions in people's minds, such as whether anything will happen, or even if the topic will be taken seriously given that most organizations make investment decisions based on as much data as can be mustered.

Investigating stress within an organization is not purely an objective research exercise. There have been many studies over recent years by academic researchers into the presence of stress within organizations. The objective of these studies was to provide a widespread database and to highlight the issues. Investigating stress within your own organization is a far more subjective and complex issue. One option adopted by some organizations is to commission external researchers to compile the data. This seems to be in the belief that bringing in external researchers maintains the collection of data as an objective, even scientific, exercise. This does not overcome the basic problem that expectations will be affected. There is a good argument that professional researchers will have the necessary skills available to conduct an investigation. It is not the research skills of the investigators which is at issue. What needs to be addressed is the implications for the organization of gathering data about stress.

Three organizations we have worked with recently provide good examples of the issues raised when considering data collection. The outcomes were totally different in each case, yet each highlights key issues in finding out if stress is present within the organization and to what extent. Local authorities are among the pioneers of stress audits in this country. Therefore they have not only reaped the benefits but also experienced the difficulties. We draw on these in the following cases.

The case of the vanishing stress audit

The first organization, a medium-sized unitary local authority, had set up a working party to investigate the problems of stress within the organization and to recommend a strategy for dealing with the problem. The working group was composed of a diverse group of people representing different parts of the organization and different roles. It was suggested early on in the working group's life that in order to set about drawing up a strategy for dealing with stress, it would be necessary to have some hard and fast data from which to work.

From then on discussion focused on collecting information on stress within the organization. The trade union people on the group were vociferous in their call for a large-scale and detailed study, bringing in outside researchers and preferably using a questionnaire. The Director of Personnel was not so taken with this idea, particularly after costing the exercise. It seemed to her that doing a study was rapidly becoming an end in itself and she was concerned to keep the attention on the strategic aspects of stress management. There were many points which emerged from the subsequent discussions, not least how to deal constructively with conflict and disagreements within a working group, but the main points which emerged related very directly to the role of the collection of data.

On the one hand the argument was made that it was vital to be in possession of all the facts before drawing up an approach to tackling the problem. It was also argued that such information would be absolutely vital when comparing progress in the future. Surely, this argument ran, all available information is needed to act as a basis for future planning and as a benchmark for future stress management work. The union view was that not until a thorough stress audit had been completed would it be possible for the working group to continue their work. What was more, the stress audit had to be completed using reputable researchers and thoroughly validated instruments. Only then would it be possible to move forward. This is a view we have heard frequently expressed in a number of organizations.

On the other hand the Director of Personnel took a different approach to investigating stress. Her argument was that when discussing how the organization should approach the topic of stress, the question of measurement was a key part of the strategy. For her it was not a case of first get the data and then design the strategy. She argued that there was information available, from summary data from the in-house counsellor and pending grievance cases, as well as softer more impressionistic data. She was not convinced of the need for such a large-scale study. She was also only too aware that asking people to fill in questionnaires raised expectations that something was going to happen, and soon. The time, not to mention the cost of a large-scale investigation would mean that nothing could happen for at least a year.

These two approaches were eventually resolved in a manner which resembled the Director of Personnel's view and a strategy, which included points about the role and the timing of collecting data was agreed. The discussion did, however, highlight how easy it can be to assume that total information is needed before movement on the topic can take place. It also raised the possibility of viewing information gathering as a strategic exercise in itself and not merely a preparatory stage.

Data as a basis for action

There is often an assumption that having hard data on stress is a necessary prerequisite for further action. It seems that somehow clear knowledge of the magnitude and location of the problem will provide inspiration for knowing how to deal with it. We would challenge that view and quote the example of the Director of Personnel who viewed data gathering as part of the strategy. We have encountered much surprise on the part of managers when we put forward our view that measurement is not necessarily a prerequisite for action. It may well be desirable, but we would question the rapid turning to data collection without serious consideration of the role that data is going to play.

Data to provide a benchmark

If data on stress levels is taken as a good indication of the state of the organization, then it can be used to benchmark and provide comparison. Stress levels on one site can be measured with another, and stress levels one year can be compared with the following year. This will give information on trends and can provide a measure of feedback for the effectiveness of stress management interventions.

Data collection as an end in itself

We will conclude this section by making the point that whenever data is gathered on stress within an organization, the reasons for the data collection need to be well thought through. This needs to take place even before decisions are made on the methodology to be used. Data collection is never an end in itself when an organization is collecting data on itself. It needs to be a purposeful activity and one linked into future action, which is appropriate for that organization. At the risk of widening a gap which is often reported to be too wide at present, collecting data to add to the wider body of knowledge is essential, but that is the remit of the academic, not the manager. The question of why collect data and how they are to be used needs to be a prerequisite for considerations of how they are to be collected.

The case of the pressing deadline

The second organization was one that discovered some interesting lessons by deciding on a conventional approach, only to find that for purely pragmatic reasons it was not viable. Out of the alternative route came a great deal of learning.

This organization was a large department in a large local authority. Stress had been identified as a key issue by the Human Resources Manager and was being driven by her. Being of a pragmatic nature, she saw an opportunity for some data collection in the guise of a senior manager who was undertaking an MBA. As is customary, all MBA students have to complete a lengthy dissertation, based on data collection. Here there was no question of whether data should be collected about the incidence of stress, the question hinged on how to do it. Therefore the MBA student/manager was invited to nominate stress as the topic for the dissertation. This was agreed without any trouble. In this organization the decision was taken that data gathering was necessary to make the case at the most senior level that stress was in fact a serious issue. The expectation was that senior managers would balk at the prospect of outside researchers invading the organization, so it was a question of how to collect data without causing too many waves and still provide reliable data. So the background to the question of data collection was a very different scenario.

Unfortunately when it came to detailed planning of how to get the data, two main obstacles emerged. The proposal was to use a reliable, validated questionnaire. That led to the question of how to get a large number of completed questionnaires analysed. The decision was taken to turn to the central research facility for assistance. However, they did not have the capacity to undertake such a big job for at least six months. After exploring other avenues to get the questionnaires analysed, it was decided that it was impracticable in the timescale. There was a time limit. The department held an annual conference for the most senior managers and it had already been decided that the data must be analysed and ready for presentation at the next conference. The practical points of data collection and analysis had not really been taken into account when planning the timescale. There was flexibility in the approach of both the manager deputed to undertake the task and the Human Resources Manager and in the interests of pure practicality it was decided to limit the scope of the data gathering and treat it as a pilot. This changed the approach. Instead of going for a large-scale survey of all staff, now it was a question of interviewing a small number of people based on a semi-structured format to elicit data and running a couple of focus groups. All the usual questions of how representative would this be, how many were needed to take part to make any sort of sense, were raised. In the end two focus groups were conducted and 30 interviews were undertaken, leaving the manager with a great deal of detailed, in-depth and at times very personal raw data to make sense of. But the depth of the picture was far greater than could have been achieved with a questionnaire and carried more impact for that reason.

Data as ammunition

Data were seen in this organization to be necessary as ammunition to convince senior managers of the seriousness of the problem. Information has a key role to play and can be a key part of putting the case for organizational stress management to others. Facts and figures can carry weight. Whether it is part of the strategy to convince senior managers or any other people who are not yet convinced that organizational stress management is a key concern, data can play a very useful role as ammunition. But that is part of the necessity of taking a strategic approach to stress management and using data as ammunition needs to be seen as part of the overall strategy.

One-to-one interviews

Although in this case the decision to use interviews was made for pragmatic reasons, there were some key lessons to be drawn. The first is that conducting face-to-face interviews even with a small number of people is very time-consuming. The pay-off is that the data collected are amazingly rich and deep. Although there does need to be some focus and the use of a semi-structured format provides that, there is also scope for the person to elaborate and tell their own story. The process of the interview gives the respondent a sense of being heard in a way that cannot happen with a questionnaire. It can also leave the interviewer with some feelings in response to what is being heard. Thus the whole process is more personal and emotive than using a questionnaire.

The major disadvantage of using interviews is making sense of the rich data that emerges. There is also the possible criticism of whether a small group is representative of the organization.

Focus groups

One advantage of using focus groups is that they are not as time-consuming as one-to-one interviews. It can also emerge for the people taking part that they are not the only one experiencing stress and that can be reassuring. The discussion needs an initial focus but then the ensuing discussion can build on the ideas of others.

The disadvantage of using focus groups is making sense of what emerges. In a free flowing discussion, it can also be difficult to actually record what is emerging. An additional constraint is lack of openness. If the culture of the organization does not encourage open discussion of the stress issue, there may be reticence amongst the group.

The case of the missing response

The third organization, also a local authority, provides an example of conventional data collection with all the pitfalls as well as advantages that can bring. In this case, it was once more the Director of Personnel who was taking the initiative for stress management. At an early stage without much consideration of the alternatives, he took the decision to undertake a large-scale, thorough survey of the organization. The scale of the survey was such that it would undoubtedly be representative, but the process was cumbersome and time-consuming. A questionnaire was compiled and administered. When the date arrived for returns, it was found that the response rate was low, or at least a lot lower than expected. On asking around and attempting to get some idea as to why the response rate was disappointing, the answers came through clearly. First, the exercise was viewed with great cynicism by the staff. In fact, it was even commented that it was all just a paper exercise to protect against litigation for stress. The common view seemed to be that there had been surveys before and nothing had ever happened as a result, so why should it be different this time. The second main reason given was that although it was a well-designed questionnaire, the experience of stress is so personal and sensitive that it really does not fit into the neat forced choice format so beloved of questionnaire designers. This fitted with the perceived culture of the organization, that senior management really wasn't interested in what the staff said. A frequent complaint was that senior management just didn't listen. A very indignant Director of Personnel insisted that the questionnaire was an attempt to find out what was happening with staff, unfortunately the staff did not see it the same way.

Data gathering as raising expectations

One reason given for the low response to the questionnaire on stress was the cynical view that nothing would happen and that it was just a back protection exercise. That might have been a harsh view but it does reflect the fact that when people are asked to give information, particularly quite personal information, it does raise questions as to what is going to be done with the data and also expectations that some action will follow. In that organization the Director of Personnel saw the data gathering as a sign of concern at a senior level and expected it to be received as such. He had not thought through a strategy and was using the data as a basis for action. Therefore he was not in a position to tell people how the data would be used. This merely increased the cynicism. One further pointer was that the Director was at that stage a lone voice and although a senior one, he did not have the full and whole-hearted support of his senior colleagues. These factors came together to increase cynicism rather than raise positive expectations. In the first example, the Director of Personnel was aware that a major data collection exercise would raise expectations and realistically assessed that because of the scale and time needed, nothing would happen for at least a year. She was aware of the danger of increasing frustration at least, if not cynicism, by the process of collecting data. Therefore it needs to be clearly taken into account that asking people to take part in collecting data on stress levels, needs to be accompanied by a statement of what is going to be done with it and when.

Data collection as invasion

This may seem a rather strong way of putting it, but asking people for very personal data within an organizational context can be seen as invasive. It may well be a factor which reduces response rates to questionnaires on stress, although it was not stated as such in our third example. This links back to our earlier points about the sensitive nature of stress. There are many people who have not come to terms with the impact of stress on themselves, let alone be prepared to share it within the organization. It is such a sensitive topic that the utmost care needs to be taken when collecting data. Anonymity and confidentiality are essential. Although it might be for organizational purposes, collecting data on stress from individuals is a personal matter to them.

Using questionnaires

This is the method which is often considered first. Over many years the use of questionnaires has become more widespread in organizations as a way of collecting data, such as employee attitude surveys. In a large population such as an organization, a questionnaire is the simplest method of collecting information from a large number of people. Questionnaires are also easy to score and collate and thus provide an easily accessible numerical score. For that reason questionnaires do have an appeal. There is another reason why this method is often considered to be the best, or at least easiest. There is a whole science of questionnaire design and there are off-the-shelf questionnaires which measure stress within an organization.

On the other hand, there are some disadvantages to using questionnaires. It is not always either easy or possible to fit intensely personal experience into a forced choice format. Responses to a questionnaire do provide a skeleton, but cannot give an indication of the depth of the responses. Questionnaires ask for people's experience to be categorized and to use the questionnaire designer's categories. This obviously imposes limits on the respondent and can be resented. It leads to a key issue when using questionnaires and that is how to interpret the results.

Key issues underlying the measurement of stress in an organization

We have seen that there are difficult issues to address in collecting data on stress in the organization. They cover the question of why data needs to or should be collected. We highlighted how the myth of total information being a prerequisite to decisions on action can hinder addressing the question of whether data needs to be collected at all. We also raised the point that data can be collected in order to enhance the argument that stress is a serious issue, data can be used as ammunition. A further argument for collecting data is to provide a benchmark for comparison.

We were able to see in the examples used that there are a number of questions which hinge around the issue of how data are to be collected. We looked at one-to-one interviewing and focus groups as a method of data collection in the second example, and the use of questionnaires in the third example. In addition we saw that there are some wider process issues around the collection of data on stress. The third example showed how the activity of collecting data raised expectations that action would follow. It was also seen as an invasion. Data collection on stress is not simply an objective scientific exercise, it involves asking people about personal matters.

We have looked at some of the 'why' and 'how' issues of data collection in the examples. We will now look at the issue of 'what' is being measured.

What is being measured when data is collected on stress

The first type of data that is being collected measures the presence and prevalence of stress in the organization. When collecting data on stress we are gathering information about individuals' experience of stress in the organization. The data can then be used in a variety of ways. If we were using them to understand a particular individual's experience we would want to follow up what they said with that individual. The fact that they could be identified in the data collection would need to be understood as part of the data collection process. This way of using data is employed when people are to receive a one-to-one session, for example, on how they are managing stress or as a method of selecting people for stress management training programmes. As stress is a sensitive issue, how this sort of data collection is handled is paramount.

More frequently when data is collected on stress in the organization we are interested in the aggregated responses of the individuals who have provided information. In this case information is usually provided anonymously and in such a way that we can put together information collected in particular departments or divisions or at particular levels in the organization, so that 'stress hot-spots' can be identified. It is usual for these data to be the basis for an organizational response to stress rather than being targeted at identifiable individuals.

A third kind of data can be collected which does not directly address people's experience of stress as they perceive it. It concerns some particular behaviours, which are thought to be symptoms or representative of stress and will indicate whether stress is extremely prevalent in organizations or only exists at low levels. In this third category we would expect to see staff turnover figures, absenteeism and sickness figures, referrals to counselling schemes, take-up on stress management programmes. These indirect measures have to be interpreted in the context in which they are collected. Staff turnover figures, for example, will almost certainly be influenced by the general economic climate and the local labour market, skills shortages and so on, in addition to stress. However, when several indicators suggest that there may be a problem, further investigation is warranted.

Behind all of these three types of data collection, what is being measured is an indication that stress may be present. In the case of the aggregate data, it will also give an indication of how widespread it might be.

The second question that data collection can begin to answer is: what are the perceived causes of stress? Again data can be collected about individual or personal information or more general organizational issues. Thus some data collection may refer to individuals' experience of particular tasks, people or groups, which may or may not be shared by others. Other data will seek to collect information about general perceptions of issues of concern in the organization. So, for example, at the individual level, a cause of stress may be difficulty in dealing with a specific manager. At the organizational level people may report concerns over prevalent management styles in the organization. Data about causes may be collected at the individual level in order to identify courses of action that will support that particular person. Data collected about more general organizational concerns will usually be used as a platform for organizational interventions. As we can see from these examples, before any data are collected, it is important to know precisely what questions are of interest and how the data will be interpreted and used once collected. Organizations frequently run into difficulty with data that they know indicate a problem but have been collected in such a way that their interpretation and meaning are unclear.

For example, there is a potential confusion between what may be taken as an indicator of the presence of stress or an indicator of the causes of stress. One piece of information may be interpreted as either. For example, if it is observed that a particular team is not working well, the productivity is down and the relationships are not good, is this an indication of stress in the system or a cause of stress in the system? The answer is that it can be both or either. This can also apply when trying to make sense of the observation that a particular manager has a drink problem. Is this a personal response to stress on the part of this one person, or can it be interpreted as a cause of stress for the team. Again it can be seen as both. At the wider organizational level, interpreting a high level of staff turnover is not always as straightforward as it may appear. If a high turnover is recorded, is this to be interpreted as a measure of the level of stress in that department, or can it be also seen as a cause of stress for staff? After all if there is a high turnover, with new people joining the group, the stability of the group is uncertain and there is a need for training and bringing new people on board.

We are sounding a note of caution as to the interpretation of data. Data themselves do not provide all the answers. It is the interpretation of the data which is a crucial factor. It is particularly important when interpreting data to bear in mind that the organization is a whole system. Making sense of what is being uncovered will take time and sensitivity. Data rarely give easy to read, clear-cut answers. To remind yourself of the complexity of interpreting data, you might like to go over Part II of the book again.

There is a further issue which can confuse the struggle for clarity over what is actually being measured. One organization we worked with conducted a survey and identified a number of key issues which seemed to be of general concern as a cause of stress. For example, there seemed to be a general dissatisfaction with 'communication'. The team tasked with looking at stress spent an interesting meeting trying to work out what this actually meant. There were at least 20 possible interpretations and solutions on the table. Another organization conducted detailed discussions with a number of people, collecting verbatim transcripts. The problem in this case was attempting to make sense of the myriad of curious and detailed examples that came out of these in order to develop some coherent organizational response. In some ways, with data collection you can't win.

Asking the right questions

In recent years we have encountered the phrase 'stress audit' frequently in discussions with managers about stress in the organization. However, this phrase can sometimes obscure the actual nature of the investigation and provide a false sense of security. We can think of at least two organizations where there was a widespread feeling of satisfaction that something was being done about stress because a stress audit was being conducted. On further pressing, the managers from these organizations admitted to being unclear as to what this actually meant. When challenged with the simple question of whether causes or symptoms were the primary focus of the investigation, we were met with blank looks. The common use of the phrase 'stress audit' can be very helpful, it can also act as a hindrance to clarifying the questions that need to be asked or even are being asked.

There is a range of possibilities for the questions which can be asked. Deciding on which are the right questions is part of the strategy and needs to be based on a clear picture of what the data is being collected for. At the most basic level, there is the simple question, *is there stress in the organization*? If this is the most important question, then the methodology needs to reflect the question. An elaboration could be, *where is stress manifested within the organization*? This would involve collecting data from different parts or different levels within the organization.

However, the most common confusion we have encountered is the confusion between the questions of whether stress is present and where, and the causes of stress in the organization. In our earlier work we used the phrase 'stress audit' to refer to an analysis of the causes of stress within a particular organization. The phrase, although being used more widely, often blurs the distinction between collecting data on causes or effects. The simple question that needs to be posed to investigate the perceived causes of stress is *what are the causes of stress in this organization*?

These questions need to be kept separate when approaching an investigation. They also need to be kept in mind when deciding on which method to use to conduct the investigation. There are problems with trying to find out about the causes of stress. As we explained in Part II, these are often emotional, complex, unconscious and almost impossible to articulate in a survey or in response to a point-blank question. The information will lie in piecing together a variety of reactions, comments, behaviours and observation to form a tentative hypothesis. For example, in a survey in one police force, it was expected that attending road traffic accidents, domestic violence or other traumatic events would be the causes of stress. This in fact was not the case. Instead, 'management style' was the most frequently mentioned cause of stress. After much department discussion it emerged that there was lack of faith in the backup that managers offered officers; they felt there was a lack of boundary management (our term) with the key external stake-holders (e.g. local authority and press) and officers felt 'unsafe'.

We recognize that all of these various issues serve to complicate matters when considering collecting data on stress in the organization. There are not only the questions of how data should be collected but also the more basic issues of why collect them and what actually is being measured. This highlights the importance of the consideration of data collection as part of the strategic analysis needed. Data will not provide clarity nor will they provide reassurance that stress is being addressed. Data collection is neither a necessary prerequisite nor is it an end in itself.

Now that the strategic analysis has been done by reading the current organizational situation and making choices about gathering data, it only remains to pull it all together in a way which takes account of the new approach and will work in your organization.

Key points in Chapter 10

- The first issue to consider is whether to collect data.
- The second issue is what to collect data about.
- When considering what data need to be collected, it is important to ask the right questions.
- The third issue to consider is how to collect the data you want.
- Taking all these points together it is important to view data collection as an integral part of the stress management strategy.

Moving forward: pulling your strategy together

The organization within which you work is unique. It may share a market with other organizations, it may share a worksite with other companies, it may even be part of a larger group or conglomerate; however, it is the only place where the exact ingredients of product, structure and most importantly personnel and culture come together. That makes your organization unique and special. The particular combination of history, current situation and future prospects all adds to the melting pot of what makes your organization different from any other.

We emphasize the unique nature of your organization because it is very important to bear that in mind. We have counselled against simply importing stress management initiatives from other organizations. We do suggest that you find out what other organizations have tried and what has worked well. But what has worked well in one organization with its own set of characteristics may not be ideal for your organization.

You are now in a position where you are aware of the many different facets of organizational stress management. Whatever you were 'carrying' personally, whatever your views and position when you first ventured down this path, by now, hopefully, you feel better informed and have a clearer perspective on the various facets which warrant exploration. You may, of course, simply be feeling confused and rather at a loss as to how to proceed. You may be wishing that we would provide all the answers in this book and that you had no more thinking and planning to do. However appealing that is, unfortunately the nub of success of an organizational stress management strategy is the way it is designed to fit the particular organization. It is vital strategically to tailor your proposals and interventions to increase the chance of success in your organization.

You will need all your political skill with you for this final stage. You will need to read the organization and the various groups and players in the scenario and learn to read events as they unfold. You will need to be clear what it is that you are carrying with you, and whether there is anything which is getting in the way of you being focused and clear in your approach.

S trategic Approach
for
T op Performance
and a
R evitalized Organization
depends on
E motional Focus
with
S ystemic Thinking
to develop a
S upportive Environment

Pulling the strands together

We started by outlining the importance of stress management as an absolutely crucial area for organizations to take seriously for today and for the future. We introduced a model which highlights the main factors which need to be taken into account as you progress with stress management organizationally, and used the word STRESS to represent the key factors.

The key factors are the need to keep your eye on the outcome; that is aiming for a *top performing* and *revitalized* organization. In order for that to happen there needs to be a *strategic* approach, one which is designed for your organization. To widen understanding of how to tackle stress organizationally we explored the importance of gaining a *systemic* understanding and an awareness of the *emotional* side of organizational life. The final piece was to consider the options available for providing *support* to the organization, to managers and to individuals. Hopefully you are even clearer now as to why organizational stress management is needed. The aim is to ensure an organization which is a top performer and where people are revitalized. By now you will have grappled with gaining an understanding of some of the less obvious ways in which stress comes about, by looking at the emotional side of working life and viewing the organization systemically. You will be aware of support and the role it plays in reducing stress and the various ways it can be provided.

By now you will be clear about the benefits which organizational stress management can bring and aware of the many changes in organizational life which make this even more important a topic. The history of work in this area over the last few decades will be clear to you and how it brings us to where we are today. You will understand what stress is, how it is manifested in individuals and how this links to the organization. You will have insight into how an organization works systemically and by now will have stopped being surprised at how anxiety can cause strange things to happen at work. You will understand people better and know some of the ways in which individuals and the organization can collude to generate stress. The variety of ways in which support can be provided will be clearer, as will the three levels at which support needs to be given. Your early analysis will have given you much useful information about your organization and your role in this initiative. By now you will understand the importance of building a strong and supportive group around you to share the load of progressing this initiative. You will be learning what barriers you might encounter in your move forward with organizational stress management. You will have the dream of how it will be without the problems of stress. The dream of the future will be in place to give you something to aim towards. You will have grappled with the data collection questions, of why, who and how to collect data on stress.

Now we have looked at each of the STRESS areas: strategy, top performance, revitalization, emotion at work, systemic understanding and support, it is time to revisit the strategic overview and look at the final stages.

Taking a big leap forward

We are aware that what we are putting forward as the route to success in organizational stress management involves a big leap. Over the years many and varied initiatives have been put in place and many have worked well. However, in many places the stress management initiatives have not worked as well as hoped, even though a lot of time and money has gone into them.

Thus it is time for a leap of perspective. No longer is it going to work to simply prop up individuals to withstand the daily onslaught of the work pressures. No longer is it simply enough to provide counselling so that people have somewhere to chew their problems over, away from the workplace. The leap that is needed is to look at the organization from a different perspective, as a whole, a system where each part interacts and affects the others. This has been proposed as the key skill needed for leadership in a learning organization. We see it as vital for understanding how stress occurs and thus effectively intervening to manage it.

In addition to understanding how an organization works systemically, we are also inviting you to become more aware of the fact that it is a system where emotion plays as important a role as does production. We recognize that this is a lot to ask and can be difficult and at times threatening for people to take on board. However, the logical and rational can only take us so far in understanding how stress comes about and what can be done to manage it. What is needed now has been described as 'emotional intelligence', the ability to connect with the world of feeling, rather than consign it to life outside work. Emotional intelligence is very different from what has traditionally been viewed as intelligence, the type measured by IQ tests. The senior managers and key people in your organization may be very well qualified in their field and have a string of outstanding academic achievements behind them. They may have long and glittering careers and a great deal of experience of running organizations under their belts. However, neither qualifications nor years of experience necessarily develop the type of emotional intelligence that is needed to sensitively pick a way through the organizational minefield to put in place an effective stress management strategy.

Therefore the new approach which we are suggesting brings its own challenges and pressures; the challenge to take a different perspective and to incorporate awareness of what may previously have been excluded from analysis, the world of emotion. The third challenge our new approach brings and adds to our recognition that this new approach is a big leap, is the need to view organizational stress management strategically.

It is not a question of seeing organizational stress management as a matter of either focusing on individuals or on the organization. By introducing the three levels where support needs to be provided, to the organization, to managers and to individuals, we are saying it is not an either/or case, but one for a both/and approach. Therefore by reaching this final stage of developing an effective organizational stress management strategy, we recognize that we are asking a great deal and that this new approach will bring its own pressures.

Making strategic choices wisely

There are five final areas we want to put forward now to complete the jigsaw and provide the whole picture to lead to strategic choices. These are creating a supportive environment for the development of the strategy, bringing people on board, putting your argument successfully, finding out what is happening in other organizations and using the information you have gained wisely.

Creating a supportive environment

It is helpful to take steps to move the climate towards a supportive atmosphere to allow good choices to be made and an effective strategy to be developed. Initially there may be indifference, or even hostility within the organization to the notion of organizational stress management. We have heard various comments in the course of our work which illustrate this, such as: 'what are they up to now', 'not another new idea for us to have to take on board', 'stress management, haven't got time for that'. At the very least an attitude of interested curiosity will be helpful. What is far better is a climate where stress is viewed as an important issue and where there is enthusiasm to tackle it.

Creating a supportive environment also means ensuring that you are well supported in your role as champion of the strategy. Carrying a stress management strategy forward skilfully means managing yourself and the group you have built around you to manage the topic. In particular it is important to pay attention to the working of the stress management group and maintain commitment to the shared vision, while planning the way forward.

One strong recommendation we would make is to continue to pay attention to the development of the group even after the initial formation stage. We have emphasized the need for a shared vision which will act as a cohesive force. A group which may be up against strong resistance needs to have good internal strength to withstand the pressures it is likely to face. This means focusing on the working of the group at all stages. One organization we know set up a group, which did not gel together very well. In the face of the indifference of the senior team, the group simply disbanded. In that case it was an extra pressure on the person leading the group to keep any momentum going. The group had not developed the internal strength to withstand external indifference to its work.

The stress management group is an ideal place for data to be gathered and shared, where perceptions of current reality can be tested out and planning done. This will be time-consuming and therefore the commitment of each member of the group needs to be sustained. Even when one senior person pulls the group together, the burden will be too much for one person. The group needs to share the load, know how to cope with disappointment and how to celebrate success. It needs to work to maintain its profile and to ensure that the organization knows what the group is doing. It needs to communicate with the wider organization. Doing good work behind closed doors may be personally satisfying but will be organizationally unproductive. Equally the work of the group needs to be visible. If word gets round that there is a stress management group which meets regularly and no one knows what it is doing, it may lead to suspicion and rumour.

There is a lot for the group to consider. Taking forward a stress management strategy is not an easy task. Attention needs to be on the process of progressing it as well as what it contains. Equally the group needs to be aware and pay attention to how it is working, as well as planning what to work on at any given time.

The factor which will unite the group and can act to provide the energy needed is to keep in focus the shared vision for what this organization would be like if a stress management strategy were successful. This can act to inspire in the face of hostility, encourage when others discourage and comfort when the going gets rough. This means continuing to develop the stress management group you have built up and networking with people in similar positions in other parts of the organization or other organizations. Creating support for yourself is vital, feelings of isolation do not help anyone be objective and productive.

The next step, bringing people on board, will also go some way to creating a supportive environment.

Bringing people on board

If the interventions are to be successful the more people that know what is happening, understand it and are on board, the better they will be. Your reading of your organization will give insight into who the key people are, but the top team is unavoidably a key player. The senior grouping of managers within any organization is a key factor in the organizational system. They influence the culture greatly and wield considerable organizational power. To put it simply if the top team are not on board it lessens the chances of a successful strategy.

We have discussed in an earlier chapter the reasons why there can be resistance to taking stress management on board. Now is the time to apply the political skill of reading to the top team. Do you know where they stand on the issue of stress management, individually and as a team? How did you gain that view, do you need to check it out with others? It may be helpful to remind yourself of the possible reasons for resistance and to use your knowledge of your organization to identify which ones could apply to the top team. At this stage we would encourage gaining understanding of any possible resistance you may face. If you can anticipate the possible barriers, you can plan to put your case taking good account of the situation.

It is not very often in our experience that the top team come straight out and dismiss stress as an unimportant area. What we have found to be more likely is that lip-service will be paid to the topic. As it has been described to us, they say all the right things and then nothing happens. This can be rather frustrating and will call for skills in managing your response. Sensitivity is definitely required when treading in this area.

When thinking about how to bring the top group on board, there is the question of who should put the argument as well as how the argument should be put. Some organizations bring in consultants to put forward the case for organizational stress management to the top team. This may be based on the notion that external people carry greater credibility or have a wider knowledge of the area to draw on. Again there is no right answer. When considering who should put forward the argument internally, the question arises as to whether one person should meet with the team or whether the whole stress management group should do so.

In one organization we worked with, the Director of Personnel had been the lead person on stress management. She was a member of the corporate management team. The other members of the team had taken to switching off and assuming glazed expressions whenever she raised the topic. She assembled a strong stress management group who identified the importance of the senior management team and the need to get them on board. The group then discussed how to do this and came up with the idea of a meeting between the two groups. This was agreed and the stress management group worked out a way of all of them being involved in presenting to and talking with the top team. This gave the message of how strong and widespread the commitment to the topic was. The Director of Personnel was conspicuously quiet during the meeting. As the top team were unused to hearing impassioned pleas for the case for taking stress management seriously coming from either relatively junior staff or union officials, the message was received differently. It was no longer a case of the Director of Personnel being seen to be on her hobby horse. This was the turning point in that organization. A person of lesser emotional maturity might have become discouraged because her voice was not being heard. Instead the Director recognized the need for an approach which achieved the objective of taking the top team one step nearer to being on board. She managed any feelings she had about her lack of personal impact and brought about what she wanted.

The top team will not be the only people who need to be brought on board. Here an analysis of all those who are important to the topic needs to be done. It is as important to include people who can be influential in a negative sense, those who could block the process. Sometimes such people are obvious, sometimes less so. For example four groups who can play an important part and need to be on board are the personnel people, the occupational health professionals, health and safety officers and the lawyers.

The role of the personnel department varies markedly from organization to organization. In some places it takes a bureaucratic role in managing the systems involved in employing staff, such as recruitment, pensions and welfare. In others it takes a more developmental role and is concerned with organizational and management development issues. But whatever the focus of your particular personnel outfit, it is the part of the organization which is usually seen as concerned with people.

Therefore they are important people to have on board when considering a strategy such as stress management, which is so clearly aimed at improving work life for people. Occupational health again can occupy different roles, but stress is central to its sphere of professional interest. Health and safety officers are another group which need to be considered. Although stress management is now clearly within the area of health and safety legislation, that does not mean to say that every health and safety person has grasped the full implications or feels comfortable about their role being extended in this way. Lawyers may make light of the legal developments. This can be particularly problematic if you are basing your case on the legal developments regarding stress at work.

When you have used your reading skills to identify the key people who need to be brought on board, then it is time to consider how you put your arguments forward.

Putting your argument together

As we outlined in Chapter 2, there are a number of different bases from which it is possible to argue. They will carry different weight in different organizations.

If the organization is used to being taken to court and there is no fear of litigation, then using the legal defensive argument is not likely to be successful. You can outline in great detail recent legal rulings and highlight the possibility of legal action, but if this is likely to be met by a shrug of the shoulder then it is not a good idea to use that argument. Equally in an organization which has not really grasped the essentials of good management practice, using the argument that stress management is central to good management and performance output is not likely to carry much weight. If the central values do not include a concern with being seen as a good employer, that argument will not be successful. If the organization does not have financial concern at the forefront of their thinking, then arguing for the bottom line cost of stress will not be fruitful. You may choose to construct the argument and draw each of these different approaches to people's attention, but that needs to be done carefully bearing very much in mind the value system and culture of the organization.

You need to be familiar with the argument and also to check out the extent to which you agree or disagree with the argument. It is perfectly possible to put forward a convincing case with which you personally do not agree, that is one of the skills of advocacy. However, when considering putting forward the case in your own organization to people who matter, it helps if you are putting forward an argument you not only understand but with which you personally are in agreement. This is where being aware of your own convictions can add impact to your case.

Finding out what has been done in other organizations

Talking with other organizations and finding out what has been tried elsewhere gives useful information. We would again counsel against the temptation to simply import an initiative from elsewhere. The interventions which will work in your organization will not necessarily be the same as those which have worked elsewhere. Suffice it to say here that increasing your awareness of how various options have worked in practice will widen your knowledge concerning the options available to manage stress organizationally.

Using data wisely

We have discussed the different methods of gathering data internally and the different ways in which they can be used. Here we add the information you have gained from other organizations. These data need to be fed in skilfully and with maximum impact. Again, your reading of the situation and knowledge will help you to construct a good platform. If there is a strong competitive streak within the organization, it might be worth mentioning that the closest rival is undertaking a particular initiative. This may be all that is needed to ensure that the same happens in your organization. If, however, there is a strong air of complacency, knowledge of what the rivals are doing is more likely to be met with, what rivals?

Bringing internal data to the attention of senior people is likely to be a threatening activity from their point of view. It is not comfortable for many senior managers to be made aware that the level of stress is high, and even less comfortable to be told that they are to blame. Bearing in mind the example we gave of half an hour being given by one management team to considering the outcome of a data gathering exercise which had taken many weeks, there may well be defensive behaviours at work. Understanding this may help you to plan the way through it and persist, so that little by little senior people are able to hear and take on board the data and consider them well.

Therefore creating a supportive environment, bringing key people on board, putting your argument together well and using data wisely will all allow the conditions to be right for the organization to make strategic choices which are right for them. The final point to consider is that the strategy is co-ordinated and stands as a whole.

Pulling it all together

There are three aspects that need to be considered when moving into the final stages of pulling it all together. There is a need for a co-ordinated approach which encompasses all three levels of possible intervention, the timings of the proposed actions and the costings. No organization in our experience, however committed to dealing with stress management, has an unlimited budget to devote to it.

We would argue strongly that each of the three levels must be considered and a strategy needs to include appropriate actions at each of the levels. It must be co-ordinated. We have already argued against a piecemeal approach, it has to be seen as a whole. This involves considering each level and how possible actions to provide support at that level will have systemic implications for the rest of the organization.

In terms of the timing of possible actions to include in the strategy, it is useful to bear in mind the desired outcome and to set a time limit for the dream to become reality. It is tempting in this area, as in much of organizational life, to want it done yesterday. But bringing about lasting changes in how support is provided in the organization, be it to reduce unnecessary pressure or increase buoyancy aids, cannot happen overnight. For example, we have emphasized the importance of providing time and space for the processing of experience to take place in the organization. If this is an unfamiliar way of doing things, it will take time for people to get used to the idea and begin to use processing time well. The dream cannot be realized immediately. Therefore the strategy needs to incorporate separate steps which together build on each other to move the organization forward. This may mean counselling patience in some quarters where impatience may throw up some resistance. Here we are suggesting that the strategy includes a good dose of hard reality. Changing an organization takes time.

Another area where hard reality needs to be added is when considering costing. As the presence of stress in an organization costs money, doing something constructively about it also costs money. Many of the options we put forward in Chapters 7 and 8 are not that easy to cost tightly. Some options lend themselves to tight costing, such as access to counselling or training programmes. But many are less easy to put a clear money figure beside, such as providing processing time with consultants for individual managers, working groups or the executive team. However, it would be unrealistic not to recognize that costing is an important aspect of the strategy.

Figure 11.1 provides an overview of the aspects that need to be considered at each of the three levels of possible intervention: the organizational, managerial and individual.

	Awareness and recognition	Sourcing stress	Actions
Organization level (Top team/ stress project team)	What is stress? Why it is beneficial? Why it is increasing? Role of organization as system	Understanding use of data collection: benefits and limitations Understanding stress from a systemic emotional perspective: organization and group dynamics	Strategy and commitment Resources for work with organizational process and structures
Managerial level (Top team and all managers)	Recognition of stress in self and others Effects on performance	Necessary and unnecessary pressures Job fit and staff Managing boundaries Role of emotions as well as 'obvious' pressures in stress Group behaviour	Working with staff groups on management and roles and experience of work (consulted to) Work on self as manager Referral of staff for training/ employee assistance programmes (EAPs)
Individual (all staff including managers)	Importance of reducing stress Recognition of personal checklist of symptoms	Personal history and attitudes Personality, characteristics and work preferences Roles adopted Lifestyle and life balance	Managing self in role Acquiring necessary skills: training & development. Self referral to EAPs etc. where appropriate. Changing lifestyle and life balance

Figure 11.1 Levels of intervention for addressing stress in the workplace

Carrying the strategy forward with skill and energy

Working on a strategy for stress management in your own organization is not supposed to be stressful in itself. However, it would be unrealistic to ignore the fact that there will be pressures involved in the process. It needs to be tackled with skill. An awareness of the situation and good management of the feelings carried at any time will go a long way to ensure that stress management is carried forward successfully in your organization.

The effort needs to be sustained. It is not a matter which can be sorted out overnight. Sustaining that effort will make demands on your energy and that of the people involved in the work of tackling stress management from an organizational perspective. The one requirement for sustained effort is that you plan how to maintain your energy. Too often we have seen managers who start out with almost a crusading zeal to tackle stress in their organizations, only to leave the organization themselves shortly afterwards. The main reason has been because they have either not been able to or not considered building a group around them. They have carried the responsibility alone, and that is demanding. They have also underestimated the emotive nature of stress and its management and have not been prepared for the demands of dealing with the emotional aspects of getting a strategy in place. Whatever the reason, managers in other places and other organizations have found organizational stress management a stressful topic, we do not want that for you in your organization.

In order to use your skills to maximum effect, in order to plot your way through this complex area, in order to bring the dream nearer to reality; for all those reasons, you must pay attention to maintaining the pressure balance in your work and life. Managing your own pressure level is a priority for anyone involved in managing stress in the organization.

Stress is not going to go away of its own accord. Nor is it just a passing fad in organizational life. Discomfort, lack of productivity and legal actions will all conspire together to ensure that the organizations who want to keep up in the future have to take this topic seriously. There are resistances, worries and sensitivities surrounding the topic. The time will never be totally right to tackle it. But for organizations of the future to be working well without unnecessary pressure and stressed staff, a step needs to be made. That step can only be taken from where you are now. Only if enough people take that first step will the momentum build to move towards the time when stress in your organization is merely a matter of historical concern.

It is by taking time to understand the topic, to allow the new perspective to provide new insights, by looking strategically as well as systemically at the issue and planning an appropriate way ahead for your organization, that you will progress towards the dream of a healthy organization, working at top performance and staffed by revitalized people. Only in small strategic steps will the time come for the dream of a world where people work at their optimum level, feeling good and energized, looking forward to going to work for an organization which is productive and successful. We hope this book has helped you towards making this come true in your organization.

Key points in Chapter 11

- Moving forwards means pulling all the strands together.
- Moving forwards involves a big leap of perspective.
- Creating a supportive environment to allow the necessary discussions and planning to take place is important.
- Setting up support for yourself and paying attention to the group you have around you matters.
- Bringing key people on board is essential.
- Putting forward a suitable argument which will work in your organization is important.
- Using the data wisely is a key element in moving forwards.

■ Political skill is needed to move forwards effectively.
■ You need to manage your own pressure level to ensure that you are in a good state to contribute your best and use the STRESS approach to good effect.

Endnote: our STRESS model in action

We have covered a lot of ground in this book. We introduced a psychological approach for dealing with stress in the workplace and emphasized the need for tackling it strategically. So let us finish by summarizing our approach to good organization practice in stress management.

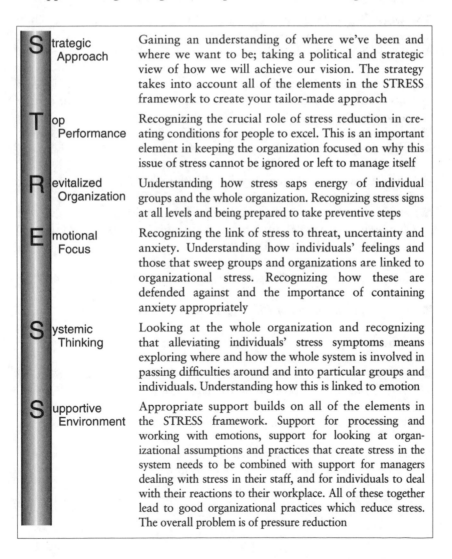

S trategic Approach	Gaining an understanding of where we've been and where we want to be; taking a political and strategic view of how we will achieve our vision. The strategy takes into account all of the elements in the STRESS framework to create your tailor-made approach
T op Performance	Recognizing the crucial role of stress reduction in creating conditions for people to excel. This is an important element in keeping the organization focused on why this issue of stress cannot be ignored or left to manage itself
R evitalized Organization	Understanding how stress saps energy of individual groups and the whole organization. Recognizing stress signs at all levels and being prepared to take preventive steps
E motional Focus	Recognizing the link of stress to threat, uncertainty and anxiety. Understanding how individuals' feelings and those that sweep groups and organizations are linked to organizational stress. Recognizing how these are defended against and the importance of containing anxiety appropriately
S ystemic Thinking	Looking at the whole organization and recognizing that alleviating individuals' stress symptoms means exploring where and how the whole system is involved in passing difficulties around and into particular groups and individuals. Understanding how this is linked to emotion
S upportive Environment	Appropriate support builds on all of the elements in the STRESS framework. Support for processing and working with emotions, support for looking at organizational assumptions and practices that create stress in the system needs to be combined with support for managers dealing with stress in their staff, and for individuals to deal with their reactions to their workplace. All of these together lead to good organizational practices which reduce stress. The overall problem is of pressure reduction

Background reading

You may like to follow up on the areas of research which have informed our book. This list is intended to provide background reading, rather than an exhaustive set of references.

Organizational stress management

The work being done on organizational stress management frequently appears in journals; a series which brings together a variety of current research issues was published by the American Psychological Association:

- James Campbell Quick, Lawrence R. Murphy, Joseph J. Hurrell (eds) *Stress and Well Being at Work: Assessments and Interventions for Occupational Mental Health* APA: Washington, DC 1992.
- Lawrence R. Murphy, Joseph J. Hurrell, Steven L. Sauter and Gwendoline Puryear Keita (eds) *Job Stress Intervention* APA: Washington, DC 1995.
- Steven L. Sauter and Lawrence R. Murphy (eds) *Organizational Risk Factors for Job Stress* APA: Washington, DC 1995.
- Gwendoline Puryear Keita and Joseph J. Hurrell (eds) *Job Stress in a Changing Workforce: Investigating Gender, Diversity and Family Issues* APA: Washington, DC 1994.

A longstanding, still relevant work by the pioneer of stress research:

- Hans Selye *The Stress of Life* McGraw Hill: New York 1956.

For a different perspective on the concept of stress:

- Tim Newton with Jocelyn Handy and Stephen Fineman *Managing Stress: Emotion & Power at Work* Sage: London 1995.

On the benefits of having an organizational stress policy:

- Cary Cooper and Jill Earnshaw *Stress and Employer Liability* Institute of Personnel and Development: London 1996.

Personal stress management

Walk into any bookshop and you will find an array of books on stress. Finding coping strategies for dealing with personal stress can vary between instant 'solutions' to long-term personal growth. Books which help you to relax and calm down may be very useful to you. Books which help you take a different perspective on life can have a long-term effect. We recommend:

Tanya Arroba and Kim James *Pressure at Work; a Survival Guide for Managers* McGraw-Hill: Maidenhead 1991.

Susan Jeffers *End the Struggle and Dance with Life: How to Build Yourself Up When the World Gets You Down* Hodder and Stoughton: London 1996.

Thomas Moore *Care of the Soul: How to Add Depth and Meaning to Your Everyday Life* Piatkus: London 1992.

Anne Wilson Schaef *Meditations for Women who Do Too Much* Harper: San Francisco 1990.

Paul Wilson *The Little Book of Calm* Penguin: London 1997.

Paul Wilson *Calm at Work* Penguin: London 1998.

Systemic and psychodynamic thinking

This is a difficult area to launch into but there are some books which are both accessible and give good applied case examples of organizations.

Anton Obholzer and Vega Zagier Roberts (eds) *The Unconscious at Work: Individual and Organisational Stress in the Human Services* Routledge: London 1994.

Larry Hirschhorn *The Workplace Within: Psychodynamics of Organizational Life* MIT Press: Massachusetts 1993.

Larry Hirschhorn and Carole K. Barrett (eds) *The Psychodynamics of Organizations* Temple University Press: Philadelphia 1993.

William Czander *The Psychodynamics of Work and Organizations: Theory and Application* Guildford Press: New York 1993.

Seth Allcorn and Michael Diamond *Managing People During Stressful Times: The Psychologically Defensive Workplace* Quorum: Westport 1997.

Individual differences

We particularly like two frameworks for understanding individual differences. The first, Myers-Briggs Types, is based on some aspects of Jung's psychology related to individual cognitive preferences. The second, Transactional Analysis, looks at the role of personal history in influencing our current feelings, thinking and actions. Useful books to start on are:

- Isabel Briggs Myers with Peter B. Myers *Gifts Differing: Understanding Personality Type* Consulting Psychologists Press: California 1993.
- Gordon Lawrence *People Types and Tiger Stripes* Centre for Applications of Psychological Type: Florida 1993.
- Muriel James and Dorothy Jongeward *Born to Win: Transactional Analysis with Gestalt Experiments* Addison-Wesley: Massachusetts 1985.

Data collection

There are many commercially available instruments for indicating levels and sources of stress. A 'tried and tested' version is

- Cary Cooper, Stephen Sloan and Stephen William *Organisational Stress Indicator* ASE/NFER Nelson Publishing Company: London 1994.

Strategy management

We have placed this book at the strategic level for organizational thinking. A valuable text for this, covering strategic analysis, choice and implementation is:

- Gerry Johnson and Kevan Scholes *Exploring Corporate Strategy: Text and Cases* Prentice Hall: Hemel Hempstead 1997 (4th edition).

We have referred to political skills in this book as part of developing your strategy. A model developed by the authors with a colleague, Simon Baddeley, is now widely used for understanding the personal dimension of organizational politics. Our first article on this was:

- Simon Baddeley and Kim James 'Owl, Fox, Donkey or Sheep: Political Skills for Managers' *Management Education and Development* Vol 18 Pt 1 1987 pp 3–19.

Two additional books which we have drawn on and you may find helpful as you think through your whole approach to this area are:

- Stephen Covey *Principle Centred Leadership* Simon & Schuster: London 1992.
- Daniel Goleman *Emotional Intelligence*: *Why it Can Matter More Than IQ* Bloomsbury: London 1996.

Index

THE SECRET
OF SKYTOP HILL
and Other Stories

THE SECRET
OF SKYTOP HILL
and Other Stories

by
ENID BLYTON

Illustrated by
Pythia Ashton-Jewell

AWARD PUBLICATIONS LIMITED

For further information on Enid Blyton contact www.blyton.com

ISBN 0-86163-765-8

This edition first published 1998
Fourth impression 2003

Published by Award Publications Limited,
27 Longford Street, London NW1 3DZ

Printed in Singapore

CONTENTS

The Secret of Skytop Hill

"Where shall we go today?" said John. "It's jolly cold. We'd better go for a brisk walk."

"Well, let's show Harry the old ruin," said Molly. "The one at the bottom of Skytop Hill."

Their cousin Harry looked at Molly. "What a lovely name for a hill! And what's this old ruin? Let's go!"

"Come on, then," said John, pulling on his coat. "Look, you can see Skytop Hill from here – it's that steep hill sticking up into the sky. It's so wild and steep that nobody ever goes there. The old ruin is near the bottom of it. It was once an inn."

They set off, walking quickly in the frosty air. It took them nearly an hour to reach the old inn, which was indeed nothing but a ruin now.

"People say that smugglers used to run this inn," said Molly, climbing over a tumbledown bit of wall. "It's terribly old – don't you think it *feels* old?"

It did. All the children thought it had a

7

strange feeling. They wandered about in the ruined building, which had most of its roof off now except for one piece over what had been the big old kitchen.

"Once we played keeping house here," said Molly. "We even made a fire in that old fireplace, and we kept bread and butter in the larder. It was fun!"

"Let's light a fire today and keep ourselves warm," said Harry. "I'll go and get some dead twigs and bits of wood."

But the fire wouldn't burn. John dragged out the twigs and put his head into the grate, looking up the chimney to see if anything had fallen down to block it.

"Sometimes birds build their nests at the top and the bits fall down and stop up the chimney," he said.

"But it's such an enormous old chimney!" said Harry. "Surely no bird's-nest could stop it up?"

"Well – there is something blocking it," said John. "A few bricks have fallen in or something. Wait – I'll poke a stick up and see if I can move them."

He found a long stick outside and poked up the chimney. The bricks were lodged very loosely across the chimney and they fell down into the grate with a clatter and a cloud of dust, making the children jump. When the dust had settled John put his head up again to see if the chimney was clear.

"I say – there's a big space where those bricks fell from," he called to the others. "And I believe I can see something there. Got a torch, Harry?"

"Here you are," said Harry and handed John a small torch. John shone it into the empty space.

"It's a box!" he said, excitedly. "Hidden up the chimney! Whatever's in it?"

"Treasure!" said Harry and Molly together. "Quick, get it down and we'll see."

John managed to get down the box. It was of some kind of metal but it felt fairly light. The children put it on the windowsill, and looked at it. It was locked.

"We must break it open," said John. "Gosh – what a find! I bet there's some kind of secret inside!"

"What shall we break the lock with?" said Harry, red with excitement. "I say, isn't it old and rusty! Whatever was it hidden up the chimney for?"

"There's an old broken poker somewhere," said Molly, looking round. "Yes, there it is. John, smash the lock with that."

Crash! The poker came down on the box. The rusty lock gave way, and the lid hung loose. John opened it.

Inside was a roll of thick, yellowed paper. John picked it out of the box and smoothed it flat. There was nothing else in the box at all.

"It's just an old paper," he said in

disappointment. The others bent over it.

"It's a rough kind of map!" said Harry. "Look – there are the points of the compass shown in that corner – north, south, east, and west. And here's what looks like a road – it seems to fork here and there – but one piece is marked very thick in black ink. That road must lead somewhere."

"Yes – but what road is it?" asked Molly. "It's got no name!"

"Here's something written in this corner," said John. "It's very faded. Wait a bit: Y-E-W-T-R-E-E – that's what it looks like. The road seems to start from there."

"Yew tree!" said Molly. "Well, this was called Yew Tree Inn, wasn't it? But there's no road at all from here except back to Lanning village, where we've just come from. Why should anyone make a map of that and hide it?"

"It's not that road, silly," said John. "We know it doesn't wind like this, and fork here and there – and anyway, on this map the road shown runs in the opposite direction."

"It's strange," said Harry, looking through the window to the north where the road or path on the map was supposed to run. "There's not even a footpath there."

"Listen – there used to be an enormous old

tree, a yew, growing at the corner of the inn!" Molly said suddenly. "It's gone now but the stump is still there. It grew out of the corner of the stable. I remember Daddy telling me about it."

"Let's go and look," said John. So out of the old kitchen they went, and into the tumbledown stable. Broken mangers were still on the wall. The floor was cobbled. A great heap of straw lay in one corner of a loosebox, flattened and brown.

"Here's the stump of the yew," said John, and he pointed to a rotting stump at one end. "Look, they had to make the wall bend in just here, so as not to spoil the tree."

The stump was by the old heap of straw. John kicked some of the straw away – and then saw something odd.

"I say! Look! The floor isn't cobbled here! There's a wooden trapdoor. Do you suppose the road marked on that old map goes underground – could it be a smugglers' way to somewhere?"

"Heave up the trapdoor!" cried Harry. "We'll soon see!"

The trapdoor had an iron handle let into it. John tried to pull it to open the trapdoor, but it would not budge.

"I've got a rope," said Harry, who always carried extraordinary things about with him, just in case they were needed. He undid a rope from round his waist. He slipped it double through the iron ring and threw the two ends over the low wall between the loose boxes. Then the children could pull on it together.

"Now – heave ho!" yelled Harry, and they pulled hard. The trapdoor came up so suddenly that all three of them sat down hard and lost their breath.

John was up first. He peered down into the space uncovered by the trapdoor.

"Steps down!" he cried. "Stone steps. I bet this is the entrance to the secret way marked on that map. It runs north on the map, doesn't it? Well, that means we go right into Skytop Hill!"

It certainly looked as if it did. The steep, rocky slope of Skytop Hill rose up directly in front of them and any underground path must lead into it. How strange!

"Shall we go down?" asked Molly, feeling scared as she peered down into the darkness. "John, do you think it leads to a smugglers' hiding-place – caves or something – you know, where smugglers kept their goods?"

"Perhaps," said John. "Of course we're going down. But if you're afraid, Molly, you needn't come."

"I'm as brave as you!" Molly said, crossly. "Of course I'm coming."

One by one they went down the stone steps. It was a good thing Harry had a torch. There were twelve steps and then a tunnel, dark, narrow, and low in places.

"This is the way marked on the map all right!" said John in excitement. "Shine your torch here, Harry – I want to have a look at the

14

map and make sure I know the right direction. We don't want to go wandering off into any of the wrong forks."

"I hope we don't get lost," said Molly, suddenly feeling afraid. "Harry, have you got some white chalk? You've usually got your pockets full of everything. We could make white crosses on the wall of the tunnel as we go, then if we miss our way we shall be able to find it again by following our chalk marks back to the stable."

"Brilliant idea!" said Harry, and fished a piece of chalk from his pocket. Then on they went again along the tunnel, Harry marking bold white crosses every now and again.

The passage opened out widely after a bit, and here and there other ways ran from it into the hill.

"It's absolutely honeycombed with tunnels!" said John. "Natural ones, too – not hacked out by men. This one looks as if it'll lead right to the very heart of the hill. I say – isn't this exciting?"

The three children groped their way along the passage by the light of Harry's torch. Sometimes the air smelled horrid. Harry kept on marking the wall with his white crosses as he went and the children were glad to think they would be able to find their way safely back again if they were lost.

The passage kept more or less level. John stopped and looked at the map whenever they came to a fork so that he would know which one to take, the one going to the right or to the left.

"We must be getting very deep underground," he said. "The hill must be rising right over us now. We shall soon come under its top."

"I bet that's where we shall find something," said Harry, marking another chalk cross. "I bet that's where the old smugglers hid their goods!"

"We may find some!" Molly said excitedly. "Oh, do come on!"

Suddenly they came into a place that seemed at first to be a great cave – but daylight shone down into it! The children looked round and then up in amazement.

"Why – we're in a sort of deep, deep pit – and that's daylight shining in from the top. There's a hole in the top of Skytop Hill, and it drops right down to where we stand!"

They were quite right. There was a peculiar opening in the top of Skytop Hill, a shaft that went right down to the heart of it, ending

where the children stood. And in the caves round about were many interesting things.

"Boxes!" said Molly. "Crates! Awfully old they look. I'm sure the smugglers hid their things here."

"Look here!" said John, suddenly, and he pointed to the ground. "A cigarette end – and an empty cigarette packet! Now who in the world can have left these here?"

It did seem odd to see the cigarette end and packet lying there among all the old boxes and crates.

"Who comes here – and why?" said Harry, suddenly dropping his voice to a whisper.

But before the others could answer, they heard something that made all of them jump violently. They heard a man's whistle – someone whistling a tune!

"There's someone coming," said John, in a low tone. "Look – from out of that cave over there. Hide, quick! We'll watch what he does."

The children crouched behind a big, empty crate in the darkness of an overhanging rock. They waited, their hearts beating loudly.

A man came into sight. A broad young fellow, kicking a stone in front of him as if he were bored. He sat down on a box.

The children didn't make a sound. Somehow

they felt that the man wouldn't be at all pleased to know that they were there. They were afraid. "He can't be up to any good," thought John. "We'd better try and find out what he's doing here."

The children crouched silently behind the big crate, keeping their eyes on the man. After a while he left his place and climbed a little way up the side of the pit, where a great rock made a kind of shelf.

Here he tinkered about with something, for the children could hear metallic sounds. There was evidently some kind of machinery up there.

"Molly! Harry! I think that man's a spy or something!" John said in a whisper. "If I get a chance I'm going up on to that ledge to see what he's got there. I can't imagine what it is. If I get caught you must both go back down the secret passage and tell someone about this, and get help."

"Oh, John, don't," said Molly, scared. "Don't climb up to that ledge."

"Shh!" said John as the man climbed down again. He disappeared into a cave. "Now's my chance," said John and darted out from his hiding-place. He climbed quickly to the ledge and stared in surprise. A strange kind of lantern or lamp was there, its face tilted upwards to the sky far above.

"What's it for?" wondered John – and then he heard a warning whistle from Harry. The man was coming again. John tried to scramble down.

But he was too late! The man saw him, made a dart at him and caught him. He shook him so fiercely that poor John thought his teeth would fall out.

"What are you doing here? You'll be sorry for yourself soon!" said the man, and flung John into a small cave. He moved a great crate in front of it. "You'll see what happens to nasty

little boys who snoop around! Have you done anything to that lamp up there?"

The man climbed up to see. Harry ran to free John but there was no time. "Go for help, idiot!" said John. "Quick, before he sees you."

Harry and Molly fled into the secret passage without being seen. How glad they were to know that they had the white chalk marks to follow.

John was left behind. The day went slowly by. He was hungry and thirsty but the man gave him nothing to eat or drink.

And then at night, when it was quite dark, a strange and powerful glow gradually filled the shaft, coming into the cave where John was a prisoner. And, at the same time, there came the drone of an aeroplane engine overhead!

"That glow is from the lamp on the ledge halfway down the pit," said John to himself, filled with excitement. "It can only be seen by anyone flying directly overhead. It's a signal of some sort. What a clever idea – yes, that man is signalling with the lamp – the light keeps going on and off."

The aeroplane droned overhead for a little while, and then made off. The red glow died away.

Darkness came again, and poor John trembled in his gloomy prison. If only the others would come.

What had happened to the other two? They had hurried away down the dark secret passage by the light of Harry's torch. Harry held the torch and Molly followed close at his heels.

And then they suddenly lost their way. They took the wrong turn, and when they tried to make their way back, they found they were lost. "I thought we were following your chalk-marks on the wall?" said Molly, almost in

tears. "How did we miss the way?"

Both children were frightened. They sat down to have a rest and to work out which way to go. At last they set out again and after a long time, to their great delight, they came across Harry's chalk crosses on the wall.

"Now for goodness sake don't let's lose them again!" said Molly. "It's getting so late – and I'm starving hungry! It will be dark before we get home."

It was almost dark when the two children staggered in at the back door, and Molly called loudly for her mother. Very soon she had told her the extraordinary happenings of the day.

"I'll ring up the police," said Mrs Johnson, who was astonished and worried. "This is serious. We must certainly rescue poor John!"

Soon the police came in a big car, and off they all went to the old ruined inn. "We had better get to the pit by way of the underground passage," said the inspector. "Something funny is going on inside Skytop Hill!"

They all crept as silently as possible down the secret passage. When they came to the part that opened into the pit they stopped in wonder – for a strange red glow lay all round. It was the glow cast by the powerful lamp hidden inside the hill. Its light shone up, and

could be seen by the aeroplane which was even then droning overhead – but nothing could be seen of the glowing lamp by any watcher out in the countryside!

"A very clever idea!" said the inspector, under his breath. "A fine way of signalling. We've often wondered how it was done. Well, you children have done a splendid job of work for us today!"

Then the inspector and his men took charge of affairs, and things began to happen. The men by the lamp were captured. Other men, hidden in comfortable caves, were routed out and taken prisoner. A radio transmitter and receiver was found that could send and take messages, and these had been flashed to the aeroplane that came twice a week to fly over Skytop Hill. It was a very clever idea.

"Nice little nest of spies!" the inspector said grimly. "Well, well – that aeroplane will have a bad time over here next time it comes. Come along, children – you've had enough excitement for one day!"

"What an exciting adventure," said John, happily, as they went to bed that night. "We never guessed that anything like that would happen when we went to look at the ruin at the foot of Skytop Hill!"

It Happened
One Afternoon

Mike went whistling into his father's study to borrow a map. He and his friend Joe were going on a weekend bicycle tour, and Mike wanted to work out the best way to go.

Mike felt happy. It was a wonderful day, and looked like being a wonderful weekend. He and Joe were to go off that evening, after Joe had finished at the office where he had just started work.

It was half-term. His bicycle was cleaned, ready for the weekend. His mother had already packed him up a bag of food. His father had given him twenty pounds to spend on himself and Joe over the weekend. Everything was fine.

He found the map and slipped it into his pocket. Then he caught sight of a new golf club that his father had bought himself. It stood by the table, neat and shining.

"Ha! Dad's got a new club!" said Mike, and he picked it up. "I bet I could hit a golf ball as far as he can. Wheee!"

He swung it up behind him and brought it down. *Crash!*

Mike turned in fright. He had smashed a lamp and a very valuable vase. There they lay on the floor in hundreds of pieces.

Mike did the first thing he thought of. He shot out of the room, down the passage to the

garden door and out to the shed. He hid there, trembling.

"Dad would be furious if he thought I'd done that," he thought. "So would Mum. They wouldn't let me go away for the weekend with Joe. I wouldn't be surprised if Dad stopped my pocket money."

He stayed there for a long while. He could hear excited voices and knew that the breakages had been discovered. He wondered what to do.

He didn't think of owning up and facing up to his punishment. Let them think it was the cat! Tabs was always breaking something.

He stayed in the shed till teatime. He knew his mother would have gone out by then to see his grandmother. Dad didn't seem to be about either – maybe he had gone for a walk. He wouldn't bother about tea. He would just scribble a note to say he was sorry they were out when he set off for his weekend.

"I don't want to face them so soon after the things got broken," he thought. "I'll just let them think I couldn't say goodbye because they weren't here when I left – and by Monday perhaps they'll have forgotten all about the accident, and won't ask any awkward questions."

He scribbled his note, crept out and snooped around to see where everyone was.

"No sign of Mum, and no sign of Dad either," he thought. "That's good. I'll leave the note on Mum's chair and she'll see it when she comes back."

He left the note, jumped on his bicycle and rode off down the path and into the lane to go to Joe's. His rucksack was on his back, with the things in it he would need. It would be fun!

He rode in at the gate at the bottom of Joe's garden. He gave the whistle that he and Joe used – but Joe didn't seem to be there.

"Blow! There's his bike, all ready – where on earth is Joe?"

He heard a movement behind the little summerhouse nearby, and then a scared and anxious face looked round the corner at him. It was Joe's sister, twelve-year-old Jane.

"Jane! What's the matter?" asked Mike at once. "You're crying. What's happened? Is somebody ill?"

"No," said Jane, with a gulp. "Oh, Mike! It's awful!"

"What's awful?" said Mike, going round the summerhouse, feeling very worried. He was fond of Jane. "Have you gone and got yourself

into trouble, Jane? What have you done? Lost
your homework again?"

"No, Mike – nothing like that. It's poor Joe,"
said Jane, and began to cry again.

"What's happened to him?" asked Mike,
impatiently. "He ought to be here, ready to
start out with me. Don't say something's
happened to stop him!"

"He's not coming," said Jane, almost in a
whisper. "He's in awful trouble. He's lost his

job at Mr Frost's office. Dad's furious with him and he might have to go to the police station!"

"Gosh – but what's he done?" asked Mike. "Do tell me, Jane. This is awful."

"I don't know exactly what he's done, nor where it all happened," said Jane. "They wouldn't let me stay in the room. All I know is that Joe was sent out to deliver some important papers from the office this afternoon – and – and they say he went to deliver them, climbed in at the window, because he saw a gold watch there – and stole it!"

Mike listened, absolutely amazed. Joe! Why, Joe was as honest as the day. "It can't be true," he said at last. "It's a wicked thing to say about Joe."

"Yes, I know," said Jane, wiping away her tears. "But he was found standing in the room and the watch was gone. They think he must have thrown it out of the window as soon as he heard someone coming. That's what they say."

"But they must be mad," said Mike. "Joe couldn't do a thing like that! He simply couldn't. He must have been in the room for some quite good reason. I know Joe!"

"Joe said he heard a peculiar noise and jumped in to see what it was," said Jane.

"They didn't believe him, of course."

"Look here!" said Mike, feeling very fierce all of a sudden. "I'm going to find out where this place is that Joe's supposed to have stolen the watch from. I'm going to go and see these horrible people there. I'm going to tell them that Joe's my friend and couldn't do a mean thing to save his life! Okay, Jane?"

"Oh, Mike!" said Jane, looking at him with the greatest admiration. "Would you really be brave enough to do all that? You would be a good friend to Joe."

"He's my best friend – and I won't let anyone treat him like that or say things like that about him," said Mike. "What's more, when I've seen these people and told them what I think of them, I shall go and see your father and mother, and tell them they ought to know better than to think Joe would ever do such a thing as steal a gold watch, and tell lies about it."

He got up and Jane got up, too, drying her eyes. "Perhaps they'll let you and Joe go off for the weekend after all," she said. "Oh, Mike – I do think you are wonderful."

"Where's Joe?" said Mike. "Come on – let's find him."

Joe was in his room, feeling very miserable.

Mike went up to him and slapped him on the back.

"Cheer up! I'll go and face these people who say things like that about you! Tell me all about it."

"Haven't you heard all about it?" asked Joe, looking astonished.

"Well – only what Jane's told me," said Mike. Joe went on looking astonished, and didn't say a word. "Do tell me what happened," said Mike. "I want to know so that I can march straight off to these people and tell them what I think of them."

Joe looked at Mike doubtfully. "Well – it seems odd that you haven't heard all about it yet," he said. "I'll tell you exactly what happened. I was told to take some important papers to a client this afternoon. So off I went. Well, as I was walking up to the front door I passed a window and I suddenly heard a most terrific crash. I nearly jumped out of my skin. I looked in at the open window and saw a frightful mess on the floor."

"What was it?" asked Mike.

"I don't really know," said Joe. "Anyway, I stood there wondering what had caused all the noise and mess and thought I'd better investigate. So I jumped in at the window – but

34

I hadn't been there more than a moment before in came the owners, and shouted at me to know what I was doing there, and what had I smashed."

"Go on," said Mike. "What horrible people!"

"I was just explaining that I'd jumped in merely to see what was happening when somebody called out that a gold watch was missing – it had been left on the table and it wasn't there. So they thought I'd taken it – got in at the window, you see, knocked over a heap of things, and then got frightened and chucked the watch away."

"I call this all absolute rubbish!" Mike said fiercely. "If they knew you they'd never say things like that about you, Joe."

"Actually, they did know me," said Joe. "But it didn't make any difference. They rang up Mr Frost and told him what they thought I'd done, and when I got back to the office, he was very angry at my behaviour and sacked me – gave me my money and sent me off straight away. My father's furious."

"I'm going to see these awful people," said Mike. "Who are they? Tell me their name and address, Joe."

Joe didn't say anything. He went very red and looked at the floor.

"Go on, Joe – tell me quickly," said Mike.

"Mike," said Joe in a low voice, "it – it was your house and your family. You see, I thought I knew you well enough to leap in at the window to see if anything was going wrong – I didn't realise they'd think I'd smashed those things, and taken the watch."

Mike sat down suddenly. He stared at Joe. A horrid sick feeling came over him, and thoughts raced through his mind. He knew at once what had happened.

Joe had just been passing his house when he, Mike, had smashed the vase and the lamp with his father's golf club. Joe had leaped in to see what the noise was – and had found nobody there, because Mike had run straight out of the room and hidden. The gold watch? Yes, it had been there all right – but probably Mike had hit that, too, and quite likely it was in some dark corner of the room, smashed to bits.

He sat staring at Joe, feeling wicked and very miserable. Joe had been punished for something he, Mike, had done and had run away from. Joe had lost his job. Joe was in disgrace. Their weekend was ruined. What was to be done?

"You see – you won't go and face those

people now," said Joe miserably. "They're your own parents. They wouldn't believe even you!"

Mike stood up, very pale. "They will believe me," he said. "And you'll get your job back, and your father will be very sorry he was angry with you. You'll see! But we shan't go off for our weekend. And shall I tell you why? It's because you'll never want to see me again after today!"

He went off, leaving Jane and Joe very surprised and puzzled. He knew what he had to do. He had to do the thing he had run away from that afternoon. He had to go and own up and take his punishment.

He went straight home and found his father. "Dad," he said, "ring up Mr Frost and tell him to take Joe back at once. I'm the one to blame."

"Now, what exactly do you mean, Mike?" said his father, astonished.

Mike told him. "I came in here and saw your new golf club. I swung it – and smashed the lamp and the vase. And I was a coward and ran off to hide in the shed. I hoped Mum would think it was the cat who had broken the things. I didn't know Joe was going to be blamed."

His father listened in silence, his face very

grave. "What about the gold watch?" he said. "That's missing, as you know."

"It's probably lying in the grate, or under the bookcase, smashed," said Mike. "I may have hit that too and sent it flying. I'll look, Dad."

He looked – and sure enough the watch was under the bookcase, badly damaged. He laid it in front of his father in silence.

"Punish me twice," said Mike. "Once for

doing all this and once for making the blame fall on someone else. I know I'm a coward and you're ashamed of me. I'm ashamed of myself. I've lost your good opinion, and I shall have lost Mum's trust – and I've certainly lost Joe's friendship. I'm a – a worm."

"Yes. I rather think you are," said his father. "The only good thing in the whole affair is that you owned up when you saw that Joe was being punished. I'm very disappointed in you. It will take you a long while to get back my trust and make me proud of you – and your mother will think the same. Now go and tell your mother I need to speak to her."

Mike was in for a very bad time indeed. His father would hardly talk to him. His mother looked as if she was going to burst into tears each time she looked at him. Mr Frost turned the other way when he met him.

But would you believe it, Joe didn't turn against him! He was just the same as usual, friendly, kind and generous.

"Idiot!" he said, when Mike thanked him for being so decent. "Aren't I your friend? You're in trouble and you want help. All right, that's what a friend is for. Come on, we'll face this together, and when everyone sees us about as usual, they'll soon forget what's happened.

You were a coward – but you were jolly brave, too, to go and own up just for me."

Things will work out all right, of course, but what a good thing for Mike that he had a friend like Joe!

A Circus
Adventure

One day the circus arrived at Little Carlington. As it came by all the village children ran beside it, cheering and shouting in excitement.

"Look at the great big elephant pulling that caravan! See him waving his trunk about!"

"I say, is that a chimpanzee? Why, he's all dressed up! He's wearing a jersey and trousers and a straw hat!"

"Look at the monkeys peeping out of their cages! Oh, there's one sitting on that man's shoulder – it's dressed like a little old woman!"

"Here come the horses – aren't they beautiful, and don't their coats shine?"

A caravan passed by – very smart, painted in yellow with blue wheels and a blue chimney. A boy sat at the front, driving the horse. Beside him was a girl with curly hair and brilliant blue eyes. Between them sat a terrier, a bright-eyed dog with a tail that never stopped wagging!

The boy was Jimmy, the girl was Lotta. Both

belonged to the circus, and Lucky was Jimmy's clever little dog, who went into the circus ring with him each night.

Lotta waved to the cheering children, smiling. Then she suddenly made a face at them. Jimmy saw her and gave her a hard nudge with his elbow. "Stop it, Lotta! I've told you before it's silly to make rude faces. You only make people cross."

Lotta made a rude face at Jimmy. Then she laughed, and patted Lucky. "I expect I'll still be making faces when I'm an old woman," she said.

"You'll be a jolly ugly old woman, then," said Jimmy. "Well, here's our field. We've been on the move for two whole days and nights – it will be good to stay in one place for a few weeks!"

All the caravans went slowly in through the big field-gate. Here the circus folk would put up the great circus tent, with the big ring inside, and the scores of benches for the village people to sit on.

Oona, the acrobat, came up, walking on his hands as usual, his hat on one foot. The village children loved him. Some of the boys tried to walk on their hands, too, but they fell over at once.

Lotta leaped down, and went over to the
children. "This is how you do it!" she said,
and turned herself lightly upside down. She
walked cleverly on her hands, and then turned
cartwheels over and over, first hands, then
feet, then hands again, just like a turning
wheel!

"Oooh!" said all the watching children, staring in amazement.

"You come to our circus and you'll see me doing this all round the ring," cried Lotta. "And I'll be riding horses, too, standing on their backs – and jumping from one to another!"

Sticky Stanley, the clown, came up. He pretended to fall over his feet. He bent down, put his feet straight, and fell over them again. The children roared.

"Come and see Mr Galliano's Circus!" shouted Sticky Stanley, and began to walk on his hands just like Oona, the acrobat, and Lotta.

"Where's Mr Galliano?" cried the children. "Where's the ringmaster? We want to see him."

"There he is!" shouted Jimmy, pointing to a big caravan in front. "Look – he's getting out now. Look out for his whip – it's half a mile long!"

Sure enough, there was Mr Galliano getting out of his magnificent caravan. He was a big man, dressed in a bright red coat, dazzling white breeches, and big black top-boots. He wore a black top hat well on one side, and he smiled through his long, pointed moustache.

He carried a whip with a very long lash. He raised it and cracked it loudly, with a noise like a pistol shot. *Crack!*

All the children jumped. What a whip! Galliano pointed to a spray of leaves at the top of the nearby hedge; then he cracked his whip again and the end of the lash neatly took off the spray of leaves!

"Do it again, do it again!" cried the children, but Mr Galliano shook his head. He raised his big top hat and strode through the field-gate, smiling.

He was the ringmaster, strict, hot-tempered, warm-hearted and generous. When things went well with his circus he wore his hat well on one side. When things went badly, or something displeased him, he wore his hat straight upon his head. Then the circus folk went carefully, not knowing who would get into trouble next.

"Jimmy – help Mr Volla with the bears," called Mr Galliano. "His caravan has got stuck in a rut, and the bears are upset."

"Take the reins, Lotta, and drive the caravan into the field," said Jimmy, giving the reins to Lotta. "You know where to put it – next to your father's. I'll take Lucky with me."

Jimmy jumped down from his caravan and

ran to help Mr Volla. The bears inside the cage behind the caravan were grunting loudly. What had happened? Why had they stopped? What was all the excitement?

Mr Volla was trying to get his caravan to move. "Hup, then, hup!" he shouted to his horses. "Hey, Jimmy – go into the bears' cage and keep them quiet. I can hear Dobby getting in a fine old state!"

Dobby was the youngest of his five bears, a funny, clumsy, loving little bear. Jimmy was very fond of him. He undid the doors of the cage and went in, closing them carefully

behind him. Lucky slipped in, too. All the animals loved Lucky, and not one of them had ever tried to harm her.

"Dobby, don't be silly! What's up?" said Jimmy, going to the little bear, who was padding up and down, scared. The other bears grunted. Dobby went over to Jimmy and hugged his leg. Jimmy sat down in a corner and the little bear clambered all over him, grunting happily.

Grizel, a big bear, lumbered over, half jealous. She tried to push Dobby away, but Jimmy gave her a friendly punch.

"No, keep off. You're too big to clamber over me too. Play with Lucky!" Lucky ran round Grizel, pretending to snap at her. It was a game she knew well. The other three bears sat and watched, forgetting their alarm.

"Jimmy – are you all right? We're getting Jumbo to pull us out," called Mr Volla. "It's the thick mud that's holding us back."

"Yes, we're all right," called back Jimmy. "Dobby's all over me as usual, and Grizel is playing with Lucky. I'll stay in the cage till we're safely in the field."

Jumbo, the great big elephant, was brought up by Mr Tonks, his keeper. "Soon have you out of this, Volla," said Mr Tonks. "I'm sure I

don't know what this circus would do without
Jumbo!"

"Hrrrrumph!" said Jumbo, quite agreeing.
A little girl pressed near, and Jumbo raised
his trunk. He blew hard down it and the little
girl's hat flew right off her head. She squealed
and all the other children laughed.

"Now, now, Jumbo, no tricks," said Mr
Tonks. "That little girl won't come and see
you in the circus if you do things like that."

"Oh, but I will, I will!" cried the little girl, in
delight. "Do it again, Jumbo, do it again!"

But Jumbo was now busy heaving the
caravan out of the mud. One big heave and out
it came, followed by the bears' cage behind.
The bears were jolted, but they didn't mind.
Jimmy was there and he wasn't frightened, so
why should they be frightened?

Jimmy was a marvel with the animals. They
all loved him, and he loved them. Mr Galliano
had once said that even tigers would eat out of
Jimmy's hand!

Soon the whole circus was safely in the field.
Two village boys followed. Mr Tonks shouted
at them.

"Now then, you! No kids allowed in the field
except circus kids. Get out!"

The boys took no notice and walked

defiantly over to the monkeys' cage. Mr Lilliput, their owner, was there. He shouted at the boys too.

"Clear off! You heard what was said. No kids allowed here while we're settling in."

"Why? We shan't do any harm," said one of the boys, sulkily. "Think you own the earth, do you?"

Jimmy appeared out of the bears' cage. The two boys eyed him. As he passed them quickly to go to his own caravan, one of the boys put out a foot and tripped him. They laughed. "Must be blind," said one.

"Or some kind of clown," said the other. Jimmy leaped up and swung round, red with rage. He shot out his fist at the boy who had tripped him up and the blow landed on the boy's ear as he swiftly turned his head away.

Then they both turned on Jimmy, and down he went in the mud. But not for long! Old Jumbo, who was nearby, lumbered up, picked up one of the boys with his trunk, neatly threw him aside and then picked up the other boy. He held him squirming in his trunk, yelling out in fright.

The circus folk gathered round, laughing, not attempting to rescue the boy.

"Well what are you going to do with him,

Jumbo?" said Mr Tonks. "Like to throw him into the stream over there?"

" No, no, no!" yelled the boy, wriggling. "Let me go, let me go!"

"Drop him, Jumbo," ordered Mr Tonks, and Jumbo did what he was told, dropping the boy neatly into a thick patch of churned up mud.

The two boys ran off, one almost in tears. "We'll pay you back, you dirty circus crowd!" yelled one boy when he was well out of reach. "You look out – we'll jolly well pay you back!"

"Bah!" said Mr Tonks scornfully, and Jumbo lifted his trunk and sent a loud jeer after the boys. "Hrrrrumph!"

"Now, get busy!" shouted Mr Galliano, suddenly appearing round a caravan. "Where's Brownie? Oh, there you are. Jimmy, go with Brownie and help him arrange the caravans round the field. Lotta, go to your mother's dogs. They want quietening. Bless us all, do I have to tell you what to do, yes, no?" Soon the two village boys were forgotten as the circus folk settled into their new camping-place. Brownie, Jimmy's father, hurried round the camp, giving a hand to everyone, for he was carpenter and handyman to the circus. Jimmy helped.

Lotta stood with her mother's troupe of dogs round her, looking happy. It was fun being on the road – but it was even better fun to be in camp again. The circus would soon be performing once more, and everyone would be happy.

In three days the circus was ready to give its first show. The big top was up, the great tent in which the show was given. Jimmy's father had set out the benches as usual, and done many repair jobs. Lotta's mother and Jimmy's had been busy washing and mending the clothes of the circus folk. However dirty and untidy they looked in the camp, they always looked spick and span in the ring.

"You look such a dirty little grub, Lotta," said Mrs Brown, Jimmy's mother, as the little girl came into her caravan. "Nobody would ever think you were the same little girl when you go into the ring with your silvery wings, fluffy dress and shining hair!"

"Oh, well – that's different," said Lotta. "What about Jimmy? He looks grand enough in the ring, too, when he takes Lucky in to perform. Did you know Lucky is learning a new trick, Mrs Brown?"

"And what's that?" asked Mrs Brown,

sewing silver buttons on to a little green cape.

"Well, Jimmy's got ten skittles, each num-bered," said Lotta. "And when Jimmy sets them up he calls out a number and Lucky fetches the right skittle!"

"Oh, yes – and she fetches it because Jimmy has rubbed it with a sausage or something!" said Mrs Brown. "Not much of a trick, that! Still, she's a clever little creature – the cleverest dog I ever did see."

"I've just been grooming my horse, Black Beauty," said Lotta. "She's shining like a mirror! Mr Galliano has given me some new plumes for her to wear. Won't she look lovely, Mrs Brown, tossing her head with its big black feathers?"

" She certainly will," said Mrs Brown. "Now, if you're going to chatter for hours, Lotta, just thread a needle and help me sew on these buttons."

"Oh, I'm just going," said Lotta, at once. "Hello – who's snooping round your caravan?"

A boy's face was looking in at the window. "It's one of those awful boys again!" cried Lotta, and shot out of the caravan.

"What are you doing, prying round?" she shouted. "You've been sent away before, you and your ugly friend there!"

"We don't let girls talk to us like that," said the first boy. "You're a dirty little grub. Go and wash your face!"

Now, Lotta didn't in the least mind being called a dirty little grub by Mrs Brown, but she wasn't going to have these boys calling her names! She rushed at them at top speed, and took the first one so much by surprise that he sat down in a puddle. She stooped and picked up a clod of earth and threw it at the second boy. It hit him on the arm.

"Here!" said the boy, angrily. "Stop it!" He swung round at Lotta and caught her arms roughly.

She yelled at the top of her voice and who should come to her rescue but Sammy the chimpanzee! He had been sitting peacefully outside Mr Wally's caravan peeling an orange, and when he heard Lotta's yells he sprang up, dropping his orange in fright.

What! Somebody had got hold of his friend Lotta? Sammy was furious. He raced clumsily over to where the two boys were shaking Lotta vigorously. He flung himself on one of the boys, making an angry chattering noise.

"Oh – who is it – what is it?" yelled the boy. "Here, you, girl – call him off!"

Lotta hesitated. She was very tempted not to

call off Sammy, but she knew he might bite the
boys and maul them. He was so very strong.

Then she grinned. All right – she would call
the chimpanzee off – but she would give him a
little treat!

"Sammy! Stop!" she commanded. "Stand
away! You can chase them if they run."

Sammy didn't want to let these boys go,
but he obeyed Lotta. He stood beside them,
dressed in his jersey and shorts, but his straw
hat had fallen off. He looked very fierce indeed.

"Let's go," said one boy to the other, and
they turned away.

"Wait," said Lotta. "Sammy, go through their pockets!"

Now this was a trick that Mr Wally had taught Sammy to perform in the ring. He kept a packet of cigarettes in his pocket, and a box of matches, and he had taught Sammy to take these from his pocket when he was not looking. Then Sammy lit a cigarette, and the audience always roared with laughter at Mr Wally's comical look of surprise when he suddenly turned round and saw Sammy.

Sammy was delighted to go through somebody else's pockets! He ran his black fingers through the pockets in the two boys' clothes. They stood still, trembling, not knowing how gentle the big creature's nature was, or how friendly he usually was to everyone.

Out came a dirty hanky, a notebook, a stump of pencil, some toffees wrapped in paper, an apple, some bits of string and a penknife; Sammy put them all into his own pockets, grunting in delight. He unwrapped one of the toffees and offered it politely to Lotta.

"Those are our toffees," said one of the boys, angrily.

"Well, they're not now," said Lotta, rubbing

58

her arm where the boys had held it. "They're Sammy's. Look, here comes Mr Galliano with his whip. I'll tell him about you!"

But the boys were even more scared at the look of Mr Galliano than of Sammy the chimp, and they took to their heels and fled to the hedge, which they scrambled through at top speed.

They felt safer on the other side. They stood and yelled at Lotta. "You look out! There's trouble coming to you, Miss Dirty Grub! You look out for yourself."

Lotta didn't bother to reply. She considered that she had paid the boys back well. They wouldn't come near the circus camp again, she felt certain.

She went to find Jimmy to tell him about the boys. He had been taking the performing dogs for a long walk over the hills. Lotta usually went, too, but she had been very busy getting her horse, Black Beauty, ready for the opening performance that night.

She saw Jimmy coming down the distant hill and ran to meet him. The dogs were let off the leash as soon as Jimmy saw her coming, and ran to meet her, tumbling over one another in their eagerness to reach her.

"Down, Pincher! Down, Toby! Oh, Lucky,

don't prance round in that muddy patch! I'll
have to spend ages bathing you, you dirty little
dog – and you were only scrubbed yesterday!"

Lotta told Jimmy about the two boys. He
frowned when he heard how they had held
her by the arms. "I'll look out for them and tell
them a few things," he said. "I wonder if
they're planning any mischief? Do you
remember, Lotta – a boy got into the camp
and let the horses loose one night?"

"Yes. And one of them plunged into the
stream and broke its leg," said Lotta,
remembering how upset she had been. "Well,
if those boys try any tricks like that they'll be
sorry. I think I'll have Black Beauty tethered

by my caravan while we're here. You've scared me, Jimmy! I wouldn't like anything to happen to her!"

The circus opened that night, and the villagers from miles around came trooping to see it. Mr Galliano's Circus. Why, it was famous all over the country!

"I hope they've got those monkeys," said one of the visitors. "I saw them before, when the circus came to a town I stayed at. They had a tea party, and they were so funny. One poured a cup of milk down another monkey's neck!"

"It's the horses I want to see," said another. "They dance, you know – waltz in time to the music. Circus horses are always such beautiful creatures."

"I want to see the clowns," said a child. "There's one called Sticky Stanley that my aunt remembers seeing. He put stilts on one day under long, long trousers, and walked into the ring looking like a giant!"

The circus folk were always excited when the first performance came along. Lights blazed out, the band struck up, the ring was freshly strewn with sawdust. People poured in and filled up the benches.

Lotta and Jimmy peeped round the curtains which soon would be swung back to allow the performers to go into the ring.

"It's a full house!" said Jimmy. "Lucky, look out there, little dog. You've got to do your best tonight, for all those people."

"Wuff, wuff," agreed Lucky.

"I shall put on your little soft rubber socks," said Jimmy, "and you can walk your own little tightrope."

"I love to see her do that," said Lotta, patting the excited little dog. "She does so love it too – she's a proper circus dog, Jimmy, isn't she?"

Lucky certainly brought the house down whenever she walked on the little low tightrope specially put up for her by Jimmy. She had a wonderful sense of balance and had never once fallen off. Jimmy was sure she boasted about it to all the other dogs!

Trumpets sounded, and the circus folk sprang into their places behind the curtain, ready for the grand parade round the ring. Tan-tan-tara! TAN-TAN-TARA!

In went the horses first of all, stepping proudly, tossing their plumed heads. In went Sticky Stanley and all the other clowns, tripping each other up, performing ridiculous

somersaults, hitting each other with balloons. In went the performing dogs with Lal, Lotta's mother, and in went Mr Volla with his bears, little Dobby shambling along hand in hand with him.

Lotta went too, on her lovely Black Beauty. Jimmy followed, with Lucky prancing round him, a bright pleated ruff round her little furry neck. What a brave, happy show they were, and how the people cheered and clapped.

That first performance was a grand success. Everyone clapped till their hands were sore. Jimmy and Lotta had to come on again and again and bow.

"Everyone loves my little Lotta!" said Lal, proudly. "Everyone is clapping her."

But she wasn't quite right. Two people were not cheering for Lotta, or clapping her. Two people were angry at her success that evening.

They were not in the big tent. They were outside, peering through a hole that they had made with a knife. Nobody saw or heard them. They were the two boys who had worried Lotta that morning.

"Bah!" said one, when they spied Lotta through the hole in the tent. "That dirty little grub again!"

The boys watched right to the end of the

show. The night was very dark, and they were well hidden in the shadows. "Better look out now, Ed, in case anyone sees us when they come out of the show," said one.

"We're all right, Jeff," said Ed. "We can mix with the crowd."

They did mix with the crowd, sauntering along as if they, like everyone else, had paid for their seats and had sat in the big tent.

They followed Mr Lilliput as he took his monkeys to their cage, and shut them in. He put Jemima with them, too, because he knew he would be busy for a while.

The two boys stood back in the little crowd and watched. They saw Mr Wally come along with Sammy the chimpanzee, and go to his caravan too.

He put Sammy in. Sammy lived with Mr Wally. He had a bunk in his fine caravan, and Mr Wally treated him just as if he were a child. Sammy dressed himself each day, brushed his fur and washed his face. It was really marvellous to watch him.

Sammy didn't want to be left by himself in the caravan. He was excited by the circus performance. He loved the crowds, the lights, the cheering and the clapping. He sat on the bunk, picking at the sheet there.

He should have begun to undress himself, but he didn't.

Ed and Jeff watched Mr Wally shutting the chimpanzee into the caravan. They noticed that he didn't lock it, but merely slid an outside bolt to keep the chimpanzee inside.

Ed looked at Jeff, raising his eyebrows. Jeff nodded. A little shiver of excitement ran down his back. He and Ed were always on the lookout for mischief – and now, here was some, right under their noses!

They could slip the bolt and open the chimp's door! Nobody would know. It was dark just there, and the people had now gone to see the beautiful horses being led out of the big tent.

Ed climbed up to look into the window of the caravan, but it was dark inside and he could see nothing. Sammy could see him, though, dark as it was! The chimpanzee had eyes as sharp as a cat's at night. He sat quite still, his eyes on the window.

He heard a little noise at the door, and he looked there. Was it Mr Wally coming back? No, it didn't sound like him. He heard the bolt outside being slid back slowly and carefully.

Then the door moved a little, and was left

slightly ajar. Sammy sat and listened, puzzled. Who was out there? He didn't like it. He made a small grunting noise and bared his teeth. If any enemy was going to come in, Sammy was ready for him!

But no enemy came. Instead, stealthy footsteps moved silently away, as the two boys left the caravan, nudging each other as they went, delighted with the mischief they had done.

They came to the caravan where the monkeys were. From inside came an excited chattering and bickering. The monkeys, like the chimpanzee, were excited. They were talking over the thrills of the evening. Little Jemima, Mr Lilliput's greatest pet, watched eagerly for him to come back.

Then she would throw herself at him, sit on his shoulder, cuddle into his neck and nibble his ear lovingly. But Mr Lilliput didn't come. He was always busy on the first night of the circus opening.

The two boys heard the excited monkeys. They nudged one another. Was this caravan unlocked, too? Could they open this door and hope that the monkeys would all escape?

"We mustn't be caught," whispered Ed to Jeff. "We'd get into terrible trouble if we were."

"We could always say that we saw that girl and that boy – what's his name? – Jimmy – we could say we saw them opening the vans," whispered back Jeff. "Feel along this door, Ed – is there an outside bolt?"

There wasn't, but, on the other hand, the door was not even locked. It was just closed, for not one of the monkeys could open it from inside. Mr Lilliput knew that none of the circus folk would go to his van, and he rarely locked it when he knew he was coming back in a short while.

Jeff found the handle. He turned it quietly. Although it seemed to make no noise at all, the monkeys inside heard it, and stiffened. Who was coming in?

Nobody. The door was simply opened a little way and left ajar. The monkeys, silent now, stared at the door. Through the crack they could see the lights that flared over the entrance of the big tent some distance away.

Not far off there came a bellowing snort from Jumbo. He was tethered to a great tree. His sharp little eyes had seen the two prowling boys, and he knew them at once. How did he know them? He couldn't see them clearly, he couldn't smell them, nor could he hear them, and yet Jumbo knew these two boys, and knew too that they had been up to mischief. Clever old Jumbo!

He tugged at his strong rope. It would not break. He gave a mighty "Hrrrrumph!" and made a lot of people jump. But nobody took much notice.

Sammy got out of his caravan first. He went cautiously to the door and pushed it open a little more. He wondered where Mr Wally was. He wanted him. He wanted to be fussed and praised and given the titbits he always had after a show.

He muttered to himself. He would go and find his master. He must be somewhere out there. Sammy could easily sniff him out.

Sammy slipped out into the darkness. He crossed over to the monkeys' caravan and

stopped. What were the monkeys doing? Sammy knew them all and liked them, though they sometimes teased him unmercifully – especially little Jemima, who had taken his straw hat from him dozens of times!

Sammy stuck his nose in the door, opening it wider. He made a few friendly noises. The monkeys knew him at once and Jemima bounded over. She landed on his shoulder and felt for his hat, but he was not wearing it. So she gave his fur a sharp tug and then threw herself to the ground, scampering away in her little coat and skirt at top speed.

All the other monkeys followed, except one who was too tired. They followed Jemima – and she followed big Sammy.

Sammy kept away from the crowds. He was looking for Mr Wally among the caravans, but he couldn't find him anywhere. He came at last to Jimmy's caravan, clambered up on a wheel and peered through the window.

Was his beloved master there, talking with that nice boy, Jimmy? No, he wasn't. Jimmy's mother was there, though, cooking something on her little oil-stove. She looked up suddenly at a noise from the window, just as Sammy slid away from it.

"Good gracious – for a moment I thought

that was Sammy!" she said to herself. "But he'll be safely in Wally's caravan. I'm imagining things."

Sammy lumbered over to the hedge. On the other side he could see people going down the lane. Was Mr Wally with them? He decided to go and see.

He squeezed through a gap and found himself in the dark lane. The people were all going home together, chattering and laughing. Some carried torches, and shone the beams on the ground to make sure they did not walk in muddy patches.

Sammy walked with them. It was so dark that nobody knew he was a chimpanzee. He lumbered along between a man and a boy, with two women in front.

A woman behind shone her torch on his legs, but he was wearing trousers, so the woman thought he was a little man. Not a single person guessed that a chimpanzee was mixing with them, walking back to their village!

Sammy began to feel excited. This was fun! He hadn't been in such a crowd before, like this, all on his own. He longed to take someone's hand, just as he so often took Mr Wally's.

He slid his hand through the arm of the boy next to him. The boy thought it was some friend of his and took hold of the hand. It was furry! He gave a yell and pushed the surprised chimp away.

"Dad! Dad! Who's that? He's got fur on his hands!" cried the boy. His father laughed.

"Oh, you've got the circus on your brain. You'll be thinking it was the chimpanzee next!"

Sammy slid away, frightened by the boy's

shout. He longed for Mr Wally. He stopped by
a bush and wondered what to do. He was lost
now, so the only thing was to follow the
crowds. He padded on again.

Behind him, scampering along in the
shadows, came Jemima. The other monkeys,
frightened, had bounded back to the circus
field, and were sitting on the roof of their
caravan, waiting for Mr Lilliput to come. They
cowered down, feeling that they were naughty
– they shouldn't have left their caravan! But
they couldn't get back into it because the wind
had blown the door shut.

Soon Mr Lilliput came, still dressed in his
colourful circus ring suit. He was whistling
softly, pleased with the evening's success,
pleased with his clever troupe of monkeys. He
opened the caravan door and shone his bright
torch inside.

Only one monkey was there, the tired one,
who had fallen asleep. She opened her eyes
now and blinked. Mr Lilliput stared round
the van in alarm.

"Linda! Where are the other monkeys?"
he cried to the only one left. "What has
happened?"

Linda chattered and came over to Mr
Lilliput. And then the other monkeys on the

top of the van chattered too. Wally went out and flashed his torch over them. "What are you doing there? Who let you out? Come in at once, all of you!"

Down they all came, leaping and scampering. Mr Lilliput watched them. Then he called anxiously, "Jemima! Jemima, where are you?"

But his favourite little monkey was not there. No amount of calling brought her to the van. Mr Lilliput shut the door, locked it, and turned round, sick at heart. What had happened to little Jemima?

And then he heard a loud shout nearby. It was Mr Wally. He had gone into his caravan and found it empty. Where was Sammy?

"Sammy's gone!" he yelled. "SAMMY'S GONE! Come out and look for him, all of you. He's gone!"

"So has Jemima!" called Mr Lilliput, running up. "Get Mr Galliano, Wally. This is serious. If they've gone with the crowds, there'll be trouble. Where can they be?"

What a to-do there was at once over the whole of the camp. Everyone came from their caravans to hear the news. Mr Galliano strode over in his white breeches and no coat, and with his hat straight on his head. Bad luck of any sort always made him put his hat on dead straight instead of on one side.

"Sammy gone?" he said, astonished. "Wally, we must get him. He'll get scared and might go for someone. We don't want him to be shot by some idiot."

"Oh, no, no!" wailed poor Mr Wally, in the greatest alarm. "Don't say such things, Mr Galliano. Jemima's gone, too."

"Search every corner of the camp," commanded Mr Galliano. "Put on all the brightest lights. Hurry!"

Jimmy was half-undressed when he heard the disturbance. Lotta came to fetch him. "Jimmy! Sammy's gone, and Jemima too. Do come!"

"Sammy's gone?" said Mrs Brown, Jimmy's mother, suddenly remembering the face at the window that night. "Did you say Sammy? I'm sure I saw him peeping in my window tonight. He must have been looking for you, Jimmy."

"Mum – did you really see him?" said Jimmy, an idea coming into his mind at once. "Where's Lucky? – Lucky, come here. You can help. Lotta, nip over to Mr Wally's caravan and bring something of Sammy's here. Quick!"

Lotta was very quick. She came back with Sammy's pyjamas. He slept in pyjamas just as his master did. Jimmy took them.

He bent down to Lucky. "Smell," he said. "These are Sammy's, Lucky – you can smell they are Sammy's. Now come outside with me. We'll find out if you can smell whether Sammy was really here tonight, peeping in through the window – if he was, you can sniff his trail for me, and show me the way he went."

"Oh, Jimmy – that's clever of you," said Lotta. "We must find him. He escaped once before, and he was nearly shot. Sniff about, Lucky, sniff well!"

Lucky knew the pyjamas were Sammy's. He smelled Sammy's footmarks outside the van too. He sniffed round, found the trail and set off.

"He's got it!" said Jimmy, excited. "Wait, Lucky – I must slip your lead on or you may go too fast for us."

Lucky led the two children here and there, and then made for the hedge. He came to the gap where the chimpanzee had squeezed through, and went through it himself, followed by Jimmy and Lotta. Then off he went down the lane, tugging at the lead, following Sammy's fresh, strong scent.

"Clever dog, good dog," panted Jimmy.

"Take us to Sammy. Oh, Lotta, I wonder where he is – and Jemima, too."

Sammy was at that very moment wandering through the town, still followed by Jemima. He had bumped into a very scared old gentleman, who had immediately rung up the police and reported that a "very big monkey followed by a very small one" had just bumped into him round a corner.

"Ah," said the policeman, "is that so, sir? That was a chimpanzee, the big one, sir – just reported lost from the circus."

The old gentleman nearly fainted. A chimpanzee! Worse and worse. He decided to remain in the street telephone box until the animal was caught, even if he had to stay there till morning.

Sammy was frightened and very tired. So was Jemima. Neither of them had the faintest idea of the way back to the circus. Jemima gave a little whimpering cry and Sammy turned round. She leaped on to his shoulder, cuddling into his neck, and the two went on again together.

They came to a wall. Sammy leaped to the top and looked down into the dark garden below. There was a shed or hut at one side. It looked a little like a caravan without wheels to the chimpanzee, as he peered through the darkness. He decided to go to it and creep in there. Perhaps Mr Wally would come and find him.

So he made his way to it and pushed open the door. Inside were some sacks and old boxes.

Sammy thankfully curled up on a sack with Jemima cuddled against him.

Not far behind were Jimmy and Lotta, with Lucky tugging at the lead, going at top speed up and down the streets where Sammy and Jemima had wandered. "What a way they went!" panted Lotta as they both ran after the excited little dog.

Lucky came to the wall on the top of which Sammy had jumped. The trail came to an unexpected end there, of course. Lucky stopped and sniffed all round. No, there was no scent after this.

"Better go into this garden and snoop round," said Jimmy. "Perhaps Sammy jumped up on the wall. That would break his trail, of course."

They cautiously went in at the gate. It creaked and somebody standing under a tree not far off heard it. It was a policeman, and he swung round at once. He thought he saw two shadowy figures by the gate, and went silently over to it. Was it burglars?

Jimmy and Lotta felt themselves pulled along by Lucky at once, as soon as they got into the garden. He had picked up the trail again, of course! He made for the little shed, whining with excitement. He knew he was near to Sammy and Jemima now!

Just as the three got to the shed, and Jimmy was feeling for the door, there came the flash of a strong light full on them, and a stern voice said, "And what do you think you are up to? You just come along with me!"

It was the policeman who had come in at the gate, had heard the noise they made, and now

had caught them in his torch's light. Jimmy almost jumped out of his skin, and Lotta gave a gasp.

"We're looking for a chimpanzee," said Jimmy. "He's quite near here – my dog's on his trail."

"Ho – a chimpanzee!" said the policeman, most disbelievingly. "That's a fine tale, I must say. You're a couple of bad children, no doubt about it – going to break in somewhere, weren't you?"

"No, of course not," said Lotta, indignantly. "We are looking for a chimpanzee. I believe he's in this shed."

"What do you two take me for!" said the policeman, coming right up to them. "Fairy-tales don't go far with me. You wait till my chief comes along in a minute or two, and try that tale on him. I'm going to take you to the police station, and we'll meet my chief on the way."

Lotta shook off his hand furiously. "Don't! We must find Sammy. Jemima's gone, too. You don't understand how important it is to find them both. I'm sure they are in this shed."

A voice suddenly came from the gate. "What's all this going on? Is that you, Jones?"

"Yes, sir," said the policeman, glad to hear

his chief's voice. "I've got two kids here, sir – about to break into this shed, I should say. Stuffing me up with tales about looking for a chimpanzee they are! Says he's about here somewhere – I don't think!"

"A chimp? That must be the one reported to us a few minutes ago," said the chief. "He's dangerous, Jones. Have you got a weapon of some sort?"

"There's a heavy spade here, sir – and a chopper," said the policeman, startled. He picked up the chopper and gave the spade to his chief. Jimmy was scared. Nobody – nobody must try to kill Sammy – why, he was as gentle as Jemima!

Sammy and Jemima heard the voices. Sammy came to the door of the shed, blinking in the light from the torch.

"There he is – that's a chimp all right!" shouted the chief. "Throw the chopper at him – get him, quick, before he gets us!"

"No, no!" shouted Jimmy and Lotta at exactly the same moment, and they flung themselves on the alarmed Sammy. But to his delight they were his friends, Lotta and Jimmy, and he put his great arms round them at once.

"Stand away from that chimp," ordered the chief. "You'll get hurt. We've got to get him

somehow. And good gracious – is that a baby
chimp behind?"

"No – it's Jemima!" cried Jimmy, in delight.
"Oh, Jemima, you went with Sammy, did you?
Now we've got you both. Please, sir, let us
take them back to the circus. We've been
hunting for them before they came to any
harm. Their owners will be so glad to have
them back."

"I can't let you two children take a dangerous animal like that through the streets," said
the chief of police. "He ought to be tied up.
Here, now, here – what do you think you're
doing?"

"Just taking Sammy home," said Jimmy,
firmly, pushing past the two burly policemen.
"Don't try to stop us – he may bite you. And
don't try any funny games with the chopper or
the spade, because you might hurt us. That's
right, Jemima, you ride on Lotta's shoulder.
Goodnight, sir!"

The policemen couldn't do anything but let
Lotta, Jimmy, Lucky, Sammy and Jemima
pass. The two men drew back in alarm as
Sammy showed his teeth at them, but he was
only smiling!

"Better follow them to the circus to make
sure they're going there," said the chief,
uneasily. So they walked behind the strange
little company, still carrying the spade and
the chopper!

"Wally, Wally! We've got Sammy!" yelled
Jimmy as soon as they reached the camp. "And
Jemima, too! Lucky trailed them for us!"

Sammy leaped on Mr Wally in delight, and
almost strangled him in his joy at being
with him again. Jemima cuddled against Mr

84

Lilliput, getting right under his coat and vest and against his chest. "Do you feel safe there?" asked Mr Lilliput, fondling her. "How did you get loose? Naughty little Jemima!"

"You did well, Jimmy and Lotta," said Mr Galliano, suddenly looming up in the camp lights. "Always, always you do well, yes! Good children. You shall come to my caravan and share a supper with me, yes, no?"

"Oh, thank you, sir," said Jimmy. "I hope it's sausages!"

"It is sausages," said Mr Galliano. "You like them, yes?"

"This is a nice, happy ending," whispered Lotta, as she walked beside Jimmy to Mr Galliano's grand caravan, from which came a magnificent smell of fried sausages and onions.

It wasn't quite the end of the adventure though – not for the two bad boys, anyhow! They came up the next day to hear what had happened because of their mischief – and who should see them but Jumbo the elephant.

Jumbo looked at them. He remembered their curious behaviour of the night before. Jumbo didn't forget things like that. He didn't in the least like these boys, and he knew they should not be in the circus field.

He lumbered over to them. Before they knew what was happening first Ed was taken up in Jumbo's big trunk and thrown up into a tree – and then Jeff was taken up. He was thrown high, too – but he didn't land in the tree – he landed on top of Mr Galliano's caravan!

And out came Mr Galliano in a rage, his great whip in his hand. "What do you think you are doing, climbing on my caravan?" he roared. "And you, up that tree? You think the camp belongs to you, yes, no?"

And then he began cracking that long whip of his. *Crack!* The lash swept Jeff's boots as he ran at top speed over the field. *Crack!* It caught Ed round the middle of his legs and stung him well and truly.

"Run, yes, run – and come back for more whip if you want to!" bellowed Mr Galliano, bringing everyone out to watch in astonishment.

Crack! The lash whizzed through the air again and caught Jeff on the hand. He yelled.

Crack! It caught Ed on his right ear, and he howled, too. How it stung! And how clever Mr Galliano was, sending the tip of his lash to ears and fingers and ankles as the two bad boys stumbled across the field!

"They won't come back again," said Lotta, pleased. She was right. They didn't!
How everyone laughed – yes, even Sammy!

The Mystery of
Melling Cottage

"Your Uncle Thomas is coming to stay for a day or two," Mrs Hollins said to John. "He's an inspector, you know, in the police force, and a very clever man."

"Goodness!" said John. "Will he tell me stories of how he catches burglars and thieves?"

"I dare say he will, if you ask him," said his mother. "And you mind you behave yourself when he comes! He thinks that young boys ought to be taught how to behave when they're small – then, he says, they wouldn't get into trouble when they're older, and appear in the courts."

John grinned at his mother. He wasn't a bad boy, and he knew his mother was proud of him. "Well, I'll try not to burgle anybody's house or steal anybody's chickens, Mum," he said, "at any rate, not while Uncle Thomas is here!"

Uncle Thomas arrived. He was not in his

uniform because he was on holiday and John felt rather disappointed. He had hoped to see a very grand-looking policeman in an inspector's uniform. But Uncle Thomas was in a tweed suit and, except that he was very big and had a very clever face with a pair of sharp eyes, he looked quite ordinary.

He liked John at once. "Now there's a smart boy for you," he said to John's mother, when the boy was out of the room. "Asks me sensible questions, listens quietly to my answers, and takes it all in. And when I took him out for a walk this morning he noticed quite as much as I did."

"I'm glad," said Mrs Hollins. "He's a good boy too, honest and straight. I'm lucky!"

John heard a lot of his uncle's tales. How this thief was caught, and that one – how a burglar was traced and the stolen goods found – how bad boys are dealt with and punished.

"We learn to use our eyes, our ears, yes, and even our noses, in the police force!" said his uncle. "You would be surprised if you knew how many times a very small thing has led to the capture of criminals."

John made up his mind to use his ears, eyes, and even his nose too, in future, just in case he might happen on something interesting. But although he kept a sharp look-out as he went about, he couldn't really seem to find anything suspicious or strange that needed looking into.

"John dear, take this bundle of old clothes along to Mrs Browning, will you," said his mother, two days later. "She's a poor old thing and lives all alone in Melling Cottage. You know where that is."

"Yes, I know," said John, and put down his book. "I'll go now." He took the bundle of clothes and set off to Melling Cottage. He knew where it was, at the end of a little lane.

On the way he met old Mrs Browning herself. She was a little, bent old woman, with a pale worried face. She had a basket in one hand, and her purse in the other. She was so thin that John felt sure she didn't eat enough.

"Oh, Mrs Browning, good morning," said John. "I was just going to your cottage with these clothes from my mother. Will there be anyone there?"

"No, no, there won't," said Mrs Browning. "It is empty, and I've locked the door. I'll take the clothes with me now, thank you, John, and carry them back home when I've done the shopping."

"Oh no, they're too heavy," said John. "Haven't you got a shed or anything I can

91

just pop the bundle into, till you come back? I could run along to your cottage, put the clothes in the shed, and you'd find them there when you got back."

Mrs Browning hesitated. "Well, yes, there is an old shed," she said. "It's halfway down the garden. You could slip down there, open the door and put in the bundle. Thank you very much."

John said goodbye and went off with the bundle. He came to the deserted lane where Melling Cottage stood. He went down it and saw the little cottage, a tiny wreath of smoke coming from its chimney.

He pushed open the rickety gate and went along the side of the cottage into the garden. Yes, there was the shed, halfway down. He went to it, opened the wooden door and looked inside. It seemed to be full of rubbish, a broken chair or two, a few pots, a spade, and some firewood. John put the bundle of old clothes down on a broken chair and then made his way up the garden again, towards the cottage.

Growing beside the wall was a very tall foxglove. A bumble-bee crawled into one of the flowers, and John stood still to watch it. And then, as he was standing there, he heard a sudden noise from inside the cottage.

It was the sound of people talking! It started
up quite suddenly and made him jump. Who
was in the cottage? Mrs Browning had distinctly said that it was empty and locked up.
Then who was there?

The voices went on. Then suddenly they
stopped and a band began to play, loudly at
first, and then softly.

"What an idiot I am!" said John to himself. "It's not people. It's only the radio."

He was about to go on, when a sudden thought struck him. Surely the radio had started up quite suddenly – it hadn't been on when he first stopped to look at the bumble-bee in the foxglove. And then the programme had been changed to another one – well, then there must be someone in the house playing about with it!

It was very puzzling. John wondered what to do. He decided to go and knock at the door and see if anyone came. So he went round to the little front door and knocked loudly. He waited, but nobody came. There was not a sound from the cottage except the radio, which was still playing music.

John left the cottage, still feeling very puzzled. He met little Mrs Browning hurrying home from her shopping. She stopped and spoke to him.

"Did you find the shed all right? Thank you, John, you're a kind boy."

"Oh, Mrs Browning, I hope there isn't any-one in your cottage," said John, anxiously, "because when I was coming back from the shed, I suddenly heard the radio being switched on."

Mrs Browning looked startled. Then she smiled. "Oh, I must have left it on when I went out for my bit of shopping. I'm that careless! No wonder it gave you a start, John. I'm always doing that."

"Oh," said John, thinking that he must have been mistaken. "Well, that explains it, then."

He walked back home. But on the way he remembered that he had distinctly heard two programmes, one after the other, as if the radio had first been on one, and then had been changed to another.

He thought about it. "Perhaps, though, it was just one programme," he said to himself. "I might have heard the end of one part, and then the beginning of the next, which was music. It could easily have been all one programme. And anyway, Mrs Browning seemed quite certain she had left it on."

All the same there was a little nagging doubt going on at the back of his mind. It did seem as if the radio had suddenly been put on – else why hadn't he heard it when he first went down the garden? He decided to look at the *Radio Times*, and see what programmes were on at that particular time.

"It was about ten-past eleven when I was there," thought John, looking at his watch.

He looked up the programmes. On one there
was a talk, lasting from eleven o'clock to a
quarter to twelve. On another there was a
half-hour of dance-band music.

"Well, then, I *did* hear a bit of two
programmes," said John to himself. "It's jolly
strange. I wonder if I ought to find out a little
more! I wouldn't like Mrs Browning to find a
burglar waiting for her in her cottage!"

So that afternoon John went along to
Melling Cottage again. The smoke was still
coming from the chimney. The radio was silent
now. There seemed to be no one about at all.

96

Feeling a little bit uncomfortable, John knocked at the door. He heard a sudden scraping noise from inside, and then silence. Somebody was there, no doubt about it. He knocked again. He heard another little noise, this time from upstairs. Then he heard footsteps coming to the door. He held his breath, wondering who was going to open it.

And, after all, it was little Mrs Browning, looking quite scared! "Oh, John, it's you!" she said, sounding relieved. "Not many people come along here, and I couldn't think who it was. You must excuse my being so long in answering, but I was in the middle of my cooking."

"That's all right," said John. "I – er – I just came to see if you'd found the clothes all right in the shed."

"Oh yes, thank you," said Mrs Browning. "Won't you come in?"

"Well, I don't think I will," said John, feeling rather foolish. "Goodbye, Mrs Browning."

He went away, still feeling foolish. All the same, he was feeling puzzled too. Why had he heard a noise downstairs when he had first knocked, and a noise upstairs when he had knocked a second time?

"I'm making a to-do about nothing!" he

thought at last. "Absolutely nothing. I'll forget about it."

But that night, in bed, he began to worry about it again. He felt sure something was not quite right at Melling Cottage. Mrs Browning did look very white and worried and frightened. And recently she had gone very thin, too. Was there anything the matter?

All at once John threw off the bedclothes, dressed himself quickly, put on his shoes and slipped quietly downstairs and out of the back door. He was soon making his way to Melling Cottage. It was about eleven o'clock, and dark, for there was no moon at all.

Down the little lane went John, and came to Melling Cottage. It stood there, a small dark mass by the side of the lane. There was no light in it at all, and no sound from it.

"I'm an idiot," said John to himself. "What did I expect to find? I don't know! There isn't a thing to be seen or heard. I expect old Mrs Browning is in bed and fast asleep. Well, I'll just creep quietly round the cottage once and then go back to bed. I'm really being very silly."

He walked quietly along the side of the cottage, and then round to the back. There was still nothing to be seen or heard in the

black night. John walked softly over the grass at the back of the cottage.

And then he stopped suddenly. He hadn't seen anything, or heard anything – but what was this he smelled?

He stood and sniffed quietly. Somebody quite nearby – sitting at the cottage window perhaps – was smoking a very strong pipe tobacco. John knew it well, because old Taffy the gardener smoked the same, and John had smelled it time and time again when he had sat with Taffy in the shed during the old man's dinner hour.

And now he could smell that same tobacco being smoked again! It was quite certain it could not be Mrs Browning. It was some man, sitting there quietly in the dark, smoking by himself.

It was all very odd and puzzling. Did Mrs Browning know there was a man in her house? She had said she was all alone, a little, bent, old woman living by herself. Perhaps she didn't know there was a stranger there.

John sniffed the tobacco smoke once more and then turned to go home very quietly. He let himself in at his back door and wondered what to do. Should he go to Uncle Thomas and wake him and tell him? Or would Uncle think he was silly?

"I'd better wake him," said John. "Better to be thought silly than to leave an old woman in danger. That man might rob her!"

So he woke up his uncle. The inspector roused himself at once, and sat up, alert and wide-awake. He listened to John's strange little tale. "You did quite right to come and tell me, John," he said. "We'll investigate in the morning. There's something unusual going on in Melling Cottage, no doubt about that. Sharp work, John!"

"But oughtn't we to do something tonight?" asked John. "Suppose that man robbed Mrs Browning or hurt her?"

"I don't somehow think we need worry

about that," said Uncle Thomas. "Get back to bed. We'll tackle it in the morning."

The next day Uncle Thomas went along to see the local police and make a few inquiries. Then he called back for John. "Come along with us," he said. "Then you'll see what the mystery was."

Two policemen were with him. Awed and a little scared, John went along to Melling Cottage with them and his uncle. They knocked loudly at the door. Mrs Browning opened it. She gave a scream when she saw the policemen.

"Oh! What do you want?"

"Madam, I'm sorry – but we have reason to believe that you are hiding your son, who is a deserter from the army," said one of the policemen. "I have a search warrant here. I must search your house."

They went in. John stayed outside with his uncle, looking scared. Presently the two policemen came out again – and this time they had a great lout with them, sullen and cruel-looking. Behind came Mrs Browning, weeping bitterly.

"He had got a hiding-place under the boards of the bedroom floor, sir," said one of the policemen to Uncle Thomas. "He's frightened his poor old mother terribly – made her hide him – and as far as I can make out she's been giving him all her food and half starving herself."

"I told him to go back," wept Mrs Browning. "I begged him to give himself up. But he's never done as I told him, never. I was too scared to say anything. I knew he'd be found sooner or later. I wanted him to go back and give himself up."

"Oh, shut up, Ma," said the sullen youth. He was led off between the two policemen. The inspector stayed to comfort the poor old

woman a little, and John looked at her miserably. How awful to have a son like that!

Mrs Browning saw him. She patted his arm. "You be a good son to your mother," she said. "Don't you turn out like my boy. He's been cruel and unkind to me ever since he was so high. I spoiled him, and this is my reward! Oh, Inspector, sir, I didn't mean to do wrong, hiding him like that but I was downright scared of him and what he might do to me."

"Now, now, don't you worry any more," said the inspector. "You did what you could. You get somebody to come and stay with you for a few days, and you'll soon feel better."

He and John walked home. Uncle Thomas was pleased with his nephew. "How old are you, John – just gone twelve? Well, I'm proud of you. Good, smart work, that. The police have been looking for that young man for some time and have even searched the cottage once before. But he must have heard they were coming and hid in the woods till the coast was clear again."

"Uncle, I did what you said," said John. "I tried to use my eyes, ears and nose!"

"You did very well, Detective John!" said Uncle Thomas. "I shall expect to hear of more cases you have solved in the future!"

The Lonely Old House

Harry, Cathy and Dick had come to stay at their little seaside cottage, not far from Kelty Cliffs. They loved it, because it was so near the cliff-path that led down to the beach, and had such a glorious view of the sea.

This was the third year they had come there, but this time their parents hadn't come. They had gone to Ireland to see the children's aunt, who was ill. So Miss Truman, their mother's old governess, had come to be with them in the cottage.

"I like Miss Truman, but she doesn't really seem to listen to anything we say," complained Cathy. "She's so busy with the cooking and the shopping and the mending that she just says 'Yes, dear, really,' or 'No, dear, really,' all the time."

"Well, never mind," said Harry. "It suits me! We can do just what we like. Miss Truman never seems to mind anything. Anyway, it's gorgeous here."

So it was. The weather was fine and hot, the bathing was good, they had a very old boat of their own, and there were lovely walks all round.

There were no houses near them at all except one. This was a big old house set in tall trees not very far away. Each year it had been empty, and the children now took no notice of it at all. It just stood there, silent and gloomy, with no one going up the drive or down.

And then one day something happened that made the children suddenly take an interest in the old empty house. They went for a walk with Kim, their Airedale. They passed near the empty house, set round with high walls. Then Kim suddenly ran off, barking.

"A rabbit," said Harry. "Poor old Kim. He never will learn that rabbits won't wait for him. Hi, Kim! Come here."

But Kim didn't come, and from his excited barking the children imagined that he really did have hopes of a rabbit. They walked on a little way, and then whistled Kim again.

"Blow him!" said Harry. "Now we'll have to go and drag him backwards out of a rabbit-hole. One of these days he really will get stuck halfway down."

They went to look for Kim, and then
suddenly they came on something they had
never seen before. It was an odd little
tumbledown house made of the white stone of
the district. It stood there among the trees,
covered with ivy and moss, its roof gone, and
its one window without glass.

"What a funny little place," said Harry, going up to it. "Whatever was it built here for?"

"This wood once belonged to that old empty house," said Cathy. "Mummy told me so. I expect it was a summerhouse or something, built for the people who used to live there long ago."

"Kim's inside!" said Dick. "He must have chased a rabbit there. Kim, come here."

But Kim was very busy scratching hard at the floor of the little stone house. The rabbit had run into the house and disappeared. Therefore it must still be there, and Kim meant to scratch up the whole floor rather than lose it! He was a very persistent dog.

He had scraped away the moss and earth from part of the floor. Dick went up to take hold of his collar and then stopped in surprise. Kim had scratched away quite a hole – and at the bottom of it was a flat stone – and in the stone was an iron handle!

"Look – that's a bit funny," said Dick, pointing it out to the others. "See? Kim's scraped away the earth and come to the stone floor – and there's an iron handle in that particular stone flag. I wonder why?"

"Ooh – it's jolly strange," said Cathy at once. "Usually stones with iron handles in them are meant to be lifted up – like trap-doors. Oh, Harry, don't let's go for a walk – let's dig down and explore a bit."

"No. We shan't find anything and we'll just get dirty and tired out," said Harry. "There's probably nothing in it at all. Come on."

"Oh no, Harry, do let's just scrape away all the earth and see if there is anything exciting," begged Dick. "I've read heaps of adventure stories, but I've never had an adventure myself. This might lead to one."

"Don't be silly," said Harry. He was thirteen, and thought the twelve-year-old Dick rather babyish. "Come on, Kim."

"Well, you go for a walk alone!" called Cathy, crossly. "I shall stay with Dick – and maybe we shall have an adventure – and we'll jolly well have it without you!"

Harry snorted and, with Kim at his heels, he went on by himself. Silly kids! Let them stay and make themselves into a mess if they wanted to.

Cathy and Dick stared down at the stone with its iron handle. "Shall we go back and get our spades?" said Cathy, eagerly. "We can't do it with our hands."

"Yes, let's," said Dick. "And we'll bring a torch too."

"What for?" asked Cathy.

"Well – you never know," said Dick. "It's a very good thing to have about you, if you're expecting an adventure."

They soon got their spades and went back again to the little stone house. What a tumbledown place it was! People could not have been into it for years and years.

They began to dig away the earth and moss from the floor of the house. They cleared it all from the stone flag beneath, and then saw that it was indeed meant to be lifted, for it distinctly moved a little when both children tugged at it!

"Gosh! Isn't this exciting?" said Dick, pushing his hair back from his dripping forehead, and smearing his face with dirt. "Wait – I've got a rope. We'll double it and slip it through the iron handle. Then we can both get a good grip on the rope and pull together. We'll never be able to pull the stone up with the handle. It's much too difficult."

Dick unwound a rope from round his waist. He always wore one there, in case of an adventure. Harry often laughed at him, but Dick didn't mind. One day, he knew, the rope would come in useful – and now it had!

He doubled the rope and slipped it under

and through the iron handle. Then he and Cathy pulled with all their might, panting and groaning with their efforts.

Nothing happened. They sat down to get their breath. "Let's run our spades all round the edges of the flagstone. It's stuck fast with soil, I expect," said Dick. "If we loosen that, the stone might come up more easily."

So they dug their spades all round the edges of the stone and cleared out the dirt. Then they took hold of the rope and tried again. And, quite suddenly, the stone moved! It first moved upwards, and then slid sideways and downwards in a peculiar way. It left a hole, dark and mysterious.

"Gracious!" said Cathy, speaking in a whisper, though she didn't quite know why. "Look at that!"

Dick took out his torch. He flashed it down the hole. "Steps!" he said. "Look – stone steps – awfully steep and narrow, though. I say, Cathy – isn't this exciting? Shall we go down?"

"No," said Cathy, half afraid.

"Well – I'm going, anyway," said Dick, and he put his foot down to the first step.

"I won't let you go alone," said Cathy. "If you're going, I'm coming with you. Oh dear – I do wish Harry was here."

"Well, I don't," said Dick. "He wouldn't stay and help so he doesn't deserve to share in this adventure!"

He went down to the next step. Then to the next. There appeared to be a missing or broken one after that and Dick missed his footing and fell. He gave a yell and Cathy jumped in fright.

But Dick hadn't far to fall – only two or three more steps. He landed on some soft earth, afraid that he might break his torch. But luckily he didn't. "It's all right," he shouted up. "There's a step missing, so look out. I'll shine my torch for you."

Cathy got down without falling. Dick flashed his torch round. A dark, narrow passage ran downwards at the end of the steps.

"It looks horrible," said Cathy, with a shiver. "Wherever does it go to?"

"Goodness knows," said Dick. "Come on. Let's find out."

"We shan't meet anything awful, shall we?" asked Cathy, nervously, not quite knowing what she expected to meet.

"Well, we might see a worm or two," Dick said, cheerfully. "Do come on. Can't you *enjoy* an adventure, Cathy? Just like a girl – scared of everything."

"Well, I'm jolly well not scared, then," said Cathy, in a brave tone. "Only – I'd like you to go first, Dick."

Dick had every intention of going first. Down the narrow, sloping passage he went, with Cathy close behind him. It smelled musty and damp. Dick suddenly wondered if the air was good. He had read somewhere that if the air underground was not good, explorers fell down in a kind of stupor and died. Still, he felt quite all right, so maybe the air was all right.

The passage stopped sloping downwards and went along on the level. It no longer wound about but ran practically straight. Dick tried to puzzle out what direction it could be running in – towards the sea, perhaps? But he could not make up his mind.

He kept the torch pointed towards the ground so as to see where to tread. He did not realise that the roof of the passage suddenly sloped down, and he got a terrific bang on the head as he walked into it. He stopped suddenly with a cry and Cathy bumped into him.

"Oh! What's the matter?"

"Look out for the roof – it gets low here," said Dick, and bent his head down to walk under the low part. Soon he came to a halt. His torch showed him more stone steps – this time going upwards.

Up them went Dick, followed by Cathy, who was now wishing to goodness they could see daylight again. They came out into a great, wide, dark place, and could not imagine where they were.

"It's a cellar!" said Cathy, suddenly. "Look, there are old cobwebby bottles over there. Oooh – look at that enormous spider. Dick, don't let it come over here."

"It won't," said Dick. "It's much more scared of you than you are of it! Yes, you're right. We're in a cellar – and if I'm not mistaken, it's the cellar of the old empty house!"

"Do you really think so?" said Cathy, astonished. "How can we get out then?"

"Up the cellar steps to the kitchen, I should think," said Dick, and began to flash his torch here and there to try and find out where any more steps were. He soon found them, in a distant corner. This time they were made of wood, not stone. The two children went up them to a door at the top. It was shut.

Dick turned the handle. It opened into a great kitchen, with a huge range at one end for cooking.

"Yes, it is the old house," said Dick. "I say – what fun! We can come here and play. We'll explore it from top to bottom."

"Will it matter if we do?" said Cathy. "Won't anybody mind?"

"Why should they?" said Dick. "We shan't do any harm or damage. I say, it's good to see a bit of daylight, isn't it, even if it has to come through such dirty windows."

It *was* good to see daylight. A few rays of sunshine straggled through the window nearby and lay on the floor. It was these that showed Dick something which astonished him. He gave an exclamation.

"Look there! Footprints in the dust on the floor! They're not ours, they're too big. I wonder who comes here."

Cathy stared at them fearfully. They looked freshly made. She didn't like them. Suppose there was somebody in the house now. "Let's go back," she whispered. "Somebody might catch us. I don't like it."

Dick was beginning to feel he didn't much like it either. It was scary to be in an old, old empty house – and see fresh footprints in the dust on the floor. The house was so quiet too – as if it was listening for something. Dick clutched Cathy and made her jump.

"Come on. We'll go back. We've seen enough. We'll come back with Harry sometime."

They hurried to the cellar door and down the wooden steps. They found their way to the hole where the other stone steps began and went down those into the dark passage. And then somebody jumped out at them from the passage with a yell that almost frightened the life out of them.

The somebody clutched hold of them tightly and yelled again. Then Dick struck out crossly and yelled back. "It's you, Harry, you beast! Scaring us like that. You really are horrible."

Harry laughed. He was very, very glad to find the others. He and Kim had come back to the little stone house and discovered the hole where the stone had been, and the steps leading down. Cross to think that Dick and Cathy had actually discovered something exciting, Harry had gone down after them.

But he had no torch and it was not at all pleasant groping about in the darkness. He longed to hear the cheerful voices of the others – and at last he did hear them! He had waited to jump out at Dick, and had given both Dick and Cathy a terrible fright.

"Sorry," said Harry. "Did I really scare you so? Get down, Kim. Dick, where does this lead

117

to? You found an adventure after all!"

"Rather!" said Dick. "One up on you! Gosh, I'm glad you're here, Harry, even though you did scare me stiff. Do you know, this passage leads to the cellar of the old empty house! And we've been up into the kitchen – and there are fresh footprints there in the dust of the floor!"

"Whew!" said Harry. "That's strange. Who comes here then? Perhaps it's just some tramp at night."

"But we *know* the place is locked and barred," said Dick, "because we've often tried to get into it ourselves from the outside, just to see what it was like. And we never could. It can't be just a tramp!"

"Let's go back again and I'll have a look," said Harry. So back they went and, once they were in the kitchen, Harry saw the big footprints too.

"Yes – they're freshly-made all right," he said. "Listen, there's somebody opening the front door! Quick, down to the cellar!"

Their hearts beating fast, the children made for the cellar door. They stood there and listened for a moment. They heard the front door open, and then to their great amazement they heard a voice they knew well! It was old Mrs Harriman, who went out doing housework, and who came to them every Saturday to help Miss Truman. Whatever was she doing here?

Kim whined, for he too recognised Mrs Harriman's voice, but Harry's hand tightened on his collar. No, he must not give them away. Mrs Harriman was talking to somebody.

"Well, here we are, Liza, and I must say it's a dreadful place, enough to give you the creeps. Fancy somebody coming along to live in it after all this time. Well, you and me's got our work cut out to clean the place up a bit, and scrub them filthy floors."

Kim whined again, and the children retreated down the cellar.

"Funny," came Mrs Harriman's booming voice as she entered the great kitchen. "I thought I heard a dog whining then. Shows you what your imagination can do!"

Harry shut the cellar door softly and went down the steps after the others. They made their way to the hole and went down the steps into the passage. Soon they had arrived inside the little tumbledown stone house, glad to see the sunshine coming through the trees.

"Well – it wasn't so mysterious after all – seeing those footprints," said Harry. "They must have been made by somebody who came to look at the house. Fancy people coming to live here after all those years! I wonder who they are. Perhaps Mrs Harriman will know."

"Don't tell her about the underground way into the house," said Cathy. "Let's make it our secret. I like secrets like that."

"Course we won't tell her," said Dick. "Let's shut the stone door and pull bracken over it to hide it. It might be fun to use it again before the people come in."

They went home with Kim, who looked very disappointed. He had hoped to find plenty of rabbits down that wonderful dark rabbit-hole

– and there hadn't even been a smell of one!

Miss Truman did not seem to mind their coming home so dirty. She did not even ask where they had been. So long as they were in good health and hadn't hurt themselves she didn't really bother much about their doings.

The next day was Saturday, so the children asked Mrs Harriman, when she came to do some cleaning, if anyone was coming to the old house.

"Yes, there is," said Mrs Harriman, beginning to clean the floor with a large bucket of water and an outsize mop. "My, my, look at this floor! Doesn't anyone wipe their feet in this house?"

"Only Kim," said Cathy, with a giggle. "Who's coming to the old empty house, Mrs Harriman?"

"Well, that I don't rightly know," said Mrs Harriman, beginning to mop vigorously. "Mind your feet, miss. The house agent, he called on me, gave me the key, and said I was to go up and clean, with Liza. All he said was that a gentleman was coming to live there, a real recluse, he called him, though what that is I don't know."

"Nor do I," said Cathy. But the boys knew.

"It's somebody who wants to live away from

121

everyone and not be bothered by visitors or anything," said Dick. "Well, he won't be bothered much there. When's he coming?"

"Next week, so I hear," said Mrs Harriman. "Mind your feet again, miss. And if anybody treads on where I've just cleaned they won't get any of my chocolate buns for tea, and I tell you that straight."

Everyone immediately went away from the gleaming wet part that Mrs Harriman had mopped. There didn't seem to be much more information they could get out of her, so they retired to the garden where they picked and ate a large amount of purple plums.

"We could watch each day and see who comes," said Dick. "We can see the furniture vans. They will have to pass our cottage."

"So they will," said Cathy. So each day the children watched, and on the next Wednesday they were rewarded by seeing two great vans come lumbering by. They followed the vans up to the old house.

Mrs Harriman was there with a paper in her hand, directing proceedings. "All furniture marked D is to go into the dining-room," she told the foreman. "I'll show you which it is. And all marked K is to . . ."

"It's just the furniture – not the recluse

man," said Cathy, disappointed. "Blow! We shan't see him now."

The children were not interested in the furniture, so they went away. They found their bathing things and went to bathe. They then took out their leaky old boat, got caught in a current, and had to row so very hard back to shore that they were absolutely tired out.

They crawled back to their cottage, groaning and stiff. "Done too much, I suppose?" said Miss Truman. "Well, I'll get you some supper and then off to bed you must go. You'll be asleep in two shakes of a duck's tail, I should think."

The boys were, but Cathy was too tired even to go to sleep! She tossed and turned. She heard the church clock down in the distant village strike ten, eleven and even twelve. She dozed a little and then heard it strike one.

And just as it had struck, she heard another noise. It was a car coming slowly and quietly along the lane by their cottage! Cathy was most surprised. No cars ever came along there, for the lane was a dead end, going only to their cottage and then a little distance on to the old empty house. Was the car going to stop at the cottage?

No, it was not. It went straight on past it, up

the lane. Cathy listened. How very peculiar! Was it going to the old house? But how late at night to arrive!

She lay down again. The car did not come back. She listened for it for some time and then quite suddenly fell asleep.

In the morning she was not quite sure if she had dreamed it. So before she told the boys she went into the sandy lane and had a look round. Yes, there were the marks of the tyres. So she hadn't dreamed it.

"The recluse man has arrived at the old house," Cathy announced to her brothers at breakfast.

"How do you know?" said Harry, disbelievingly.

"Because I heard his car going by last night at about one o'clock," said Cathy.

"That's morning, not night," said Dick.

"Well, it was one o'clock in the morning, in the middle of the night," said Cathy. "And anyway, there are tyre marks in our lane this morning."

The children went for a walk up to the old house after breakfast to see if they could see any sign of the "recluse man", as Cathy would keep calling him. But the great iron gates were not only closed but padlocked, and, as there were high walls all round the grounds, the children knew there was no way of getting in at all. Except, of course, by the underground passage.

"But we can't possibly use that again," said Harry. "Not now the house is occupied. It didn't matter when it was empty. My word, the recluse, whoever he is, means to keep everyone away, doesn't he?"

"What about food and milk and stuff?" wondered Cathy.

"Oh, he's probably got good stores," said Harry. "Come on – let's go and lie on the sand. I'm so stiff with rowing yesterday that I don't even want to bathe today!"

So, with Kim bounding along beside them, the children went down to the beach and forgot all about the peculiar old house. They spent a happy, lazy day together, and went off to bed, yawning, at nine o'clock.

Cathy had tossed and turned for hours the night before, so tonight she fell asleep at once. Dick did too, but Harry lay wide awake, listening to the owls hooting in the woods round the lonely old house. He was glad he was in his cosy cottage, not imprisoned in that great house, surrounded by high walls and tall trees.

He lay so that he could look out of the window. It was very dark outside for the sky was clouded over, and there was no moon at all. He faced in the direction of the old house, which was a good way away, hidden by trees.

Harry lay there, gazing out for a little while – then he became conscious of some far-off light somewhere. Was it a light? He tried to focus his eyes in the direction from which he thought it came, and waited. Yes, it was some kind of light – faint and far off – and coming in flashes. How odd. Where did it come from?

He thought for a minute. It could come from the top windows of the old house. He could see those indistinctly through the tops of the trees in the daytime, if he looked out of his window. But why should a light come and go from there in the middle of the night?

He decided to get up and investigate. He pulled on his shorts and jersey and went out, Kim running beside him, surprised and pleased to have a night walk.

Harry made his way towards the old house. He could not see in the dark, and almost bumped into the trunks of trees as he made his way between them.

And then he saw the light quite distinctly. It came from the topmost window of the old

house, a pin-prick of light, flashing on and off, on and off, as if the owner was trying to signal to somebody. But to whom would anyone want to signal at night, in that lonely place? Nobody would ever see that pin-point of light, except by accident.

Then the light became fainter, and finally the flashes stopped altogether. Harry made a note of exactly where the window would be and made up his mind to look for it the next day. Then back he went to bed and quickly fell asleep.

He told the others the next morning and they felt very excited. "It's a mystery," said Dick. "There really is some sort of mystery. We must solve it!"

They went to have a look at the window. It was the topmost one on the eastern side of the house – and it was barred.

"Well, that's nothing. It's always been barred, as long as we can remember," said Dick. "It was once a nursery, Mrs Harriman said."

"Do you think there is anyone there now?" said Cathy. "I mean – somebody we could see, if we climbed a tree, say?"

"Cathy, that's an awfully good idea!" said Harry at once. "If I climb this tall tree here, its top will be about level with that window. I'll do it."

The tree was a chestnut, and it grew just outside the wall that ran round the grounds of the old house. Harry climbed it easily. He went steadily to the top and then slid out on a broad branch to get as near as he could to the barred window. But he was still so far away that he could not possibly see inside.

And then, just as he was going to get down, somebody came to the window and looked out. Harry expected to see an old man – but instead he saw a young boy with a shock of dark hair, enormous dark eyes and a pale face. Harry was most surprised, and stared across at the window in astonishment. He gave one of his

129

piercing whistles to get the boy's attention.

The boy heard it and looked out. He suddenly saw Harry on the branch of the chestnut tree and was so amazed that he could only stand and stare. Harry yelled to him:

"Who are you?"

The boy put his finger to his lips and looked thoroughly scared. Harry did not shout again. Then the boy made a sign to Harry to wait, and disappeared from the window. He was away for a minute or two then came back.

He put his finger to his lips again, to tell Harry not to make a noise. Then he began to hold up sheets of white notepaper, on each of which he had printed in bold black letters one letter of the alphabet. He held them up one after another for Harry to see.

Harry jotted them down in his notebook as the boy held them up. I-A-M-A-P-R-I-S-O-N-E-R. It was not until he had got them all jotted down that Harry suddenly saw what words they spelled. "I am a prisoner."

"Golly!" thought Harry. "So that's what the light meant last night. He was signalling with his torch, I suppose, hoping someone would see the light, till the battery failed. Gosh, what am I to do about this? How can he be a prisoner?"

Harry waved reassuringly to the boy, and was just about to begin climbing down the tree when he saw that the prisoner had disappeared very suddenly indeed from the window. Then a furious face appeared and looked out. It was the face of a bearded man wearing big glasses, with black frames.

Harry slid out of sight at once. He climbed down as quickly as he could and told the others what he had seen. They listened breathlessly.

"Then it is an adventure," said Dick. "I had a feeling we were in for one. We'll have to rescue this boy. Perhaps he has been kidnapped."

"Yes. I never thought of that," said Harry. "We'd better look in the paper and see if there's anything about kidnapping. We never usually look at the paper, so we wouldn't know."

They went back to the cottage, and on the way they met Mrs Harriman, going to clean at the old house.

"Mrs Harriman – have you seen the man at the house?" asked Harry. "Is he all alone?"

"Yes, not a soul there besides himself," she answered. "Says he's writing a book and has to be quiet and by himself."

"Are you sure there's nobody else?" asked Dick. "Have you been all over the house?"

"Of course I have," said Mrs Harriman. "Not on the top floor, though, because there's nothing there, so Mr Cordery says."

"Oh – that's what he says, is it?" said Harry. "Well, Mrs Harriman – just suppose I told you there was a prisoner up there?"

Mrs Harriman laughed loudly. "Now don't you go playing any more of your jokes on me, young Harry. I've had enough of them. If you

132

think you're going to make me climb up those steep stairs to the top, just to look for an imaginary prisoner, well, you can think again. You and your imaginings!"

And she went on her way, chuckling. It was no good trying to get any advice from Mrs Harriman, or any help either. They went in at their cottage gate and went to look for the paper.

And there, the headline, big and black, stared them in the face: JACKIE MACARIO, SON OF FAMOUS FILM STAR, KIDNAPPED. The children gazed at the words as if they couldn't believe their eyes.

"Do you think," said Cathy at last, in a whisper, "do you think that's the boy – the one Harry saw?"

"Yes," said Dick. "Miss Truman, did you see this in the paper this morning – about the kidnapping? Well, we know where the boy is."

"Now, don't tell silly stories," Miss Truman said placidly. "If you want to pretend things and play games like that, you can – but really you can't expect me to believe them!"

And the more the children told her about what they knew, the more she pooh-poohed it all. She could not realise that they were no longer small children, and she wasn't going to be bothered to go into their ridiculous tales.

"It's no good," said Harry, at last. "We'd better do something ourselves. We'll rescue him tonight."

"How?" asked Dick at once.

"We'll go through the underground passage, into the cellar, up into the kitchen, and up to the top floor," said Harry. "The door will be locked and bolted – but the key and bolt will be on the outside, and we can easily undo them."

"Oh – I'd be afraid!" said Cathy.

"Well, don't come then," said Dick. "I'll go along with Harry – and we'll take Kim too."

"Oh no, I must come if you go," said Cathy bravely. So they laid their plans, and waited anxiously for the night to come.

At eleven o'clock they set out with their torches. Kim went with them. He had been warned not to bark and he quite understood. The three children came to the little tumbledown summerhouse and removed the flagstone that hid the entrance underground. Down they went, one by one. Cathy was trembling. It was so dark and spooky. She was glad to feel Kim's tongue on her bare legs now and then.

Along the passage, up to the cellar, up the wooden steps to the vast dark kitchen, where a winking red eye showed where the great range was almost out. Then out of the kitchen and into the hall.

The wide stairs lay before them, well carpeted. Where was Mr Cordery? In his room, probably. There was no light to be seen anywhere.

The three went up the stairs with Kim beside them. It seemed as if he, too, was walking on tiptoe! Up one flight of stairs – up

another – and then a third. Now they were at the very top of the house.

Harry quickly swung his torch around the top landing. All the doors were open but one. The prisoner must be in that!

They tiptoed towards it. It was bolted. There was a large key in the lock, and the children felt sure the door was locked too.

Cautiously Harry turned the key. It gave a slight click. Then he slid back the bolt. It creaked a little, and the children held their breath as they waited to see if anyone had heard. No, there was no sound.

Harry turned the handle and pushed the door open. The room was in darkness. Then a scared voice came from somewhere. "Oh, what do you want? Why do you keep me here like this? Don't hurt me, don't hurt me!"

It was a boy's voice. Harry switched on his torch and spoke in a whisper.

"Are you Jackie Macario?"

"Yes, yes. Who are you? Oh, don't scare me so!"

"We are your friends," said Harry. "We've come to rescue you. I'm the boy you saw in the tree – the one you showed those letters to."

"Oh, yes – I got beaten for that," said the boy. "Have you really come to rescue me? Let's go then, before that horrible man discovers you."

Without waiting to put on even a dressing-gown the boy went to the door with the others. He jumped violently when Kim licked him for he had not known there was a dog there.

"It's only Kim," whispered Dick. "Come on. Down the stairs."

They went down the stairs as quietly as possible. But suddenly, in the darkness, Cathy bumped into something and it fell over with a crash. Scared almost out of their skins, the four children ran swiftly across the landing to the next flight of stairs.

And then suddenly a door was flung open, a light flashed on, and there was Mr Cordery, black-bearded and fierce, glaring at them in the greatest astonishment.

"What's this? Who are you? Come here, you, you, you . . ."

He was in such a rage that he could not get his words out. He caught hold of Dick and shook him hard.

The others paused, afraid for Dick. Kim gave a growl and flung himself at Mr Cordery. The man gave a shout and tried to fend the dog off.

"Come on, Dick!" shouted Harry, running

down the next flight of stairs. "Leave Kim to settle him." They had enough time to dart into the kitchen. Then Kim came after them, his head bleeding from a savage blow. Then came Mr Cordery raging with temper, an iron bar in his hand. The children ran to the cellar door and down the wooden steps. Kim followed them.

The door slammed above them. They heard Mr Cordery's loud laugh. "Ha! You want to be prisoners, too, do you? Well, you shall all stay down in the cellar, in the dark and cold, with the spiders and the bats!"

Then the key turned in the lock of the cellar door. Harry began to laugh weakly. "He thinks we're his prisoners. He doesn't know it's our way of escape. Come on, quick, before he smells a rat!"

They dragged the surprised and frightened boy with them. Down the steps, into the underground cellar, along the passage and up into the old summerhouse. Then through the woods and home. Cathy was terribly worried about poor Kim. Was he very badly hurt?

They went into the house and banged on Miss Truman's door. "Miss Truman! Come quickly!"

Miss Truman came, looking most astonished. When she saw the three bedraggled children, and a fourth one, quite strange to her, and poor Kim bleeding from his wound, she was quite astonished.

The children poured out everything to her.

139

"Oh dear, oh dear, why didn't you tell me before?" she said, as she bathed Kim's head.

"But we did, and you thought we were making it all up," said Cathy, quite crossly. "Miss Truman, oughtn't we to tell the police? Jackie Macario's mother and father ought to know where he is, and the police ought to know about Mr Cordery."

"Of course, of course," said Miss Truman, putting her arm round the shivering Jackie. "You go and get a dressing-gown for him, Harry. Kim will be all right now. I'll go and phone. Dear me, what a night, what a night! I can scarcely believe it!"

Neither could the local policeman when Miss Truman telephoned him. But he did believe her tale at last, and said he would telephone his superior officer in the next town and get instructions.

And before very long a police car came roaring up with a detective and three big policemen in it, all very anxious to see for themselves if the little prisoner the children had rescued really and truly was Jackie Macario.

Nobody had much sleep that night, except little Jackie who was tired out with excitement.

The police left the cottage and roared on to

the old house. Mr Cordery was astounded to hear loud knockings on the front door, and only when he heard that it was the police who were demanding entrance did he open the door.

And then it was Mr Cordery who was taken prisoner!

"I tell you I know nothing about Jackie Macario," he kept saying. "Nothing at all."

But when he was faced with the boy the next day, he could no longer go on with his tale. "All right," he said, sullenly. "I'll tell you everything. I didn't kidnap him – the others did that. I just brought him here and put him in that barred room to wait till the ransom was paid. That's all I did. And then some interfering kids got him away – though how they got into the house, and out of the cellar I locked them into, beats me!"

"Yes. A clever lot of kids," said the detective, smiling round at the three children. "Well, Jackie, your parents will soon be here, and you'll be safe again."

"I'd like to stay with these children if Mum will let me," said Jackie. But alas, she wouldn't. She took her precious son away with her, thankful to have him safely back – but she left behind three things that thrilled the children tremendously.

One was a great rubber ball for playing about with on the beach or in the sea. That was for Harry. Another was a shrimping net almost as big as the one the fishermen used when they went shrimping. That was for Dick. The third was a funny rubber horse that could be ridden in the waves. That was for Cathy.

"Gracious!" said Cathy, in delight. "What great presents – and all for taking part in a really exciting adventure. Miss Truman, you can have a ride on my horse if you like, next time you bathe."

"No, thank you," said Miss Truman, eyeing the big rubber creature in horror. "I know what would happen to me! I'd be pushed off it at once – that would be your idea of a joke!"

The children laughed and raced off to the beach with their presents. "Let's hope for another adventure soon!" said Dick. "They're *fun*!"

Number
Sixty-two

Ever since John had solved the mystery of Melling Cottage he had been on the lookout for another. But mysteries didn't seem to come along very often – and some mysteries turned out not to be mysteries after all!

There was the time when he had seen a man and a woman quarrelling in a garden, and suddenly the man pulled out a knife, but when John yelled out that he was going for the police it turned out that the two were only rehearsing their parts in a play.

John had felt very foolish over that. And another time he had reported a mysterious sack on the other side of a hedge, apparently full of stolen goods. But it was only a sack of potatoes left there by the farmer for his brother to fetch as he passed by on his way to market.

"I'd better be careful next time," John said to himself. "I won't report anything unless I'm absolutely sure about it."

Now one afternoon he went by himself to Oaktree Wood. There was a big tree there he liked to climb. It was an easy one and he could get almost to the top. From the top he could see a very long way indeed.

It was like being in a ship, because the wind swayed the tree, big as it was, and the movement was like a boat going over waves. John liked it. If he shut his eyes he felt as if he were right out at sea.

So this afternoon up the tree he went. He was soon at the top, looking out over the countryside, which lay smiling in the summer sunshine. John had a book with him. He opened it, settled himself comfortably on a branch and began to read. Sometimes he looked out from his high perch, and saw the lorries, buses and cars going along the roads.

He saw a car stop and pull off the road on to the grass verge. A man got out and disappeared. John waited idly for him to come back, but he didn't. Surely he hadn't gone for a picnic all by himself? John went on reading his book, occasionally glancing up to see if the car was still there.

After half an hour the car was still parked there, empty. John began to wonder about it. Then he suddenly heard the crack of a twig in the wood below, as if someone had trodden on one and broken it.

"There's somebody coming through the wood," thought John, and glanced down through the leaves. But the tree was too thick for him to see anything below on the ground.

He heard a match being struck. Somebody was lighting a cigarette. Perhaps he was waiting for someone! John heard a slight cough down below. The man was under the tree. Another twig cracked.

Then there came the sound of someone making his way through the bushes, and a low voice said, "That you, Lou?"

"Yes," said the man under the tree. "Number 62, tomorrow."

"Okay," said the other voice and its owner made his way back through the bushes again. That was all. Not another word was said. The man under the tree went off and in about ten minutes' time John saw him come out of the wood and get into the car.

John strained his eyes to see the number of the car. He could make out the beginning – L39, and the last two letters, which were ST, but that was all. He wrote it down in his notebook.

Car number L39 . . . ST, he wrote. *Red in colour. Sports saloon. Can't see make.*

John often wrote things of this kind down but as a rule they were all wasted. Still, you never knew. Things might come in useful sometime. He began to think about the message the man under the tree had given to the other, who was, apparently, already hidden in the wood.

"Number 62, tomorrow."

What did it mean? What was number 62? And why tomorrow? John frowned, and puzzled over it. Should he report what he had seen and heard? No, better not. It might be nothing again.

"Perhaps number 62 is a house somewhere they mean to burgle," thought John, suddenly. "Number 62. Where is there a number 62? It must be a fairly long street if there are over sixty houses in it. I'll go and do a little exploring."

Before he slid cautiously down the tree, he listened to see if anyone might be about – the man hiding in the wood for instance. But he could hear nothing, so down he went, as quietly as he could. Once on the ground he sped through the trees as if he were a rabbit with a dog after him!

He went to the village. There must be a number 62 somewhere. What was the longest road? Yes, Summers Avenue must be. He went along it, looking for sixty-two.

"Forty-one, forty-three, forty-five – oh, these are the odd numbers. I want the evens." He crossed the road and came to the evens.

"Forty-two, forty-four, forty-six – blow, there are only two more. Forty-eight – fifty. There's no sixty-two."

He went down another street but there were even fewer houses there. That was no good. Then he went to Limmers Street, which was a terrace of small houses. Ah, there was a sixty-two – good! John looked hard at it.

Nobody would want to rob a tiny house like
that, surely? The people in it must be very
poor for the curtains were dirty and ragged.
Two or three equally dirty and ragged children
were playing on the doorstep. No, this couldn't
be the right sixty-two. That was quite certain.

"Well, there's only the High Street left
then," thought John, and went there. However, he felt that number 62 could hardly be
the one meant by the man, for it was the police
station! It had no number, of course, but as it
stood between number 60 and number 64, it
was clear that it must be 62, if it had a number
at all!

"I can't understand it," said John, puzzled.
"There are only two sixty-twos – and one's a
slummy little house and the other's the police
station. Perhaps the sixty-two doesn't mean
the number of a house at all."

Then he wondered if by any chance the
number might be part of a telephone number.
No – the man wouldn't have said "sixty-two"
then, he would have said "six-two" because
that was how telephone numbers were given.
People said "one-o" not "ten," they said
"seven-three" not "seventy-three" and the
man would certainly have said "six-two" not
"sixty-two".

So telephone numbers were ruled out as well. Then what in the world could sixty-two mean?

Should John go to the police now, and tell them what he had heard? No, he still didn't want to, because it just might mean nothing, and he would be laughed at.

He turned to go home. On the way he saw a man running by in a white tee-shirt and shorts. Then after a while another came past. They were practising running for races. John stared at them idly. Then he stiffened. Each man had a number on, in big black figures! The first man's number was 14. The next

man's was 34. Then a third man came padding along – he was 53.

John looked after the runners. Could the number 62 belong to one of these runners? Was it a man, number 62, that that fellow was talking about? If so, why?

He went on towards his home, thinking hard. His father was at home. Perhaps he would be able to tell him about the runners and their big race.

Yes, his father knew all about it. He had been a keen runner in his time, and he told John that there was to be a ten-mile race the next day, on a certain route, and that so far as he knew almost a hundred competitors were entered for it.

"Then there may be a number sixty-two?" asked John.

"Yes, of course. But why do you ask that?" said his father.

"Oh – I was thinking of something," said John. "Dad, is there a list of the competitors up anywhere? If there is I'd like to have a look and see if I know any of them."

"Yes. If you go along to the athletic club, you are sure to find a list there," said his father. "I didn't know you were so interested in running."

John smiled and went off. He found the athletic club and went in. The secretary was there. "What do you want, young lad?" he asked.

"Could I just look at the list of runners?" said John. "For the ten-mile race tomorrow?"

"Yes, it's over there," said the secretary, and pointed with his pen. "They start at Beamers End, each running two minutes after the last. And they end at Longfields Club Room."

"Er – do they run past Oaktree Wood?" asked John. The secretary nodded. John began to look down the list of names. He came to number sixty-two: 62. Laurie Baxter. Who was Laurie Baxter? He looked at the address: 16 Renfrew Street. That was a poor street, where factory workers lived, in the next town. Laurie Baxter, 16 Renfrew Street. Now why in the world should anyone want to bother about Laurie Baxter running in a ten-mile race?

"Who will win, do you think?" asked John. "Laurie Baxter?"

"Good gracious, no," said the secretary. "He'll be about halfway. He's not much good."

"Oh well – thank you very much," said John and went out. Now, was he right or wasn't he, in thinking that Laurie Baxter was the number 62 that the man in the wood was telling the other fellow about, for some reason or another? And was he right in thinking that the fellow in hiding was going to lie in wait for Laurie Baxter? If only he knew!

He couldn't possibly go to the police and say "I think that Laurie Baxter will probably disappear halfway through tomorrow's race, and not turn up at the end because somebody in Oaktree Wood is lying in wait for him!" It sounded too silly for words – and it might not be true. It was only what John thought, not what he knew. He wondered what to do. Then he decided that he, too, would hide at the edge of Oaktree Wood, just before the race, and he would see if anything happened. He could always give the alarm if an attack was made on number 62.

So, the next afternoon, feeling rather excited, John made his way to Oaktree Wood. He chose a tree that overlooked the stretch of road that ran by the wood, down which the runners would go, and he climbed it, making sure that there was nobody to see him.

Then he sat on a branch and waited. After a long, long time the first runner appeared. He was number 7. Apparently they were not running in their right order, but just anyhow, each starting off two minutes after the last.

Then number 16 appeared, and after him number 43. Then came 1 and 8 and 17, each some time after the other. Would 62 never come?

Then came one that looked like 62 but when he got nearer John saw that he was 63. Blow! Three or four more came – and then, surely, surely this was 62?

It was! He was a weedy youth, not a very good runner, with thin shoulders and skinny legs. He came along the road to a curve. And then things happened.

Somebody shot out from the hedge, clamped strong arms round Laurie and dragged him swiftly back into the undergrowth. His hand was over Laurie's mouth. John gasped. It was all so sudden. He caught a glimpse of a second man, and then Laurie was bundled away so quickly that except for a swishing of branches as the men forced their way into the undergrowth, there was nothing to be seen or heard.

John quickly shinned down the tree. He ran after the men but they had disappeared. Then, in the distance, he heard the sound of a car being started up. Oh, so the men had a car hidden somewhere in a glade, had they? If only he could see it and take its number!

But by the time he got to the little clearing, the car was moving away, and all that John could see was that it was red. Red! Then probably it was the same car he had seen the man in the day before. He had got part of the number of the car, but not all of it. Blow!

The car came to a road in the wood and soon the sound of its engine died away in the distance. John sat down on an old tree-trunk to think. Now he wished he had gone to the police and reported what he had thought might happen. It had happened. He didn't know why, or what the men were after – but the thing was, Laurie Baxter had been attacked and taken away in a car. He'd better go to the police and tell them about that.

So off he went. He marched into the station and asked to speak to the sergeant, who was a friend of his uncle's. Then he told him what he knew.

"Please, sir, Laurie Baxter, number 62 of the ten-mile runners, was attacked and taken off in a car, just as he was running beside Oaktree Wood," said John. "I saw it happen. I was up in a tree, waiting for it to happen, as a matter of fact."

"Waiting for it to happen?" said the sergeant, surprised. "What do you mean? How did you know it would happen?"

John told him everything – how he had overheard "number 62" in the wood, said by the man from the car – how he had looked at all houses that might be the number 62 meant – and then how he had thought it must be the number 62 of the runners.

"And it was," said John. "I wonder why Laurie Baxter was attacked, though."

"I don't," said the sergeant, grimly. "I have an idea that he was in a burglary committed three weeks ago, and that he got off with most of the goods and sold them – while the others got nothing! Something scared them in the middle of the robbery and two of them fled, but Laurie apparently didn't. He waited, then when all was quiet he took the goods and made off. I reckon the other fellows are angry with him and want to know what he's done with their share."

"Oh," said John. "But why didn't you arrest Laurie Baxter then, if you knew all this?"

"We questioned him, and put a watch on him," said the sergeant, "but we thought if we let him go free the others might make contact with him and then we'd pull in the whole lot. But now it looks as if we've lost them all."

"Well, sir – I managed to get part of the number of their car," said John, eagerly. "Look – L39 . . . ST. The car was red, sir, and was a sports saloon."

"Good boy!" said the sergeant, and took John's notebook. "This will help tremendously. We can stop all cars of this description."

Then a radio call at once went out to police patrols. "Calling all cars, calling all cars. Please

watch for a red car, make unknown, sports saloon type, registration L39, middle unknown, ends with letters ST. Three men inside. Hold for questioning. Over."

"Can I stay here and see if anything happens, please?" asked John, excited.

"Right," said the sergeant. "Seeing that you've brought us so much information, you can wait – I might want to ask you more questions, mightn't I?"

So John waited. He had a cup of tea with the sergeant and felt very important. Many telephone calls came in, but nothing exciting, until at last there came the one the sergeant wanted. He turned to John.

"They've got them! The car was stopped at Reading. The registration number is L392 BST. It's a red Ford sports saloon. Three men inside, one of them Laurie Baxter. *Now* we'll get going!"

They did. Laurie was so angry with his companions for attacking and kidnapping him that he gave the whole show away. He told where the rest of the unsold stolen goods were, and related his companions share in the various robberies they had committed together.

"So now," finished the sergeant, smiling at the excited boy in front of him, "they'll all spend a nice quiet little time thinking over their sins in prison. They'll commit no more robberies for a while – thanks to you, Detective John!"

And Detective John went proudly home. He'd solved another problem. Now – what would the next one be?

Caravan
Holiday

"Aren't we going to have a summer holiday this year?" Geoffrey asked, gloomily. "Nobody's mentioned one."

"Don't be a selfish little beast," said Ann, his younger sister. "You know Mummy's been terribly ill and Daddy's spent loads of money on her. We can't possibly mention summer holidays."

"No, we can't," said her older sister, Jenny. "All the same – we could do with one after all our worry and anxiety."

"Quite right," said Roddy, looking up from his book. He was eighteen, and kept all the others in order. "We *could* do with one. And we're going to have one. I've managed it."

"Oh, Roddy! You never said a word!"

"Well, I've only just arranged it," said Roddy. "Dad's said I can borrow the small car – and I've borrowed a small caravan from a friend of mine – and I thought we'd go caravanning for two weeks."

163

"Gosh! How super!"

"Roddy! What made you think of it?"

"I'd rather do that than anything in the world!"

Roddy grinned. "I thought you'd like it. Geoff and I can sleep in a tent each night, and you two girls can bunk in the caravan."

"It'll be great," sighed Jenny.

"That depends," said Roddy. "Caravanning isn't the same as going to stay at a hotel, you know, where all your beds are made for you, your meals cooked and everything done. We shall have to do everything ourselves."

"I can't cook," said Jenny. "I don't like that sort of thing. I'm no good at it."

"Well, you'll have to try your hand at it," said Roddy. "We'll all have our jobs. Mine will be the car and looking after it. Geoff's will be all the odd jobs of getting wood for the fire, putting up the tent, and that kind of thing. Do you good, Geoff. You're too lazy for words."

Geoffrey was lazy. He wouldn't do a thing for anyone unless he had to. But he was so excited about the idea of going off in a caravan that he was ready to promise anything.

"You and Ann will have to do the shopping, cleaning and cooking," said Roddy. "And I hope Ann gets over her fear of cows, horses, earwigs, bats, snakes, moths and caterpillars, as we are quite likely to meet a good many of them on our way."

Ann shivered. She was very silly about things like that. But she was not going to give up this holiday lightly. Perhaps they wouldn't meet so many of those awful things as Roddy thought.

"And before we go, one thing's to be quite understood," said Roddy. "My word's law, see! You all toe the line on this holiday, and nobody shirks or messes about. We've got to pull together if we're going to enjoy ourselves. And if you play any monkey tricks, young Geoff, I'll kick you out," said Roddy, still in a very friendly tone, but with a hint of sternness behind it that made Geoff remember how he had forgotten to clean his bicycle the week before, and had lost Roddy's knife only yesterday.

They all began to talk at once. What clothes to take, where they would go, how to manage about camping each night.

"I've got a campers' guide," said Roddy, pulling it out. "It gives all the fields we are allowed to camp in, and which farmer to go to about it, and the rules you have to keep. No leaving field gates open for cattle or horses to stray out of, you know. Things like that."

They all read the little guide eagerly. They decided to strike out across country, keeping close to farms, so that they could buy food easily.

"Will the car be able to pull a heavy caravan?" asked Geoff.

Roddy nodded. "Oh yes – easily. It's not one of those monster caravans, you know. It's arriving tomorrow."

Sure enough it did. The children rushed to the drive to watch it being towed in. It was painted blue and yellow, and was quite modern. They opened the door and went inside.

"A sink! With taps to turn! Where does the water come from – a tank in the roof?"

"Look at all the cups and plates and things. And it's even got a cooking stove."

"Look at these bunks. They fold up flat in the daytime. They look jolly comfortable."

"Bags I the top one."

They were all delighted with it. They wished their mother and father were there too, but they had gone away. Their mother was convalescing now, and the children had been left in the charge of old Hannah, the cook-housekeeper, and Roddy.

Hannah spoilt them and Roddy didn't. Roddy was quite determined to take his father's place and keep them in order. Lazy Geoff, fussy Jenny, and timid Ann were all in awe of their big brother.

"We're starting off tomorrow, don't forget," said Roddy to Jenny. "See that everything is packed into the caravan – all the things we'll need, I mean. Hannah will help you. You ought to be able to manage that."

"Well, Ann must help," said Jenny, who hated jobs of this sort. She had made up her mind she was going to be an actress when she was grown up, very beautiful, very much sought-after and spoilt. She didn't mean to do all the things her mother did so well. She wasn't going to bother about dull things like mending and making beds, cooking, cleaning and washing. Let somebody else do those!

Ann and Jenny set to work to pack, though actually Hannah did most of it. Geoff was sent to clean the outside of the caravan. It was beautifully clean inside but had got splashed with mud during a rain-storm on the way. Roddy went to fill the car up with petrol and oil, and to pump the tyres up, too.

They were all ready to start out the next day. Hannah waved goodbye, thinking with relief that now she really *could* get on with a bit of cleaning. The car started up with Roddy driving it and Geoff sitting beside him.

The girls were looking out of the back windows, waving to Hannah. The sun shone down brilliantly. It was going to be very, very hot.

"Here we go!" said Roddy, and the car started moving. The caravan jerked and followed. Down the drive they went, the caravan running docilely after the car.

"Goodbye, Hannah!" shrieked Jenny. "We're off! We're going to have a simply wonderful time!"

Soon they were several miles on their way.

The sun was now very hot. They went on until they came to the place where they had decided to have their lunch. It was at the top of a hill, and there was a magnificent view from where they sat, munching sandwiches hungrily.

"This is lovely," said Geoff, lying down on his back. "I wish I could eat some more. But I can't. I feel like a nap."

"Well, pick up your sandwich bag first, you lazy kid," said Roddy. "Don't leave litter about."

"Can't just now," said Geoff, sleepily. "Will in a minute."

Roddy said no more. Geoff's sandwich wrapper did a little dance in the wind and then flew off down the hill. Roddy didn't do anything to stop it. Ann took a look at his face and grinned. She knew what that look meant!

"Half an hour's rest and we'll go on," announced Roddy, taking out a book from his pocket. The girls wandered off and Geoff did a little light snoring.

When the girls appeared again Roddy poked Geoff with his foot. "Wake up, Geoff. Pick up your rubbish, and come to the car. Hurry up!"

Geoff sat up and looked round. "Where is it?" he asked. "Can't see any rubbish."

"Down there," said Roddy, pointing far down

the hill. "Come on! If you'd picked it up when you were told to, you wouldn't have had to go miles after it."

"Well, I'm not going to climb all the way down there this hot afternoon," said Geoff, indignantly.

"Don't, then. But you're not getting into the car till you've picked it up," said Roddy. "I'll give you ten minutes."

So Geoff sulkily climbed down to fetch the sandwich wrapper, and grew very hot indeed clambering back. Roddy grinned at him. "Your own fault, old boy," he said. "One of the rules of caravanners and campers, you know – leave no litter."

They set off again. It was a lovely ride. The sun shone down, hotter than ever, but there was always a breeze blowing and Roddy had the sunshine roof open.

They missed out tea because they had had such an enormous lunch. They drove on and on for miles, passing through tiny villages, bigger towns, going up and down hills, and over bridges.

Then at last they came to where they were to camp for the night. It was a big field with a small clear stream running by one end of it. Cows stood not far off, chewing the cud.

Ann gave a scream. "Not here, Roddy! There are cows!"

"So there are. Good. We can get some milk from the farm in the morning," said Roddy, stepping out of the car. "I'm just going to arrange things with the farmer. Geoff, get a fire going please, to cook a meal. You know how to. You'll find plenty of twigs in that little wood over there. Ann, you and Jenny get a meal ready. Some bacon and tomatoes would be nice. There's a frying-pan in the caravan."

He went off, paying no attention to Ann's wailing. "But I'm afraid of the cows, Roddy, I can't stay here for the night. You know how I hate cows."

"Well, they must hate you too coming into their field and yowling about them like that," said Geoff, in disgust. "I'm going to get some sticks for the fire. You'd better stay in the caravan, Ann, in case one of the cows comes over to see what you're making a fuss about. If I were a cow I'd stick my horns in you and toss you over the hedge."

"You're a hateful boy," wailed Ann. She went into the caravan and would not stir out of it at all. Jenny was cross.

"You might help me," she grumbled. "You know I'm not much good at cooking. Oh, blow – where did we put the bacon?"

She got everything ready and Ann gave her a little help, though she would not come out of the caravan. But when Jenny was ready with the frying-pan, the bacon and the tomatoes, there was no fire!

"Geoff! Geoff! Where are you? You haven't made the fire, you lazy thing!" she yelled.

Geoff was nowhere to be seen. He had gone to the wood to get firewood and had suddenly seen a very large rabbit staring at him. It bolted off a little way then sat up and stared at him again. Geoff believed he might catch it if only he could get near enough. It seemed so very tame.

He forgot all about the firewood. So, when Roddy came back, carrying a pint of milk, some new-laid eggs and a little butter, there was no sign of a meal. He was feeling tired and hungry, and he looked at Jenny in exasperation.

"Well, I did expect you'd have the meal ready."

"It's Geoff. He went off for the firewood and hasn't come back," said Jenny.

"Well, why didn't you send Ann for some?" said Roddy. "Where is she?"

"In the caravan. She won't come out because of the cows," said Jenny.

"Right," said Roddy. "She can stay there."

He went to a copse of nearby trees and brought back some twigs and soon had a fire going. Jenny put some bacon and tomatoes into the pan.

"Wait – we shan't need all that," said Roddy. "Geoff's not here and Ann's not coming. Just cook enough for two."

Ann heard him. "I'm hungry, too!" she called. "I want some bacon."

"Well, are you going to come out here and have it then?" said Roddy. "If not, you won't get any. What a baby! Frightened of cows indeed! You're just putting it on."

Bacon and tomatoes and bread were fried for two people. Then Roddy poured out mugs of creamy milk. He and Jenny ate a delicious meal, listening to a yellowhammer somewhere that kept saying "Little bit of bread and no cheese."

Ann peered out of the caravan. She was so hungry that she thought she would brave the cows after all. "I'm coming," she said. "Cook me some supper."

"Cook it yourself!" said Jenny. "I'm not going to start all over again for you, Ann."

"Nice polite family we are," said Roddy. "Well, they say there's nothing like a caravan holiday to knock the rough corners off people."

Ann looked at the fire. It was almost out. She would have to find sticks and make it all over again. She couldn't be bothered. Besides, she would have to go near the cows to get sticks. So she had some bread and butter and milk, and made that do.

"Now, you two go and wash the things in the stream," said Roddy. "Hello, here's Geoff!"

Geoff came along carrying an armful of wood. "I say," he called as he came near. "I've been stalking the tamest rabbit you ever saw. Nearly caught it too. Hope I haven't kept you waiting for the wood."

"Well, you have," said Jenny, indignantly. "We waited ages. We've had our supper. There's no bacon or tomatoes for you because Roddy wouldn't let me cook any. You can have bread and butter and milk."

"But I'm very hungry . . ." began Geoff,

crossly. He glanced at Roddy's face and decided to say no more. He cut himself some bread and butter, and took a raw tomato.

"Come on, Ann – let's wash up," said Jenny with a yawn. "I don't know why I feel so sleepy, but I do. It'll be fun to get into those comfy bunks and go to sleep with the owls hooting around."

"I don't like owls," said Ann. "And if you don't mind, Jenny, I'm going back into the caravan. Those cows have come a bit nearer."

"You'll go and help with the washing-up, or I'll put you on the train tomorrow morning and send you back to Hannah," Roddy said suddenly. Ann stared at the cows and then at Roddy. She decided she was much more scared of Roddy. It would be terrible to go back home before the holiday had properly begun. So, pulling a long face, she walked over the grass with Jenny, keeping as far away from the cows as she could.

They washed the things in the stream. "Isn't Roddy strict?" said Ann. "I hope he's not going to be like this all the time. Oh, look at that cow. It's coming over here, I know it is!"

She fled back to the caravan. Jenny followed, grinning, carrying the washed crockery. The boys were putting up their tent. Roddy was

176

showing Geoff exactly how to do it.

"And you've got to do exactly as I've shown you, or you'll have the tent down on top of us another night," said Roddy. "This will be your job in future, Geoff – putting up the tent at night and taking it down when we leave in the morning."

"We're going to bed, Roddy," said Jenny, with a yawn. "Do you mind? I'm sleepy."

"No, you turn in," said Roddy. "And you'd better turn in too, Geoff. Put the sleeping-bags in the tent – groundsheets first, of course. That's right. I'm going for a bit of a stroll. I won't wake any of you if you're asleep. If you're too hot at night, Jenny, leave the caravan door open."

"Oh no – the cows might walk in!" cried Ann.

It was fun going to bed in the caravan. The

girls let down the two bunks and arranged the bedclothes. They washed at the little sink, and were delighted to get into their pyjamas and snuggle down into the bunks.

Ann had the top one. At the foot of it was one of the caravan windows. Ann opened it to let air into the caravan, because it was very hot.

"Oh, let's have the door open too," said Jenny, and swung it wide open. A breath of sweet-smelling air came in.

"No, Jenny. I simply won't have it open," said Ann at once. "Honestly, the cows might walk in."

"What – up the steps?" cried Jenny. "Don't be so silly."

But Ann made such a terrible fuss that in the end Jenny shut the door, grumbling hard. Ann peeped out of the open window by her bunk. She saw Geoffrey standing at the tent-opening in his pyjamas, and called goodnight to him.

"I'm just going to get into my sleeping-bag!" he said. "All nice and cosy. Roddy's not back yet, but he won't be long."

Soon the two girls were almost asleep. It was nice to hear the gurgle of the stream in the twilight. A bird gave a sudden little song. It was a late robin. Then there was only the stream, and the wind in the trees to be heard. The girls fell asleep.

They didn't hear Roddy come back, and get into his sleeping-bag. They didn't hear the sleepy voice of Geoff talking to Roddy for a while.

They heard nothing at all – until Ann awoke with a jump.

She knew where she was at once – in the caravan, of course. How lovely! Then suddenly something bumped against it and shook it. What could it be? Ann sat up and leaned over to the window to look out.

Something was looking in! Ann saw an enormous face and smelled a hot, sweet breath. She screamed at the top of her voice and everyone woke up.

"Help! Help! Something's come to get me!" yelled Ann, and stared in horror at the face still looking in at the window. It was not a very dark night, but dark enough for Ann not to be able to see exactly what it was and light enough for her to make out two big, staring eyes.

"What is it, Ann?" cried Jenny, sitting up. Ann went on screaming. Roddy and Geoff came rushing into the caravan, scared stiff.

Whatever was happening to the girls?

"Look – look – something's come to get me!" screamed Ann. "Make it go away! Kill it, Roddy."

Roddy flashed on his torch. Now the enormous face at the window could be seen clearly. It had a long brown and white nose, big eyes fringed with long eyelashes – and a pair of curving horns.

"Good heavens – it's only a cow," said Roddy in disgust. "Just a cow looking in at the window – and you scream the place down and wake everyone up! I'm ashamed of you, Ann."

The cow backed away towards the ropes of the tent. Geoff ran to shoo it off, afraid that the tent might come down.

"Just find out whether there's something to scream about before you wake us all up again," said Roddy. "No, don't shut the window, Ann, this caravan is like a furnace!"

"I won't have cows breathing all over me through the window," said Ann, in tears.

"Well, I shall leave the door open then," said Jenny. "I'm not going to suffocate in here because of your fear of cows. You can choose whether you'll have cows breathing over you, or cows trying to climb up the steps of the caravan."

"Or you can take my sleeping-bag and a groundsheet and sleep under the caravan," said Roddy, grinning to himself. Ann gave a squeal.

"What – with hedgehogs and earwigs and things running all over me! You beast, Roddy!"

The door remained open. Ann lay listening for cows again, but none came. So she fell asleep and did not disturb anyone again that night.

It was a lovely day when they all woke up at last. Ann awoke first because she heard cows mooing and she sat up in fright, thinking they were in the caravan. But they were at the other end of the field. A little dog was looking in at the door and Ann stared back at him.

Should she squeal and wake Jenny because there was a strange dog there? The little thing looked at her and wagged its tail. And, to her surprise, Ann heard herself saying, "Good little dog, then!"

Whereupon the dog came right into the caravan, saw Jenny's face nearby on the lower bunk and gave it a lick! Jenny woke up suddenly and Ann nearly rolled out of the top bunk, squealing with laughter at the sight of Jenny's astonished face.

"Golly – do you mean to say you're not

scared of this dog!" said Jenny, seeing Ann lean down to pat it. "What's come over you?"

They had breakfast out in the field. Boiled eggs, bread and butter, ripe plums and milk that Geoff had just fetched from the farm. It tasted quite different from exactly the same breakfast at home.

They got ready to set off again. Jenny and Ann washed up the plates, and looked at the map with the boys. "Over the hills and far away!" sang Ann, happily. Then Roddy put his head in at the door of the caravan.

"Just look here!" he said crossly to the girls. "Your bunks aren't made. The caravan isn't tidied up. And Jenny's clothes are all over the place. You're two lazy kids, and we shan't move on till everything is spick and span."

"We can do all that later on," said Jenny sulkily.

"Well, you won't," said Roddy. "I never knew such a putter-off as you, Jenny. I tell you, if you don't play your part properly during this holiday, I'll leave you behind somewhere!"

He went off to show Geoffrey how to fix the car to the caravan. It was quite easy but had to be done carefully. "I could do this each day for you," said Geoff, anxious to be in Roddy's good books.

"Right," said Roddy. "I'll trust you to do that. It's time you had a bit of responsibility. After all, you're not a silly kid any more."

They had a lovely day. When they came to a beautiful old village Roddy stopped at a garage to check the tyre pressures. He thought one wheel had a slow puncture.

"You kids can wander about a bit," he said. "Do you good to stretch your legs. Jenny, don't forget you're responsible for the food side of this holiday. Geoff, here's some money – get me some cigarettes, will you? And Ann, buy some postcards somewhere and send one off to Mum. You know her address."

"We'd do everything without being told so often," said Ann. "You're always telling us to do things."

"If I thought you'd do them without being told, I wouldn't open my mouth," Roddy said, with a grin. "But you wouldn't! Now cut along."

A little way beyond the village was a big field. Hearing curious trumpeting sounds from it, the three children went to explore, Ann a little timidly.

"I say, look – it's a circus camp," said Geoff, thrilled. "Let's come and sit on the fence and watch. We might see something."

"Will there be lions or tigers or bears?"

"Dozens!" said Geoff, wickedly. "And probably crocodiles and enormous snakes, and . . ."

Ann screamed and wouldn't go any nearer. In fact she decided not to look at all when she saw one of the elephants apparently going for a walk by itself round the field. She left the others and went back to the town.

She found some postcards and wrote one to her mother. Then she wandered about by herself, buying some sweets in a little shop.

Soon it was half past twelve – the time Roddy had told them all to be back at the caravan. The others came running up at the same time. Roddy looked pleased. "Good. I quite thought I'd have to sit here for ages tooting my horn for you. Get in."

Up the hills and down, once catching a glimpse of blue sea far away, went the little company of caravanners. They had tea in a tea-shop garden, and ate new-baked bread with honey, and hot scones with jam and cream. They all had enormous appetites, and the waitress had to bring them out a second supply of her scones.

"We'll be at our next stopping-place in nice time," said Roddy, looking at the map. "See – there it is – South Tollington – and we ask for Fenton Farm. There's no stream nearby though – so we can't wash in stream water – we'll have to make do with the caravan water."

They arrived at about seven o'clock. Roddy went off to the farm at once and came back in a few minutes time looking rather annoyed.

"He says we can stay for the night but he won't let us have any milk or anything," said Roddy. "Apparently the last lot of campers stole two or three of his chickens – or so he says – and now he's not going to supply anybody else with anything. Never mind – we must make do with what we've got. What are we going to have for supper, Jenny?"

Jenny suddenly looked dismayed. She stared

at Roddy, going red. "I – I don't know," she said.

"Whatever do you mean – you don't know?" said Roddy. "What did you buy this morning?"

"Well – actually Roddy – you see – what happened – well, you see . . . " began Jenny, going redder than ever.

"Answer me properly," said Roddy.

"I forgot about the shopping," said Jenny. "Geoff and I found a circus in the field – and we went and sat on the fence – and . . ."

"Do you mean to say there's no supper for us!" cried Roddy. "And I can't get anything from the farm either. Well, you really are the limit. Selfish, lazy lot – that's what you are!"

"I did buy some cards and send one to Mummy," said Ann, in rather a small voice. The others rounded on her at once.

"Yes, and why did you? Only because you were scared of looking at the circus camp!"

"Well, I'm going for a stroll," said Roddy, in disgust. "Where are my cigarettes, Geoff? I gave you the money for them this morning."

Now it was Geoff's turn to go red and to stammer. He had forgotten those too! Roddy stared at him in anger, swung on his heel, and went off by himself. The others felt most uncomfortable, but instead of blaming themselves they began to say nasty things about Roddy.

"Always flying into a temper!"

"Expecting us to do every single thing he tells us."

"Blow his beastly cigarettes."

All the same it was distinctly annoying to have no supper because they were all very hungry. The cupboard in the caravan was bare except for a hunk of stale bread and a bit of hard cheese. Jenny looked at it. "We'd better let Roddy have that," she said, and put it on a plate.

"And I'd better put up the tent," said Geoff sulkily. "Get into a row if I don't!"

He put it up carelessly. The girls, feeling hungry and cross, decided to go to bed. There were no cows to worry about tonight, but there was a large spider in a corner of the caravan that made Ann squeal. However, neither Jenny nor Geoff would remove it.

"Squeal away," said Geoff. "Go on till Roddy comes back, if you dare. He's in a mood to box your ears tonight!"

So Ann stopped squealing and got fearfully into her bunk. Geoff got into his sleeping-bag and waited for Roddy. But Roddy was a very, very long time. He had found somewhere to have a meal and he sat there for a long while. What was he to do with his lazy, irresponsible, selfish brother and sisters? He had given up a lovely holiday in Scotland to give the kids a treat – and if this kind of thing was going to happen all the time he was going to wish he had gone to Scotland after all!

He didn't see the plate of bread and cheese when he got back. A mouse discovered it in the night and helped himself. It was a good thing that Ann didn't know that or she would have squealed the place down again! Roddy got into his sleeping-bag, yawned and went to sleep.

The wind got up in the night. The rain came down in squalls. It beat against the caravan and the tent. The wind tugged at the tent and made it flap.

Suddenly something gave way and the tent collapsed completely. It fell over Roddy and

Geoff, waking them up suddenly, smothering them as they tried to push it off them.

"Good heavens! The tent's down!" said Roddy at last. "You silly little idiot, Geoff – I suppose you put it up carelessly as I wasn't there to watch you. Now we'll have to mess about in the dark and the rain for ages!"

The two boys had a very difficult time with the collapsed tent. Roddy made Geoff work

hard for he knew it was his fault. Geoff knew that too. It would have been all right if only this wind hadn't got up! Cold, wet through, and cross, the boys were at last able to get into their sleeping-bags again and settle down in the newly-put-up tent. Geoff was sulky and would not apologise. Roddy was angry.

"I had to go off and find a meal for myself tonight," he began, "and I've a good mind to go off and find a bed for myself too. Not one of you does his or her bit . . ."

"How mean of you – getting supper for yourself and forgetting all about us!" Geoff said angrily, feeling hungrier than ever.

"I didn't forget you," said Roddy. "You went hungry because it was your own faults – good lesson for you – but I didn't see why I should suffer because of your carelessness and forgetfulness. And what about this tent tonight? What about an apology for your carelessness over that?"

"You won't get one," said Geoff. "I think you're horrid. I really do think it's the limit getting a meal for yourself and –"

"One more word from you and you'll get out of this tent," said Roddy. He meant it. Geoff didn't say another word. He was angry with Roddy – but he was angry with himself

191

too for being careless over putting up the tent.

Nobody was very cheerful in the morning. For one thing Ann, Jenny and Geoff were very hungry and there was nothing to eat till they got to the next town. For another thing there was no water for anyone to wash in! That was Ann's fault! She had left the tap running a little all night long – and now there was no water left in the tank in the roof of the caravan.

"Well, I really don't expect anything else from any of you," said Roddy, sarcastically. "No food – no water – no cigarettes – tent collapsing. There's not much else you can do!"

He went off to tell the farmer they were leaving. "Come and help me fix the caravan to the car, for goodness sake," said Geoff to the others. "I'll get into another row if I don't do it just how he showed me."

"Do it yourself," said Jenny, annoyed. "I've got the caravan to tidy. I shall get into a row if I don't do that. This is a beastly holiday. I hate it. I wish it would end quickly."

Roddy came back, saw that the caravan was fixed to the car, noticed the three sulky faces, and said nothing. He felt sad. They had all looked forward to this holiday – and now, just because they couldn't pull together and each

192

play their part, it was going to be a failure.

They set off. They had a good breakfast in the next town and felt a bit better. They even began to talk cheerfully again. "Where are we going today? What are we going to do?"

"I thought we might head towards the sea now," said Roddy, opening the map. "The weather is so hot we could do with a bit of swimming. We might get permission to put the caravan up on the cliffs somewhere, so that we could get a good view of the sea."

Everyone cheered up considerably. This sounded simply lovely. "Yes, let's go towards the sea," said Jenny. "We've brought swimming costumes with us, luckily."

They set off again. They were all looking out for the first sight of the sea when they came to it. They had pleasant thoughts of bathing in the cool water and basking in the sun to dry.

"Golly! Look at this hill we've got to climb," said Jenny. "Isn't it frightfully steep?"

It was. The car groaned up it. Roddy stopped halfway and made the other three get out. "If we get rid of your weight, maybe the caravan won't be too heavy for the car," he said. He set off again, and the children followed on foot.

And then suddenly something dreadful

happened. Geoff had not fixed the caravan properly to the car and the steepness of the hill, making the van drag heavily on the car, broke the fastening between them. The caravan broke away – the car suddenly shot forward, relieved of its weight – and the caravan began to run backwards down the hill all by itself!

"Look! Look!" screamed Ann, suddenly. "The caravan is running backwards. It's broken away from the car! Look out!"

The caravan, looking most peculiar, lumbered down the hill, gathering speed as it went. The frightened children squeezed into the hedge as it passed them, afraid of being knocked down. Strangely enough the caravan kept to the roadway, though it veered occasionally from side to side.

Roddy stopped the car. He jumped out of it in time to see the caravan careering down the hill by itself. He stood in horror, unable to do anything to stop it. He suddenly felt very sick. What if it caused a terrible accident? Suppose another car was coming up the hill?

The caravan turned a corner and disappeared from sight. Roddy waited for the sound of a crash. Ann ran up the hill to him, white-faced and sobbing.

"Roddy! Roddy! The caravan's gone. Oh, Roddy!"

The others joined Roddy too, pale and frightened. "Oh, Roddy," said Geoff, his mouth quivering, "it was my fault I know. I didn't fix it properly."

They all sat down, feeling very shaky at the knees. Roddy put his arm round Ann, who was almost sick with fright.

"It's a dreadful thing," he said, in a quiet voice. "I – I hardly like to go down the hill and see what's happened. The least we can hope for is that the caravan has smashed itself – without smashing any other car or hurting anyone."

"I wished for this holiday to come to an end – but I didn't mean it to be like this," wept Jenny. "Oh, Roddy, it's awful. Will we have to pay for the caravan?"

"Of course – and for any damage it has done too," said Roddy, looking as white as the others. "I ought to have looked to see that Geoff had fixed it properly. It's my fault too. Perhaps I've tried to make you do too many things – in the wrong way. Well, this is a terrible punishment for not being able to pull together."

"Don't say things like that!" cried Jenny. "And don't look like that, Roddy. We've been awful. We haven't helped you a bit. Oh, I wish we could begin all over again, and do better."

"Well, we can't," said Roddy, getting up. "The holiday is finished. The caravan is smashed to pieces. Come on – we'll have to go and face it sometime."

In silence they went down the hill. Round the corner they went, afraid of what they might see. There was no sign of the caravan at all. They went on, looking fearfully from side to side. But there was no caravan to be seen.

They met an old man. "Have you seen our caravan running away?" asked Roddy.

The old man looked most astonished and shook his head. "I ain't seen no caravan at all," he said. "You didn't ought to let one run away. Them's not safe things running about on their own."

The children would have smiled at this any other time. But they couldn't now. They hurried on, afraid of what they might see at any moment.

Soon they came to a gap in the hedge. It looked as if something had broken through. They looked over the hedge and saw a most extraordinary sight!

There, standing in the field, was their caravan, surrounded by a circle of staring cows. It did not appear to be damaged at all. There it was, gleaming blue and yellow, standing by a little stream. They ran to it in excitement. They went all round it, their faces glowing.

"Roddy! It's not damaged at all! Not even a scratch, except just here where the thorns in the hedge caught it!"

"Oh, Roddy – it's too good to be true!"

"I can't believe it! Not a thing wrong with it!"

Ann was so delighted to see the caravan, whole and undamaged, that she took no notice of the cows at all. She slipped her arm through Roddy's.

"Oh, Roddy – aren't you glad? Our holiday hasn't ended after all!"

Roddy pulled the others down on to a bank

and looked at them gravely. "Well," he said, "it's a miracle the caravan is all right and that it hasn't smashed into anything or hurt anyone. But I think, kids, our holiday is at an end, anyhow. This is a terrible lesson to us. Because we didn't all play our parts and pull together as we should have done, this happened. We had better go home before anything worse comes."

Geoff looked at Roddy. "Nothing worse will come, Roddy. Don't break up this holiday. I'll play my part in future. You can trust me absolutely."

"And me too," said Jenny. "I'm sorry for all my temper and forgetfulness. Honestly, I'll do my bit. I feel so very, very thankful that nothing terrible has happened after all."

"I do too," said Ann. "I won't be silly or fuss any more. I won't even scream when I see a spider. I'll do everything you want me to, Roddy. But do, do let's go on with the holiday. We'll all pull together now."

Roddy smiled his nicest smile. "All right," he said. "We'll go on. I hoped you'd all want to. I do, too. We'll have a perfectly splendid time now – lovely meals from Jenny, no more squeals from Ann, plenty of good work from Geoff. And I'll keep my temper and think you're all perfectly wonderful!"

He got up. "We'd better see to the caravan now," he said. "We'll want a bit of help getting it out of this field. Then off we'll go again and make our way towards the sea!"

Two men helped them to get the caravan on the road once more. Roddy ran the car down to it and fixed the two together properly. They all got in.

"Now, off we go," said Roddy. "And this time we'll really enjoy ourselves!"

The
Lost Treasure

James, Susie and George were all feeling very sad. Not so much because they were going back to their boarding-schools in a few days, but because when they next broke up for the holidays, their lovely home, Grey Towers, would belong to someone else!

"Why can't we keep it for ourselves?" asked Susie. "Mummy, it's been our home, and Daddy's home, and Grandpa's home, and even Great-grandpa's home! Why have we got to leave? It ought to be our home too!"

"Well, dear, we're not so well off now," said her mother. "We can't afford to keep up a big place like this, even though it has belonged to us for three hundred years! Our family used to be rich, you know, in your great-great-grandfather's time. But then he offended a friend of the king and he was stripped of all his money and the famous family jewels."

"*All* of them?" said James, who had heard this story before. "I thought that Great-great-

203

grandpa hid some of his treasure."

"So the tale goes," said Mother. "But I'm afraid I don't believe that now, James. It would have been found long ago if it had been hidden. Anyway, dozens of our family have looked for it and haven't found it."

"I've looked for it too," said George, the eldest. "I've looked everywhere. I thought there might be a secret panel or something somewhere, which led to a hidden cupboard, but I never found anything."

"And all because long ago one of our family offended somebody, we've got to leave the home we love, and go and live somewhere we'll hate," said James.

"I do so love Grey Towers," said Susie. "Mummy, I can't bear to think I'll never come home to it again. I shall go and say goodbye to every single bit of it before I go back to school."

"Yes, we'd better do that," said James. "We'll go into every room and every corner so that we'll remember it always. Let's start now. Let's go up to the towers and look out of the windows, so that we can see all the country around that we know so well."

"Yes. And we'll even go down to the cellars and say goodbye to those," said George. "Not that I've ever been very fond of them, but I'm

204

not going to miss anything!"

"Well, we'll take Jumpy with us then," said Susie. "There might be rats there and I don't like them. Jumpy can chase them for us. He's a good dog for rats."

They began to say goodbye for the last time to all the places they loved so well – the rounded tower rooms at each end of the house – their own bedrooms, tucked into the roof – their big games room with its magnificent view of the nearby sea – the long dark landing where they had often hidden to pounce at one another.

"We mustn't leave out anything," said Susie, dolefully. "We'll do the cellars last. Where's Jumpy?"

"Jumpy!" called George, when at last they were ready to go down into the dark cellars. "Jumpy! Come along! We want you to come down and chase rats! Rats, boy, RATS!"

"And that's about all we shall find down in those old cellars," said Susie with a shiver. And down the stone steps they went, with Jumpy leaping beside them.

The cellars were deep down under the house. They were dark and smelled damp and musty. There was no electric light there so the children had torches. Jumpy didn't mind the dark at all. He rushed here and there, sniffing in every corner for rats.

Old barrels lined the walls. Empty bottles, thick with dust and cobwebs, stood on dark shelves. Wooden crates stood about. It was not a very pleasant place.

There were three or four cellars of different sizes. Nothing of any value was kept there now because Mother said it was too damp to store things. So it wasn't really a very interesting place after all.

"I don't feel I mind saying goodbye to the cellars, really," said Susie, flashing her torch round. "I never liked them much. Ugh, is that a frog?"

"No – a rat! Hi, Jumpy, here's a rat for you. Rat, quick!" yelled George. Jumpy raced up at once, his tail quivering in delight. The rat shot

into the next cellar and Jumpy tore after him. The children followed with their torches.

The rat ran round the cellar, looking for a way of escape, but there was none there. It went into the last cellar of all, a place so hung with cobwebs that Susie stopped in dismay, feeling the webby fingers across her face.

"It's horrid here!" she said. "I won't go in!"

Jumpy chased the rat to a corner, where a big barrel stood. Then he scraped and whined loudly, trying to get beneath the barrel.

"The rat's found a way out somehow," said James, in disgust. "I wonder if it could have gone under this barrel. Help me to overturn it, George. That's right – over it goes! There, Jumpy, is the rat under it?"

No, it wasn't. But there was a dark hole there and Jumpy suddenly fell down it unexpectedly, disappearing with a loud yelp!

"Gracious! What's happened to Jumpy?" said Susie, in alarm. The boys shone their torches on the floor under the barrel they had overturned.

"There's a round hole there! Where does it lead to?" said George. "Look, it's had a wooden lid or something over it at one time but it's rotted away. What a funny thing! Jumpy! Are you all right?"

A doleful wail came up. Jumpy was plainly not at all happy. He was very frightened. The boys shone their torches down the hole.

Far down they could see two green eyes gleaming up at them. It was poor Jumpy, looking up in despair.

"We'll get a rope and go down and get Jumpy up," said George. "What a funny pit. What can it be for? We'll go down and see, shall we? Maybe it was just a hiding-place for a smuggler!"

"Yes, that's it," said James. "We know that smuggling was carried on here ages ago. Fancy us never finding this old hole before. Come on – let's get a rope and rescue poor old Jumpy. What a noise he's making."

Soon the three children had found a rope and were back in the dark cellars. Jumpy was still howling mournfully, and the echoes of his doleful voice filled the cellars and made Susie shiver.

"I don't like it," she said. "Let's rescue Jumpy quickly and get back into the daylight again!"

"I'd better go down on the rope and tie Jumpy to it, and you must haul him up somehow," said George. "Then I'll come up on the rope myself. It's not very far down – less

than three metres, I should think."

He let the rope down after first tying it firmly to an iron hook in the wall. Then down he went, hand over hand, to poor Jumpy. The dog was thrilled to see him and barked joyfully.

George stood at the bottom of the hole, and felt for Jumpy's collar. He meant to tie the rope round his body in such a way that the others could haul him up without hurting him.

He switched on his torch – and then he gave a loud cry that made the others jump. "Look! It isn't just a hole. There's an opening here – it must lead into a passage. Gracious, how exciting!"

James and Susie almost fell down the hole in their excitement. What! An opening out of the hole? Where *could* it lead to?

"I'm coming down too!" shouted James and down he went, landing almost on top of George. Jumpy, happy now that the children were with him, had pranced out through the opening at the bottom. George shouted up to Susie.

"Wait a bit before you come down. Let me and James get into the opening or you'll land on top of us. I'll shout when we're ready."

Susie waited till he shouted. Then down she

went on the rope too, hand over hand, as she had been taught to do at gym.

She saw a small opening at one side of the wall of the hole. She had to bend down to get through it. The two boys were there, waiting, their torches switched on.

"It's a passage!" James said excitedly. "See? There it goes, down and down! Shall we explore it?"

"Well, of course!" said George. "What do you think? I'll go first. Let me squeeze by you. Golly, isn't it narrow!"

"Now Jumpy's gone again," said James. "He must be halfway down the passage by now. Jumpy! Come back, you silly, or you'll get lost."

A distant bark answered him. Jumpy was doing a bit of exploring himself. The children followed, their heads bumping into the rocky roof of the passage every now and again.

"It's leading towards the sea," cried James. "It'll come out somewhere on the shore, I bet it will!"

The passage went down and down, sometimes so steep and rocky that the children almost fell. It was all very strange and exciting. Their torches made patches of light in the darkness, and now and again they caught sight of Jumpy's wagging tail some way in front of them.

James suddenly heard a curious noise. He stopped. "Listen," he said in alarm. "What's that? Can you hear that booming sound? Whatever can it be?"

"I know!" said Susie. "It's the sea! We're coming near the sea."

"I wonder what part of the beach we shall come out on. Won't anyone walking on the beach be surprised to see us!"

Suddenly the steep little passage came to an end. In front of them the children saw a huge wooden door, studded with nails, fitting roughly into a rocky archway.

"A door!" said George. "Fancy finding a door down here! Is it locked?"

It wasn't locked – but it was bolted. Luckily the bolts were on their side of the door. With Jumpy watching impatiently, George and James tried their best to push back the heavy bolts. They couldn't – but the screws that held the bolts to the door suddenly gave way, for they were set in wood that had rotted and grown weak with the years. They fell out and the door swung open before them.

They flashed their torches beyond it. They saw a cave there, a surprisingly large one, with a high rocky roof and a smooth sandy floor. Directly opposite was a tiny opening, just big enough for a man to creep through, that looked out on the sea just below! It was a most astonishing sight.

Daylight came in through the hole in the cave wall. The children switched off their torches and looked round.

"Old trunks! Brass-bound boxes!" cried James running to where they stood in untidy heaps here and there. "Look, Susie, look, George! Do you suppose they'll be empty?"

"Of course," said George. He looked round the cave. "This must have been one of the old smugglers' caves," he said. "A well-hidden one too. You can only get into it from the seaward side by that hole there. The smugglers would have to unpack their goods on the moonlit shore and carry them to that hole, and hand them in to someone waiting in this cave."

"But George – how did these boxes and trunks get here?" asked Susie, looking at them. "If they didn't come from the shore they must have come from our house, Grey Towers, years and years ago!"

"Susie's right! They may have belonged to Grey Towers!" shouted James, and he flung himself down by one of the boxes. "Quick,

214

let's open them and see what's in them. Oh,
quick, quick, quick!"

The children couldn't open the boxes. They
must be locked! They were bitterly disappointed. But then, lying half buried in the
sand nearby, George suddenly spied an old
bunch of keys!

"We'll try these!" he cried, and was soon
busy fitting key after key into one of the
trunks. Suddenly one key turned with a

grating noise – and George flung open the lid. Packed hurriedly inside, flung in anyhow, were all kinds of jewels! Even now, after all the years of hiding, they gleamed brightly.

"Oh – look!" said Susie, in an awed voice, and held up what she felt sure must be an

emerald and diamond necklace. "And look at this – it's like a dog-collar made of rubies. And this – and this!"

"It's the old lost treasure of Grey Towers!" said George, and he looked very solemn and yet very excited. "The treasure our great-great-grandfather must have hidden when he was in disgrace with the king. And somehow nobody can have known where he hid it, and when he was taken away and imprisoned and killed, the treasure stayed here and was never, never found – because nobody ever knew about that little round hole in the cellar under the big barrel!"

After this long speech all the children sat silent, thoughts spinning round in their heads. "We shan't need to leave our dear old home now! We can stay on at Grey Towers! We can sell all these things and be rich!"

"But will it be treasure-trove? Will the Queen have to have it?" asked Susie, suddenly.

"Of course not. It's our family's riches, even though they've been lost for years!" said George. "Goodness – what will Mother say?"

"Look what's in this box – old gold pieces!" said James, unlocking another treasure hoard. "What a lovely sound they make when I run my hand through them! Let's fill our pockets

with this money, and dress ourselves up in all
the shining jewels, and go and find Mum and
Dad! What a surprise we'll give them!"

This seemed a lovely trick to play, and a
fine way to show off their discovery. Quickly
the children decked themselves out in heavy
necklaces, bracelets, brooches, pins and
sparkling belts. They filled their pockets with
the money, and took some in their hands to
fling down before their parents!

"Let's put that collar of rubies on Jumpy,"
cried George and, giggling with excitement,

they did so. Jumpy was astonished by such a heavy collar, but he didn't seem to mind.

Then off they went up the secret passage to the cellars, shouting and laughing in delight. "Here comes the old lost treasure! Here comes the old lost treasure!" they called.

And you should have seen their parents' faces when they saw three dirty, dusty, gleaming children arriving with a ruby-collared dog, flinging gold pieces about, and shouting at the tops of their voices:

"We shan't leave Grey Towers after all, we shan't, we shan't!"

And, of course, they didn't!

Great-Grandpa's Telescope

Great-grandpa was snoozing in the garden in his deckchair. He woke up suddenly. Now, who was that whispering nearby? Couldn't he even have a nap without those boys pestering him?

He couldn't see anyone and the whispering seemed to have stopped. He was just about to close his eyes again when he caught sight of a movement in the hedge. It was a good thick hedge, where birds nested and sang, and was a good hiding-place for any boy or girl who wanted to be unseen.

He watched the hedge. There – the boughs and brambles moved again. He was sure somebody was there. And he was sure he knew who it was. His great-grandson James, with his friend Malcolm. Always up to something!

He called out sharply. "James? Are you hiding there? Come out at once."

An indignant face looked out of the hedge. "Shh!" said James. "SHH!"

"Shh? What do you mean – shh?" said his

great-grandfather, crossly.

"Great-grandpa, don't make a noise," said James, in a low voice. "Malcolm and I are watching a kingfisher sitting on a bough over the stream on the other side of the hedge. You'll frighten him away!"

"Oh. I thought you were up to some joke or other," said Great-grandpa, lowering his voice. "I don't take kindly to being squirted with water pistols or being jumped at and booed. So you're watching birds, are you? Well, I used to do that long ago."

"Oh, blow! The kingfisher's gone," said

James, as a brilliant blue-green bird flew over the garden, crying "tee-tee-tee" at the top of his voice.

The two boys came into the garden. James was bright-eyed and merry, Malcolm was solemn and serious. They were great friends because they both loved birds and liked watching them.

They began to talk to the old man and tell him about the birds they had seen. He listened with interest. "You know quite a lot," he said. "Have you seen the big herons down on the marsh? They're interesting birds to watch."

"Yes. But as soon as we go near them they fly off," said Malcolm. "What we want is a pair of binoculars. We could hide in a hedge then, and look through the glasses and see the birds so clearly that they might be really close to us. But nobody will trust us with binoculars."

"Hmm," said Great-grandpa, "I'm not surprised. Binoculars are expensive and valuable things. You boys are so careless nowadays – you don't take care of things as we used to do when I was a boy. Look at your new bike, now, James – new six months ago, and it might be as old as the hills already, it looks so dirty!"

James went red. "I'll clean it this evening," he said. "I promise you, Great-grandpa. I know I've neglected it, and it's a beauty."

"Well, that's the way I like to hear a lad speak," said Great-grandpa, pleased. "And because I know you'll keep your promise, I'll do something for you."

"What?" asked James, eagerly.

"I'll lend you my old telescope," said Great-grandpa. "It's a poor thing compared with modern binoculars, but it still brings far-away things close – and I'll lend it to you to watch the birds."

"Oh, thanks," said both boys, and James beamed all over his face. "Where is it, Great-grandpa? Can I fetch it now?"

His great-grandfather told him where it was, and he ran to get it. Soon he and Malcolm were taking turns at looking through it.

"Oh, I say – it's cracked or something," said James at last. "Everything we look at seems to be cracked in two!"

Great-grandpa looked through it. "Oh, yes – I forgot it was cracked," he said. "It's this glass bit at the end here. Somebody dropped the telescope once and it got rather cracked. But once you get used to the crack, you don't notice it."

Malcolm put the telescope to his eye. "Great! I can see the church tower as close as anything!" he said. "I can see two sparrows quarrelling on it. I can see a blackbird too, sitting at the top of a hawthorn tree."

"Let *me* see," said James, and took it away. "Wow! Doesn't it bring things close? I can see exactly what clothes are hanging out on Mrs Kaley's line, and that's *ever* so far away."

"Now we shall be able to watch the birds properly," said Malcolm.

"We can hide in the hedge, stick the telescope to our eyes, and see birds half a mile away. We'll have fun!"

"Right," said Great-grandpa. "I'll lend it to you. Mind you, it's a poor thing really, old and cracked and not very powerful. You need first-class binoculars if you want to see things properly. But this will be a help, I'm sure."

It *was* a help. The boys went out bird-watching together and took the telescope with them. They didn't only watch the birds. They sat behind a bush, pushed the telescope through the leaves, and watched the rabbits playing in the evenings. They had to laugh at them, they were so comical – and then the rabbits would run away in fright. But they always came back.

225

Having the telescope made the boys want binoculars more than ever. The crack in the lens was annoying. It got a bit worse and the boys found it difficult to see clearly. But even so the telescope was great fun and brought things so close that they could watch the yellowhammer singing at the top of the bush, the sparrows going in and out of their nests under the eaves of old Mrs Hall's cottage, and even follow the swallows swooping in the air catching flies.

"Last night I heard owls," James said to

Malcolm. "We've never been able to watch owls, have we? It's going to be full moon soon and we could do a spot of owl-watching, if you liked. I'd love to see that big barn owl who screeches round the farm sometimes."

"Right. I'll watch tonight," Malcolm said promptly. "It's my turn to have the telescope."

"All right," said James, wishing he could have it first for night-watching. "Take it. You might see the tawny owl, too – I've heard his lovely hoot sometimes."

But the night was cloudy and dark and Malcolm neither saw nor heard any owls. It was most disappointing. He wanted to have the telescope for the second night but James wouldn't let him. "No, it's my turn," he said. "You've got to be fair."

James went to bed as usual that night. He took the telescope with him. He looked at his watch. Half past eight. It wouldn't be time for the owls to come out yet. It was still daylight, for it was high summer.

"I'll set my alarm clock for one o'clock," he thought. "The moon will be out then, and so will all the owls. It will be a good hunting night for them. I'll hear them hooting all over the place – and I bet I'll hear the screech of the old barn owl too."

He went to sleep. At one o'clock his alarm clock woke him up. He had put it under his pillow so that no one else would hear it. He switched off the alarm and sat up. The moon streamed in at his window.

"Ooooooh! Ooo-ooo-ooo-OOOOH!" called a beautiful voice in the night. James nodded. "Tawny owl," he said, pleased. "He's about tonight. Now – I'll train the telescope on to the farmhouse and watch for the barn owl first. Then when I find out where the tawny owl is hooting from, I'll try and see him too."

He saw nothing through the telescope except a big black bat that suddenly flitted across his view and made him jump. But he heard something.

It was a hoot. "Too-whoo, too-whoo, too-whit!" James listened. Then there came an answering call. "Too-whit, too-whit-too-whoo!"

James frowned. What owl was this calling? The hooting didn't sound like any owl he had ever heard! It came again.

Where did it come from? It sounded rather as if it came from somewhere near the old church. James trained the cracked lens of the telescope on to the church and waited for the sight of an owl.

No owl came. No more hoots came either –

but the barn owl suddenly gave one of his harsh shrieks and made James jump. It came from the farmyard. James thought he would train the telescope on to the farmhouse again.

He took one last look at the church tower – and then he stiffened in surprise. Something was moving on the roof of the church. What was it? It wasn't an owl – far too big. Could he be mistaken?

He watched intently. There was no movement for a while, and then he caught sight of another moving shadow on the farther side of the roof. Yes – two black shadows were

there. But they weren't birds – and they couldn't be animals – unless perhaps it was cats! Certainly it couldn't be human beings.

"It must be cats!" thought James, watching through the telescope. "No – it isn't! It's men – two men! They have come right out into the moonlight now and I can see them plainly. But what are men doing on the church roof in the middle of the night?"

He decided to put on some clothes and go next door to Malcolm. He would take the telescope with him.

So, dressing hurriedly, James stole down the stairs and went to the back door. He unlocked it and slipped out. The telescope was safely under his arm. Good gracious! Fancy seeing men on the church roof through it! What a strange thing.

He came to the wall that divided his garden from Malcolm's. Over he went and made his way to the path that ran below Malcolm's window. He picked up a few small pebbles. He took aim and threw one. No good. It fell back again. He threw another and it pinged against the glass pane of the window. He waited a moment, but as nothing happened he threw a third pebble.

That one brought Malcolm to the window!

James heard it being cautiously opened, and called up.

"Malcolm! It's me, James. Come on down. I've got something to tell you. Hurry up!"

"Right," came Malcolm's whisper, and he disappeared. It wasn't long before he was creeping out of his house.

"What is it?" he said to James. "Quick, tell me!"

James clutched hold of Malcolm's arm. He whispered in his ear. "I was watching for owls through the telescope. I heard some peculiar hooting which didn't really sound like owls. It came from near the church, so I trained the telescope on to the church roof, just in case owls were swooping about there."

"Go on," said Malcolm, excited. "Were there any?"

"No. But I saw something moving on the roof," said James. "It wasn't birds, of course – and it wasn't cats, either. It was men!"

"Goodness!" said Malcolm, surprised. "Men? But why should they be wandering about the roof of the church? They must be mad. Did you really see them? Here, give me the telescope."

"You can't see the church roof from down here on the ground," said James. "We'll have to go upstairs if you want to get a view of that.

But don't let's waste time, Malcolm. I want to get along to the church and find out what's going on."

"Yes – you're right. That's the best thing to do!" said Malcolm. "Come on then. Let's keep in the shadows, just in case those men have got a look-out somewhere."

They set off quietly, James with the telescope still tucked under his arm. "I think the hoots I heard were signals made by the men, not by owls," he said. "They didn't sound a bit like owls."

They came near the church. A big yew hedge, dark and thick, ran round the church-yard. The boys crouched behind it, and listened and watched.

At first they heard nothing. Then a slight noise came from the roof of the nearby church. The boys peeped out to look up to it. "There's one man – look!" whispered James, in excitement. "He's carrying something. What is it? It's all very mysterious, isn't it, Malcolm? What can they be doing?"

"What had we better do?" whispered back Malcolm. "I know what I'd like to do!"

"What?" asked James.

"How do you suppose they got up to the roof? By a ladder?" said Malcolm. "Well, *I'd* like to find that ladder and remove it! Then they would be in a great fix, wouldn't they?"

James thought this was a wonderful idea and he said so. "We'd have to make sure that there wasn't a third man or even a fourth hanging about down in the churchyard, keeping watch," he said. "We'd get into awful trouble if they caught us spying on them. Malcolm, let's creep right round the churchyard in the shadow of this yew hedge and listen and look."

So, holding their breath, the two boys made their way slowly and silently round the big churchyard, watching out for any other men that might be there.

Malcolm suddenly clutched James and made him jump. "Quiet!" he hissed in his ear. "Look over there – there's a man – a third man and he's standing at the foot of a ladder, holding it! We can't take it away after all."

"What a pity," said James. They fixed their eyes on the man, who stood with one foot on the long ladder and his two hands holding it. From above came the sounds of panting.

Then a cautious voice spoke from the roof. "You there, Eddie? Come on up for a minute. This piece is too awkward for us to manage between us. We want your help."

"Right," said Eddie, who was a big fellow. He clambered up the ladder and climbed on to the roof. Malcolm gave James a nudge.

"Come on. Now's our chance! We'll remove the ladder, and then you can run for the police while I stay here and watch what happens. We'll have to tug like anything at that ladder. It will be awfully heavy."

The two boys ran to the ladder. They both took hold of it at the bottom and pulled it as hard as they could. The top edge slid down from the roof – lower and still lower – and then the ladder collapsed and fell down to the ground with a very loud noise.

"Quick, hide!" whispered James. "In this doorway here. They won't have seen us. Just see what they say."

They crouched in the doorway and listened. Astonished voices came from the roof high above.

"What was that? The ladder! It's slipped and fallen! Eddie, why didn't you make it secure? Now we can't get down."

"It was safe all right," said Eddie's voice. "Somebody must have pulled it down. Listen!"

There was silence as the men listened. But they heard nothing, for Malcolm and James were as quiet as the church mice!

"It slipped," said somebody's voice. "Now what are we going to do? Let's chuck the stuff down and then find a way to climb down ourselves."

"It will make a noise," objected Eddie's voice, but the other men pooh-poohed this.

"It won't make as much noise as that ladder did when it fell! Nobody heard that. The church isn't near the village, and it's the middle of the night. Come on – let's heave this piece over."

There was a heavy thud not far from the two boys, who clutched one another, startled. What in the world were the men stealing and throwing down to the ground?

"I'll run for the police now, before the men get down and run off with their goods," said James. "Keep hidden, Malcolm, won't you?"

James rushed off, keeping in the shadow of the yew hedge again, his feet making no sound. He made his way up the church lane and after a while came to the village. He knew where the police station was. A solitary light burned there. One of the two policemen must be still on duty.

The door was shut but not locked. Malcolm turned the big iron handle and stumbled in. A policeman sitting asleep beside a telephone jumped up in alarm. He was surprised to see James. He knew him quite well.

"What's up?" he said. "What's happened to bring you here at this time of night?"

James poured out his story, and the policeman listened carefully. "But I can't imagine what they're stealing!" said James, out of breath at the end.

"Can't you? I can!" the policeman said grimly. "Our church has a fine lead roof – lead is worth a lot of money now. Those rogues are stripping the roof, meaning to take the sheets of lead away and sell them. And on the first rainy day we'll have the rain pouring into the church and ruining everything."

He made a short telephone call to the other village policeman, who was off duty and asleep at home, and asked him to join them down by the church at once. "Telephone through to headquarters before you leave," said the first policeman. "We'll want a few more men."

Then he set off with the excited James and they went to the churchyard, keeping as quiet as they could. A low voice came from the doorway where Malcolm was still hiding.

"How quick you've been! Those men have been chucking something down ever since you left. Now one of them is trying to find a way

237

down. I heard them say something about a lorry."

"Ah! So they've got a lorry hidden somewhere have they?" said the policeman. "Well, I'll just go and find it and let the air out of the tyres – then they can't get away if they get the wind up and run!"

He and James went to look for the lorry. They found it easily enough, hidden under some trees outside the churchyard. The policeman lost no time in letting the air out of the two front tyres.

By this time the second policeman was there, too, and a whispered conference took place. James was so excited that he could hardly keep still. What a thing to happen! Who would have dreamed that his great-grandpa's old telescope would have found out such a robbery!

There came the sound of quiet feet and a panting whisper. It was Malcolm. "James! Where is the policeman? That man called Eddie is climbing down a drainpipe."

The two policemen at once ran back into the churchyard – and the very first thing that happened was that they bumped into Eddie! He gave a yell and slipped away, calling out to warn the others. He tore across the churchyard and over the wall.

"He's gone for the lorry," said the policemen. "Come on."

Eddie was in the lorry and starting up the engine as the two men panted up. The lorry started off with a jolt – but the man realised at once that the tyres were flat. He gave a shout and leaped out – straight into the arms of the two policemen!

"There's a car coming!" yelled James, and just then a police car glided up, closely followed by a second. Out jumped four more policemen,

their buttons gleaming in the moonlight. What an excitement!

It wasn't long before the ladder was set up again and the two men still up on the roof were ordered down. Then the police cars drove away with the three prisoners, and the two village policemen examined the sheets of lead that had been stripped off the roof of the church.

"You two boys have done pretty good work tonight," said one policeman. "Those men are the ones that have been going round the country for a long time, stealing lead from all kinds of roofs. How did you say you managed to spot them?"

"Well – I was looking through my great-grandpa's telescope," began James – and then he stopped. "Oh my goodness – what have I done with it? I brought it with me – and now I haven't got it!"

"Is this it?" said a policeman, picking up something. James gave a cry.

"Yes – and oh dear, one of those sheets of lead must have fallen on it! It's bent and broken! It won't be any use at all. Whatever will Great-grandpa say?"

The boys went back home, very excited. They decided not to wake their parents up.

They would tell them in the morning.

You should have seen the faces of James's parents – and of his great-grandfather, too – when he told them his news at breakfast. They simply couldn't believe his story!

"Bless us all!" said Great-grandpa. "What boys do nowadays! Do you mean to say it was all because of my old telescope?"

"Yes, Great-grandpa – but I say, I do hope you won't be too cross with me! You see, in all the excitement of the night a sheet of the lead fell on the spot where I had put the telescope – and it's bent and broken."

"Now, don't you worry about that," said Great-grandpa, generously. "That old telescope wasn't much good except for you two boys to use. It won't be missed!"

"It will," said James, sadly. "It was awfully useful for bird-watching, Great-grandpa. We shall miss it very much."

A knock came at the door and somebody walked in. It was the rector of the old church. He loved it very much and had been horrified to hear how the lead from the roof had nearly been stolen. He looked at James.

"Ah, James!" he said. "I've heard about you and Malcolm from the police this morning. Where is Malcolm?"

"There he is – just coming in," said James. "Hi, Malcolm – how are you after last night?"

Malcolm came in, solemn as usual, but with a very pleased look about him, all the same. "My parents are awfully pleased," he said. "They seem quite proud of me! Good morning, everybody. Have you told your great-grandfather about the broken telescope, James?"

"Of course," said James. "Here's the rector, Malcolm. He's heard about everything, too."

"Yes," said the rector, beaming. "I came to thank you both for what you've done. And I wanted to say that I want to give you something as a little memento of such an exciting evening. Is there anything you would like, the two of you?"

"Oh, yes, sir – a pair of real binoculars," said James at once. "We'd like those better than anything!"

His mother laughed. "Oh no, James," she said. "You mustn't ask for those – they are very expensive."

"Oh," said James, and went red in the face. "I didn't know they were so expensive. Sorry, sir!"

The rector smiled all over his face. "Well, as it happens, you can have what you want," he said. "I've got an old pair – a good pair – which I never use. I'd be delighted to give them to you and Malcolm for bird-watching. I used to do it when I was a boy, but I don't have time now."

James and Malcolm share the glasses between them, and take the very greatest care of them. They have watched so many birds and animals and discovered so many things that they are keeping a diary about them. Great-grandpa is going to be allowed to read it first because, as he says, there wouldn't be any book if it hadn't been for him and his old telescope!

The Case of the Five Dogs

One day, when John was sitting reading in his garden, he heard his name called. He looked up and saw the face of a little girl peeping over the wall. "Hello, Meg, what do you want?" he asked.

"Oh, John – can we come in for a minute? There's Colin here and George, and me and Katie. We want to talk to you."

"Come on over the wall then," said John, surprised. They all clambered over. Meg and Katie were ten, George and Colin were about twelve. With them were their dogs.

"What's up?" asked John. "I say, keep your dogs in order, won't you, Dad's just planted out some new things in the beds."

The boys and girls settled down on the grass, each holding the collar of their own dog. "You see, John, we know you're an awfully good detective," said George. "So we thought you might help us. Something awful has happened."

"What?" asked John, feeling rather important at being called an awfully good detective.

"This morning some of Farmer Warner's sheep were chased by dogs," said George. "One fell in the stream and broke its leg."

"And the farmer went to the police and he said it was our dogs that did it," said Katie, almost in tears. "He said one of his sheep was

killed the other day by dogs, and he saw an Aberdeen like my Jock, a terrier like George's Sandy, a Sealyham like Meg's and a spaniel like Colin's in the road outside the field. So now he says it was our dogs that killed his sheep last week, and ours that chased them today."

"And perhaps they'll be shot," said Colin, gloomily. "Or else our fathers will be fined. But we know it wasn't our dogs."

"We want you to help us," said George. "You've got to prove that it was somebody else's dogs, not ours, see? You're a clever enough detective for that, aren't you?"

"Well – I don't know," said John. "This isn't quite like any case I've had before. To begin with, some dog must have killed that sheep. If we could prove that first, we'd be halfway to saving your dogs. But we don't know whose dog did it."

"Yes, we do," said Colin at once. "It was the log-man's dog – you know, the man who comes all round the district selling logs. He's got a horrible black dog, big and fierce and ugly."

"Oh, yes, I know it," said John. "It's the only dog I'm really scared of. It looks so fierce and it growls like anything if anyone goes near

247

it. I always think it looks as bad-tempered as its master."

"Yes, that's the one," said Meg.

"But how do you know it's the dog that killed the sheep?" asked John. "Did you see it?"

"No, but we know someone who did," said George. "You know, there's a gypsy caravan near that field, and there are some children living there. One's called Julie, and we sometimes speak to her. She told us she saw the big black dog chase the sheep and kill it."

"Well, then – that's easy! She's only got to tell the police that!" said John.

"She won't. She's afraid of the police. She says if we try to make her tell, she'll say she doesn't know anything," said Colin. "She says her father would beat her black and blue if she told anything to the police. They are so scared of policemen."

"I told the policeman who came about my dog that I knew it was the big black one belonging to the log-man," said George. "But when he came again he said the log-man said he wasn't in the district that evening, so it couldn't have been his dog, because it never leaves him."

"And now it's our dogs that are getting the

blame for everything!" said Meg, fiercely, putting her arms round her Sealyham. "Why, Scamp doesn't even chase cats! I'm not going to have him shot for something that isn't his fault."

"So you see, John, you *must* do something," said Katie. "We could only think of coming to you. Will you help us?"

"Yes, of course," said John, who was very fond of dogs. "But it's going to be difficult to make a man own up to his dog killing a sheep, if he's already said that neither he nor his dog were here that evening. Have you asked if anyone else saw him or his dog that evening near Farmer Warner's sheep field?"

"Yes, we've asked everyone," said Colin. "But nobody did. You know, there was a big meeting on the green that night, and simply everyone was there. There might not have been a single person anywhere near the field when the sheep was killed – except Julie, and she won't tell."

"She ought to tell," said Meg. "That dog once snapped at their baby."

"It's an awful dog," said George. "It'll end up killing somebody. John, can you do something?"

"Well, I'll try," said John. "But somehow I

just don't know how to begin. First – what day was the sheep killed?"

"Last Friday," said Colin. "I was on the green with the others. We were listening to the speaker, and I was watching an aeroplane doing stunts in the sky. It wrote 'Moon' against the blue, and we all laughed, because it was Mr Moon who was speaking at the meeting. It was a good advertisement for him. He wants everyone to vote for him, doesn't he?"

"Fancy hiring an aeroplane to write your name in the sky!" said Meg. "I wish one would write mine. I'd feel very important."

"Well, let's get back to our subject," said John. "The sheep was killed on Friday. Julie says she saw the log-man's black dog kill it. The log-man says he wasn't here and neither was his dog. Where does he say he was, I wonder?"

"He swears he was fifteen miles away," said Colin. "Out on his bicycle, he says. He'd sold all his logs that day, and went to speak to a man at Five-Mile Hill about timber, but he wasn't there. Anyway, the log-man swears he was miles and miles away from here. He says his dog loped along beside his bike all the way. So there you are!"

"Did Julie see the log-man as well as his

250

black dog on Friday, when the dog killed the sheep?" said John.

"No. But she said she heard his peculiar whistle, when he whistled to the dog to come to him," said Colin. "You know his whistle? It's awfully loud and shrill. He puts two fingers in his mouth when he does it. Julie can do it too. But I can't."

"Well – it looks as if the dog and the man were there on Friday then, when everyone else was on the green listening to Mr Moon," said John. "But how in the world can we prove it?"

"The log-man is coming again tomorrow," said Meg, suddenly. "It's his day for our village. Couldn't you talk to him, John?"

"Well . . ." said John, and stopped. He didn't like the log-man, and he didn't think the log-man would like him, either. And he certainly didn't like the log-man's dog. It gave him a horrid feeling when the big black creature sniffed round his ankles. He felt as if at any moment it might take a bite out of his leg.

"Oh, please, please do," said Meg. "We'll come and be with you, if you like. But we'd better leave our dogs at home, or that awful black dog will gobble them up!"

"Yes, for goodness sake don't bring your

dogs," said John, picturing a free fight between them and the black dog going on all round him. "All right. I'll think of something to say to him. You can all be with me and listen to what he says."

The log-man always went to the village inn, when he was near, and brought out a drink for himself. He sat down on the log bench beside the green in the evening sunshine, and ate bread and cheese and drank his beer. His dog always lay at his feet.

"He'll be there about six o'clock," said John. "I often see him there then. We'll be playing about, and I'll go up and try to get him into a conversation. You can all listen hard. But don't mention the word 'dogs' or he'll be on his guard."

"Right," said Colin. "He doesn't know any of us. Now mind, everybody – leave your dogs at home so that they can't get out."

John was a bit worried about this new problem. It wasn't like his others at all. He didn't see how to tackle it, no matter how hard he puzzled about it. He lay in bed that night and pondered over it.

Julie had seen the dog killing the sheep and had heard the log-man whistling to him that Friday evening. Therefore he must have been there. But he said he was miles and miles away. Everyone else, unfortunately, seemed to have been on the green, listening to Mr Moon, and looking at his name being written in the sky. It was fortunate for the log-man that nobody was anywhere near Farmer Warner's field that evening!

After a long while John made a plan. He didn't think it was very good – but it just might work. He'd see.

So, the next evening, about six o'clock, he, Meg, Katie, Colin and George went to the green, near the Rose and Crown Inn. They began to play a game with a bat and ball. No dog was near. All had been left safely at home!

"Here's the log-man now," said John, in a low voice. "See, there's his cart. He's driving his old brown horse, and that awful black dog is sitting up beside him just as he always does."

The cart drew up outside the inn. The man got down and went inside. He came out with a tankard of beer and went to sit in the evening sunshine on a wooden bench beside the green. He pulled a packet of sandwiches out of his pocket.

"We'll give him a minute or two, then I'll go up and ask if he knows the time," said John, and threw the ball to Colin. All the children

kept an eye on the black dog. He lay beside his
master, but they felt that at any moment he
might go after their ball.

In a little while John went up to the log-
man, followed by the others. "Could you please
tell me the time?" he asked.

"Look at the church clock," said the log-
man, in a grumpy voice. Blow! John had
forgotten that the church clock could be seen
from the green.

"Oh, yes, of course – thanks," he said. "A quarter past six," he said to the others. Then he looked at the black dog.

"Fine big dog you've got," he said, politely. "I bet he eats a lot. Can he catch rabbits?"

The log-man looked at him. "My dog don't chase nothing," he said. "He don't chase even a sparrow. He just keeps alongside of me."

"But surely he would chase a cat?" said Colin, joining in. "All dogs chase cats."

"Well, this one don't," said the log-man. "He don't chase nothing."

The dog looked at them out of bloodshot eyes and growled.

"He won't bite, will he?" said Meg, retreating hastily.

"Never bit anyone in his life," said the log-man. "Best-tempered dog I ever had."

The dog growled again and showed yellow teeth. None of the children liked him at all.

"Is he afraid of anything?" asked John. "You know – afraid of guns or noises or anything like that? Some dogs are."

"No. He ain't afraid of nothing," said the log-man.

"I knew a dog once that was scared stiff of aeroplanes," said John.

"Mine don't mind nothing at all," said the

log-man and took a long drink.

"I think I can hear an aeroplane now," said John. "Oh no – it's a car. I say – have you heard of those aeroplanes that can write in the sky? I wish I could see one!"

"You did see one – don't you remember? It wrote 'moon' in the sky," said Colin, astonished at John's forgetfulness.

"No – surely it wrote 'sun'," said John. "Wait a bit – yes – I'm remembering – it wrote 'sun', didn't it?"

"Gah – it wrote 'moon', of course," said the log-man, munching hard. "Can't you read, then? It wrote 'moon' plain as anything. That's a wonderful thing that is, to write in smoke in the sky."

"Let's see – it was a white aeroplane, wasn't it?" said John, as if he was trying hard to remember. But everyone put him right.

"No, it was one of those silvery-grey ones, it was, really!"

John appealed to the log-man. "It wasn't, was it? It was white."

"You're wrong," said the log-man, and took another sandwich. "It was grey. Saw it as clear as could be. And the markings too – LGO they were, whatever they might mean. My eyes are as good as yourn any day."

He got up, emptied the dregs from his tankard on to the grass and went into the inn. He came out again, followed by his dog, and climbed up on to his cart. Without so much as a wave he drove off.

The children crowded round John. Only Colin had seen how his little plan had worked. The others hadn't.

"John – how very, very clever of you – to lead the conversation round to aeroplanes like that – and to make him say he'd seen that one writing 'moon' in the sky, and to make him describe it too!"

"Well – but what's so clever about all that?" said Meg.

"Can't you see, silly? That plane came over on Friday evening, and only Friday evening – and the log-man said he was miles away! Well, how could he have seen that aeroplane writing in the sky, if he wasn't here?"

There was a silence. John and Colin looked round triumphantly. "There you are!" said John. "He's admitted he was here and we've got five witnesses. Come on, we'll go to the police station."

And off they all went. John's friend the sergeant was there, and he took them into his room, looking amused. He listened to their

whole story without interrupting once. Then
he made a few notes.

"Very interesting," he said, "this is very,
very interesting. And very smart work too,
Detective John. We will follow this up and ask
the log-man how he managed to see this
aeroplane doing its tricks when he was fifteen
miles away."

The children next went to Julie. They told her what had happened. "Suppose the log-man admits he and his dog were here, will you say what you saw?" asked Colin. "You must, you know – because you'll be a proper witness then."

Julie looked scared. "Will I get into trouble if I don't say?" she asked.

"Yes, awful trouble!" said John, hard-headedly. "Oh, Julie – surely you will speak up for our dogs – you wouldn't want them to be destroyed, would you, instead of a wicked dog that has killed a sheep and already scared your baby?"

"Well, all right then," said Julie. So when a policeman called, Julie told him all she had

seen, and, armed with this, and the other information the children had given him, the sergeant went off to interview the log-man.

He came back again in his car, and saw the children gathered together on the green, waiting for him. This time they had their dogs with them.

He stopped his car. The children crowded round him.

"Well, he's confessed," said the sergeant. "He was in the district, his dog was with him, it did go for the sheep, and then he whistled it off. He says he didn't know a sheep was killed at the time, and was too afraid to confess when he did hear. I don't know about that. Anyway, what do you think that dog did?"

"What?" asked the children. The sergeant showed them a bandaged leg.

"Tried to take a nip out of me!" he said. "Silly thing to do, wasn't it? He's going to be punished for all his misdeeds, you may be sure – and your dogs can now go home without a stain on their character – thanks to good old Detective John!"

"Woof," said the dogs at once. "Woof!" And they tried to lick John as if they did honestly understand what he had done for them. He really is a very good detective, isn't he?

The Wild West Kids

Peter banged on Jill's door early one summer morning. "Jill! Get up, and let's get the horses. It's a beautiful morning, really super."

Jill sat up with a jump. She looked out of the window. The sun was streaming over the fields out of a sky as blue as forget-me-nots. Hurrah!

"All right, I'm coming," said Jill and leaped out of bed. "I'll just throw on some riding-clothes."

In a few minutes she was down in the stables with Peter. Each of them had a horse of their own, given to them by their grandfather, who was a farmer, and bred cattle, sheep and horses.

"Dear old Bunter," said Peter to the lovely chestnut horse that stamped with delight at seeing him so early in the morning. Jill's horse went to her too, nuzzling his great head against her shoulder in the way she loved.

She had called her horse Nuzzler, because of this endearing habit of his. She rubbed her hand up and down his velvety nose. "Hello, Nuzzler! Are you pleased to see me so early? What about a gallop?"

Nuzzler whinnied softly, and capered round a little, his brown eyes gleaming. That was what he loved more than anything, a swift gallop over the grassy hills on a sunny morning.

Then off went both children, first cantering and then letting Bunter and Nuzzler gallop. Peter reined in Bunter a little and then called back to Jill.

"Shall we go to our circus ring this morning? We've got plenty of time. I bet Nuzzler and Bunter would enjoy it."

"Oh yes," called back Jill. "I feel as if I could do all sorts of marvellous things on a day like this."

They galloped to a little round clearing, roughly about the size of a circus ring. Both children had ridden horses since they were two years old and they were as much at home on a horse's back as on their own feet. They had found this little "circus ring" as they called it, three or four years before, and had practised quite a number of daring tricks there.

Peter stripped off Bunter's saddle. "I'm going to do some bareback riding," he said.

"Cowboys and Indians! Hooo, Bunter! Round we go, top speed!"

Bunter knew this trick. Round and round the little green ring he went, just as if he was in a circus. He didn't mind Peter's wild Indian yells in the least. He enjoyed them. He even threw back his own head and gave a loud and exultant neigh, as if he too were whooping like an Indian!

Peter stood up on Bunter's back, and stayed there while Bunter went round and round.

He kept his balance marvellously and Jill clapped him loudly. Then down he flopped, on to Bunter's back – but rode back to front!

"Jolly good, jolly good!" yelled Jill. "Now here I come too."

She galloped into the little green ring and Nuzzler began to go round and round behind Bunter. Jill was almost as clever as Peter in the way she could stand up on Nuzzler's back. But she could not ride backwards. She always slipped off with a bump when she tried.

As the two children were performing to their heart's content, letting out wild yells at intervals, two boys came up. They also were on horses – and with them was a string of shining, satiny horses, tossing their beautiful heads and champing at their bits.

Peter and Jill did not see them at first. Then suddenly the two boys cantered into the little green ring on their own horses and joined the private circus! Round and round went the four horses, and Peter and Jill stared in sudden surprise at the newcomers.

"Go on, go on," yelled one of the boys to Peter, seeing that he was about to rein his horse to a stop. "Now, when I shout – turn your horses the other way and make them canter in the opposite direction."

He gave a loud shout: "HUP then!" His own horse and his friend's at once stopped, wheeled their heads round, and tried to go the opposite way. But, of course, Bunter and Nuzzler, not being used to this sudden change, did not turn properly – and all four horses bumped violently into one another. Jill gave a shriek and fell off. Then all four of the children collapsed into laughter.

"I say! Who are you?" asked Peter, looking with admiration at the string of horses standing patiently nearby.

"We're from the circus camp," said the bigger boy. "It's arrived this morning, down in Bolter's field over there. We're in charge of the horses. I'm Sam and he's my cousin Dan. Sam and Dan, the world's wonder-riders, the real Wild West Kids."

"Gracious!" said Jill, getting up from the ground. "Is that what you're called? Are these horses circus horses? Do you ride in the ring?"

"You bet we do," said Sam. "We've got proper Indian clothes and headdresses – and you should hear us yell."

"Aren't you lucky to belong to a circus," said Jill, enviously. "Fancy having all those glorious horses to look after, too. No wonder you ride so well if you perform in the ring."

"Well, you two kids ride pretty well too," said Dan. "We watched you. Say, your brother's as good as any circus fellow, the way he stands up to ride that horse of his. Has he rubbed any resin into its back so that he doesn't slip? We always do."

"No. Never heard of it," said Peter, feeling very pleased at this unexpected praise from a real circus-rider. "We only just mess about, you know."

"Like to come and see round the circus camp sometime?" asked Sam. "And can't you come and see us do our act some night? We're hot stuff, Dan and me."

"We'd love to," said Jill. "We'd better get back to breakfast now, though. Can we come after that?"

"Right. We'll expect you," said Sam. "Come on your horses, of course. They'll enjoy having a gossip with ours."

Jill and Peter galloped back home, thrilled. "Fantastic!" said Jill. "I've always wanted to see round a circus camp. I wonder if they've got elephants this year."

After breakfast the two galloped off to Bolter's field. It had been quiet and empty the day before but now it was crowded and full of life. Brightly painted caravans stood all about, tents had sprung up, and men were busy putting up the big top in which the circus itself was to perform that night. It was a most enormous tent.

"Two elephants!" said Jill, in delight. "And look at all those dogs. I've never seen so many

tails wagging in my life, not even at a meeting of hounds! What's in that travelling cage, I wonder? Oh, Peter, isn't this fun? I wonder where Sam and Dan are. Let's look for them."

Sam and Dan were on the look out for them. They came over to the children and grinned. "Hello! So you've come. Leave your horses here with ours and we'll show you around a bit."

The circus camp was a thrilling place to wander round. They saw the two enormous elephants, Miss Muffet and Polly Flinders. Polly played a trick on Jill. She suddenly wound her trunk round her waist, lifted her up and set her gently on her head. Jill, half frightened, gave a squeal.

"Hey, Polly! Where are your manners?" called a little man nearby. He walked up, grinning all over his comical freckled face. "Sorry, Miss, if she scared you. But she only does that to people she really likes. She must have taken a fancy to you!"

He held out his arms and somehow Jill slithered down. She felt proud that Polly had liked her so much, but she thought she would keep away from both elephants, just in case they suddenly liked her very much again!

"You must come and see them in the ring

some night," said the little elephant man. "They're grand. They play cricket with me."

Someone came swiftly up to them, turning cartwheels in a most graceful and amusing way. Immediately Sam and Dan joined in, and over and over went the three on hands and feet, like living wheels.

"Oh, teach us to do that!" begged Jill, when all three stood upright again, laughing and breathless.

"That's Tickles, the chief clown," said Dan. He didn't look like a clown at all. He looked like a rather dirty and untidy young man, with a terrific shock of hair, a very snub nose, and the widest grin the children had ever seen. He was dressed in a pullover and old flannel trousers.

"Pleased to meet you," said Tickles. He jumped into the air, turned a double somersault, landed neatly on his feet, and then turned himself upside down and walked about on his hands.

"Full of beans this morning, isn't he?" said Dan. "He's a scream in the ring. Specially when he tries to ride a horse. We've got one called Toothy, who will try to pick Tickles up whenever he falls off. They bring the house down between them."

"It does sound exciting," said Peter. "I wish I could walk on my hands like Tickles does."

"Well, we'll teach you if you like," said Tickles, and walked off with the little company to see an excited crowd of dogs, who were gathering round a small woman.

"That's Madame Lilliput and her performing dogs," said Dan. "See that little white one? He's a marvel. They all play football in the ring, and Tippy's goal. You should see him bump the ball away from goal with his nose."

The dogs looked very lively and well-fed and happy. They jumped up at Madame Lilliput, trying their best to lick her hands. It was plain that every dog adored her.

Taking a big football in her hands, Madame Lilliput wandered off towards the big top.

"She's going to put in some practice in the ring," said Dan. "She doesn't like being watched, or I'd take you to see those clever dogs of hers."

They wandered round the camp, looking at the caravans. They peeped inside one or two, marvelling at the amount of stuff that was packed there. All of them looked cosy and comfortable, but one or two were rather dirty and untidy.

"Who lives in that grand motor-caravan?" asked Jill, seeing a big one by itself, painted a lovely blue.

"Oh, that belongs to Jo Martini. He owns the circus," said Dan. "He's a fine fellow, but, oh! what a temper! You'll see him in the ring when you come, with his outsize whip. You'll hear him cracking it, too. It makes a simply terrific noise."

"Do you remember when we had that bad fellow here – Jeremy Hiyo – and . . . "

"Oh, yes," finished Dan, "and Jo flew into a temper with him and chased him all round the camp, cracking his great whip so cleverly that the end of it flicked Jeremy each time. Didn't he yell!"

"I've felt the end of that whip myself," said Sam. "Makes you yell all right! Look out – there's Jo himself."

A great big man came out of the blue caravan. He wore spotless white riding-breeches and a top hat. In his hand he carried the biggest whip that Jill and Peter had ever seen. He cracked it, and it went off like a pistol shot. The children jumped. Jo grinned at them.

"Good morning. Visitors, I see. Want to join my circus?"

"Oh! I wish we could!" said Jill, fervently. "But I don't expect we'd be allowed to."

"I don't expect so either," said Jo. "You have to be born to circus life if you're to be any good, you know. Trained to it from a day old. See this whip? You wouldn't believe how often I've used it on these two bad lads here."

Sam and Dan laughed. Mr Martini cracked his whip again and strode off. "Isn't he grand?" said Jill. "I feel half scared of him, but I like him all the same."

"That's what all the circus folk feel about Jo Martini," said Sam. "He's a proper ringmaster, he is – strict and stern, not afraid of using his fists and his whip, too, if anyone needs them – but kind as your own mother at home."

Peter and Jill spent the whole morning in

the camp, seeing every animal and person there. The circus folk were friendly and kindly, and the animals all seemed to be treated as if they were humans. There was a big bear there that belonged to one of the clowns, and he was so tame that he was allowed to wander about on a leash. There were monkeys, too, that leaped and chattered on the roofs of the caravans, pointing at Jill and Peter with little hairy fingers.

"They're surprised to see you," explained Dan. "They love anything strange or new. Look out for Scamp – the one over there wearing a little red hat. He's a real bit of mischief. He ran off with Jo's whip one day, and stuck it in the chimney of Tickles' caravan."

"Look – there's Madame Lilliput coming out of the big tent with her dogs," said Peter. "Has she finished practising? Can we go and see the ring?"

"Yes. And it's time we took the horses in and gave them a bit of practice there, too," said Sam. "We've got a new horse, Ladybird. She's not quite sure how to waltz yet."

Jill and Peter helped the boys to take the horses into the great ring. Sawdust was scattered in the centre. The ring was enclosed by curved pieces of wood covered with red plush. Each piece fitted against the next, and made a great red circle.

It was fun seeing the horses canter round in rhythm, nose to tail. At a shout each turned round slowly and carefully and then went the other way. Then they had to waltz. Sam started a great hurdy-gurdy going, and when the music poured out, every horse pricked up its ears.

"They love music," said Sam. "Now watch them waltz to it!"

Most of the horses managed to dance gracefully round and round, turning themselves neatly at the right moment. Jill and Peter watched in amazement. If only Bunter and Nuzzler could do that!

"See the new horse – Ladybird – she's trying her best to do what the others do," said Sam. "She's going to be a clever little thing."

"They're all beautiful," said Jill. "Absolutely beautiful. Do they wear feathery plumes at night?"

"Yes. They're as grand as can be," said Sam. "And don't they love being dressed up too! Bad as the monkeys. They just love it."

"Now you can see our Wild West act!" said Sam. The string of horses trotted docilely out

of the ring. Then in galloped Sam and Dan, whooping and yelling for all they were worth. The things they did! Jill and Peter watched in amazement.

They stood up, they sat down, they slithered right under their horses and up the other side, they stopped at top speed and reared up alarmingly, they even leaped to one another's horses and changed places.

Jill and Peter got tremendously excited and yelled loudly. Then suddenly two brown noses appeared at the tent opening, and Bunter and Nuzzler, attracted by the yells of Jill and Peter, looked in.

"Bunter! Come on! We'll join in!" yelled Peter, and Bunter trotted over to him. Nuzzler came too. In a flash both children were on their horses and in the ring as well. What a commotion there was! The four horses enjoyed it as much as the children, and soon Peter began to do things as daring as those the two boys did. When he jumped from his own horse to Sam's, Dan gave a yell.

"Look at that! Bravo, bravo!"

At last, tired out and trembling with excitement, they slowed down and trotted their horses out into the sunshine. Sam and Dan looked admiringly at Jill and Peter.

"I say! You'd be as good as we are, if you did a bit of practising."

"Do you think so?" asked Peter, eagerly. "Could we come along and practise with you sometimes? We've got holidays now. Bunter and Nuzzler would love it."

"Yes, you come," said Sam. "Then if you're ever out of a job you could always ask Jo for one in his circus!"

Jill and Peter cantered off, their eyes shining. "What a morning!" said Peter. "Gosh, we've always enjoyed messing about in our own little ring – but to practise in a real circus ring – it's marvellous!"

"It's fantastic," said Jill. "I do hope Mum won't say no."

Their mother asked a lot of questions, but she didn't say no. "You'll get tired of it after a day or two," she said. "But I've no doubt it will do you good to see how hard the circus folk have to work. You just train your horses for fun and pleasure – to the circus folk it is a way of earning a very hard living."

So morning after morning Jill and Peter rode down to Bolter's field, where the camp lay set in its circle of gay caravans. They practised hard with Sam and Dan. Nuzzler and Bunter seemed to love it. Nuzzler even managed to learn to waltz quite well, but Bunter couldn't seem to. He would turn round the wrong way and upset all the others. Sam and Dan taught the children how to turn cartwheels and somersaults. Once they lent them old Indian suits, with fringed trousers, embroidered tunics, and great feathered headdresses. Jill had never felt so grand in all her life.

"Let's make up a new Indian game," said Sam, suddenly. "You can be a squaw, Jill, belonging to Peter. We'll be enemies and capture you. We'll tie you up to a tree, and then shoot at you with arrows – then up can come Peter. We'll snatch you up, put you on our horse, and ride off. Then Peter can come thundering behind and rescue you."

Feeling a bit doubtful about all this, Jill consented. It was certainly exciting, if a bit

uncomfortable. She made a very realistic prisoner, yelling and screaming for help so loudly that Tickles the clown looked into the ring to see if she really meant it. He stayed to watch, applauding loudly.

When Peter thundered up on Bunter, and rescued Jill from Sam's horse, everyone was too excited for anything. "If only we could do that in the ring at night!" said Sam, wiping his hot face. "Wouldn't everyone love it!"

"Oh dear – I was half afraid I was going to fall off your horse, Sam, before Peter rescued me," said Jill, sitting down on the red plush ring. "Goodness, I'm hot. Oh, Nuzzler darling, don't breathe so heavily down my neck. Look, Sam, he's worried about me. He thinks it was all real, not acting!"

So he did. He hadn't been in the game, and he couldn't bear to hear Jill yelling for help. Now he was nuzzling her lovingly, trying to find out if she was all right.

"Horses are the nicest things in the world," said Jill, stroking Nuzzler's long nose.

"Madame Lilliput wouldn't agree," said Dan. "She thinks there's nothing to beat dogs."

"And the elephant man adores Miss Muffet and Polly Flinders," said Sam. "He's always saying that elephants are the cleverest animals in the world."

"And I suppose Miss Clarissa thinks her monkeys are the best," grinned Peter. "Well, give me horses and anyone else can have the rest as far as I'm concerned."

Both children had been to see the circus show two or three times. How different the circus folk looked when they were all dressed up for the ring! They were grand and beautiful. Madame Lilliput, in her short, sparkling skirt and her plume of ostrich feathers, looked like a beautiful doll, though she was the plainest little woman imaginable in real life. Tickles the clown and his friends, Spick, Span and Soapy, the other clowns, looked lively and amusing in their circus clothes – quite different from the rather dirty, untidy youths they were in daily life.

As for Mr Martini, he was really magnificent. He was dressed in gleaming white from top to toe, and even his top hat was white. His top-boots were white and so were his riding-breeches. His whip had a vivid scarlet bow, and how he cracked it! He looked wonderful as he stood in the middle of the brilliant ring, with his performers around him.

"You know, Sam, I'd give anything to go

into the ring just once," said Peter, longingly. "Just to feel what it's like – to be one of you, and one with all the animals. There can't be anything like it in the world."

"There isn't," said Sam. "It's the finest feeling there is. In the ring we're all one big family together, doing our best. We may quarrel outside in the camp, but in the ring we're the circus, we're pulling together, we're making a grand show, and aren't we proud of it!"

"I shall be awfully sorry when you go," said Jill, with a sigh. "You're all such fun. And those lovely, lovely horses. I know every single one of them now, and I don't know which I like best. Ladybird, perhaps, because she is so sweet and tries so very, very hard to do as well as the others do."

"We're giving our last show on Saturday night," said Sam. "Then we go on to our next camp. It'll be a grand show, so be sure you come. Jo says he'll give you two of the best seats that Saturday."

"Of course we'll be there," said Peter. "Mum and Dad are coming too, but they won't want to be in the front. Mum doesn't like to be too near. Heaps of the boys and girls of our school are coming too, so be sure to do your best."

"You bet!" grinned Sam. "We'll yell to you when we gallop by in our Wild West act."

"We've told everybody about you," said Jill. "Simply everybody. They'll all be looking out for you and they'll clap you like anything."

"They'll think you're marvellous," said Peter. "Gosh – I wish they could see us performing too – we're almost as good as you are now."

Saturday morning came. Peter and Jill rode down to the camp, feeling rather sad. It wouldn't be there the next day. It would be on the road, rolling away to another field. How they would miss Sam and Dan and the horses.

"Good thing that school begins again next week," said Peter. "I should feel lost without anything to do. What fun we've had!"

When they got to the camp they noticed something strange. There did not seem to be anyone about. Where could they be?

"What's happened to everyone?" said Jill, in wonder. "Oh look – there's somebody coming out of the big top."

It was Madame Lilliput coming out of the great circus tent, hurrying as fast as she could. When she saw the two children, she ran towards them, her face screwed up as if she was crying. When she came nearer, the children saw to their horror that tears were running down her cheeks.

"What's the matter? Oh, what's happened?" cried Jill, scared.

"It's Sam," said Madame Lilliput. "He climbed up to the top of the tent to put the lamp straight – and he fell. Oh, poor, poor Sam! What shall we do? We need a doctor, quickly."

Jill's heart went cold. Sam! Cheerful, lively, kindly Sam. Tears came into her eyes.

Peter sat still on his horse. Sam had fallen from the top of the tent down to the ring below! He must be very badly hurt indeed.

"Listen," he said. "Our father is a doctor. I'll ride back home and get him to come at once. He'll be here in a jiffy. Don't move Sam till he comes."

The boy flew off like the wind on Bunter. Jill heard the thud of the hoofs as he went, but she did not go with him. She wanted to see poor Sam.

She slipped off her horse and walked on trembling legs to the big circus tent with Madame Lilliput. Everyone was inside, even the dogs and the monkeys. In the centre of the ring lay poor Sam. His eyes were shut and he was as white as a sheet. Mr Martini was kneeling over him, almost as white as Sam himself. Tickles the clown was trying to keep everyone back.

"Don't crowd round," he said in a shaky voice, not a bit like his own. "Give the poor lad a bit of air, can't you?"

Madame Lilliput went up to Mr Martini. "Jo! There's a doctor coming. He'll be here soon. Best not move the lad at all. Peter's gone for his father, who's a doctor."

The circus folk looked immensely relieved. They had been as frightened as the children when they heard of Sam's fall, but now they cheered up a bit.

286

Jill was still very worried. She had heard her father talk many times of illnesses and accidents, and she was afraid that Sam might be seriously damaged, perhaps for life.

"Poor, poor Sam," she thought. "Suppose he can never ride again? And poor Dan too. He's so fond of Sam, and they do such wonderful things together. And there's tonight too – the last night of all, when they'd planned to put on such a fine show. What a terrible bit of bad luck!"

Peter had found his father about to set out on his calls. He turned his car round at once and set off in the direction of the circus. He knew all about Sam and Dan from his children. He was at the camp in four minutes and drove his car into the field through the gate, bumping over the ruts.

Then he was in the big tent, making his way through the anxious folk. "Turn them all out," he said to Jo. "Every one of them." And out they went. Jill and Dan were allowed to stay, with Jo – and in a little while Madame Lilliput stole back to see if she could help.

Sam opened his eyes and groaned. Peter's father examined the boy quickly and carefully. Then he stood up.

"He'll be all right, thank goodness. He's not

damaged himself too much. He'll have to go to hospital and have treatment – and he'll be very sore and bruised for a few days. There'll be no riding for him for a month or two, though."

Tears ran down Dan's face – a curious mixture of tears, really. He was crying for joy because Sam wasn't seriously injured – and for grief because now he wouldn't be able to ride with Sam for a long time. Jill sniffed too. She knelt down by Sam and stroked his hand.

"You're not too badly hurt, Sam," she said. "You'll be all right. Poor old Sam!"

Sam tried to say something and couldn't. He looked very worried indeed. He tried again.

"What is it, old son?" the doctor asked
gently. "Don't worry about anything. You
won't do yourself any good if you do. Things
will be all right."

"It's tonight," said Sam, with an effort.
"See? It's the big show tonight. What about –
the Wild West Kids?"

"That's all right," said Jo. "We'll do without
them."

"No," said Sam. "No. There's Dan. Don't
leave him out. Jill, you and Peter – can't you do
it with Dan?"

"Now don't worry yourself like this," said
the doctor, anxiously. But Jill pulled at his
arm.

"Daddy! Why shouldn't Peter and I help
Dan tonight in the ring? We know everything!
We've practised it time and time again. Even
Sam says we're as good as he and Dan are!"

Peter was now back and he joined in eagerly.
"Yes, Dad – we can do the Wild West act. We've
got a very good one, with Jill as a squaw.
You've seen it too, haven't you, Mr Martini?"

Jo nodded. He had come into the ring once
while the four of them were doing it, and had
been amused and surprised. He looked at
Peter's father.

"They're good," he said. "And if it would

set Sam's mind at rest – and if you wouldn't mind, Doctor, why I'd be pleased to give your kids a chance in the ring. They'd love it – it would be a reward to them for all the practising they've done with Sam and Dan here. But it's for you to decide."

The doctor looked down at Sam. The boy's eyes were shining and colour had come back to his face. He caught hold of the doctor's hand feebly. "Give them a chance," he begged. "Let the show go on just the same without me, but with Dan and Peter and Jill. I'll feel happy then."

"All right," said the doctor, and Peter and Jill looked at one another with shining eyes. Poor Sam – it was because of him they had their chance, and they were immensely sorry for him – but they could not help feeling excited and happy to think of the coming night.

"We'll do our best, Sam," said Jill, and the boy nodded, looking happy.

"Help me to lift him gently to my car," said the doctor to Jo. "I'll take him to hospital myself. You can come with us, Dan. Not you, Jill and Peter. That would be too big a crowd for Sam. I'll look after the boy, Mr Martini, till he's better, and keep you posted about him."

"Thanks, Doctor," said Jo, gratefully. "He's

got no father or mother. There's only me and I'm his guardian. He's a good lad. Aren't you, Sam?"

Sam tried to put on a grin. He was in pain and it was difficult, but he managed a faint one. Then he was carried gently to the car and laid comfortably on the back seat.

That evening the three, Dan, Jill and Peter, were in a state of the greatest excitement. Dan, wild and lively after the shock and grief of the morning, shouted and laughed. Peter and Jill dressed themselves in their Indian clothes, and Jill found that her hands were

shaking with excitement. She could hardly do up her tunic.

All the circus folk came to wish them luck. "It's grand of you to step in like this, so that Dan can carry on," said Tickles. "Our last show in a place is always the best. You'll be fine!"

"I hope so," said Peter, feeling suddenly nervous. "You know, Tickles, all our school friends will be there. Can't think what they'll say! And Mum and Dad are coming too. I hope we shan't do anything silly."

"You'll be all right," said Tickles. "We shall all be fine tonight. We're all feeling glad that Sam isn't hurt too badly. He'll be back with us again before the winter, as good as ever, your father says. Say, he's a grand fellow, your father, isn't he? If I wasn't a clown, I'd be a doctor. Next best thing to making people laugh would be to make them well when they're ill. I wouldn't mind being a doctor at all."

Peter smiled. Funny old Tickles. Then he began to worry about his part in the show again. Would he really be able to do it all right? Would Bunter be nervous?

Neither Bunter nor Nuzzler were nervous. They were excited and happy. Somehow they sensed that for once they were one with all the other horses. They were The Circus. Bunter whinnied a little and Nuzzler nuzzled against him.

The grand parade began to the lively strains of the band. Into the ring went every performer, both human and animal, parading round in their finery, lifting their hands to

greet the clapping audience. And into the ring went Jill and Peter too on Bunter and Nuzzler, following Dan. The children were all dressed in their Indian costumes, ready for their act later on. Their hearts were beating fast. They waved their hands too, and tried to see the faces of their parents in the vast audience.

"Hey, there's the Wild West Kids!" shouted a shrill voice. Peter knew that voice. It belonged to Bobby, a boy in his form. "Hey, look! There's three of them, not two, tonight."

Peter waved his hand to Bobby. Bobby did not recognise him in his Indian clothes, but he was thrilled that one of the Wild West Kids had actually waved to him.

"See that," he said proudly to his companions. "He waved to me. Gosh, wouldn't I like to be in his shoes tonight!"

The grand parade was over. The show began. In came the beautiful horses to canter round and round, and to waltz and do their tricks. How they enjoyed every moment. Everybody clapped wildly at the sight of the sleek, shining creatures, and Mr Martini cracked his whip and looked at them proudly. This was his great moment. He was the grand man of the circus, the ringmaster, and these beautiful horses were his. He wouldn't have changed places for anyone on earth at that moment.

"Good old Jo!" whispered the watching circus folk to one another.

Crack! went his whip, and the horses changed round and went in the opposite direction, while the band kept time to their cantering.

One after another the turns came on. Tickles and the clowns sent the audience into fits of laughter. They had never been so funny before. When Tickles tried to ride a horse and fell off every time, Bobby and the others from Peter's school cried with laughter. It made Jill and Peter laugh to see them.

The elephants played cricket with their trainer, and the dogs played football with Madame Lilliput. Their eager barking filled the ring, and when the little goalkeeper dog saved goal after goal the audience cheered and clapped with admiration!

"What a fine show!" said Bobby to the others. "What's next? Oh, the Wild West Kids. Good!"

And into the ring rode Dan, Jill and Peter! As soon as the time came for them to appear, all their nervousness went. Instead they were filled with a wild excitement and they galloped

in, whooping and yelling as if they really were Indians!

The children in the audience clapped and stamped vigorously. This was what they liked. They shouted and yelled as much as the Indians did, when they saw the tricks they performed.

Round the ring they went at top speed. Then up on the horses' backs they all stood. Then down they sat, facing their horses' tails. Yes, even Jill could manage that now without sliding off. Then up they stood again, and Peter and Dan changed horses by jumping from one to the other.

"Good gracious!" said Peter's mother to his father. "I didn't know they could do this kind of thing! Is it safe? Oh my goodness, there they go again. Well, I never thought Peter and Jill would go careering round a circus ring, performing like that!"

Then the three did their act where Jill was the squaw. Dan rode off with her and then tied her up to a post. He shot arrows at her, missing her cleverly, and she screamed so realistically that her mother almost went into the ring to rescue her herself!

Then up thundered Peter, whooping for all he was worth. How the audience cheered him!

Dan snatched at Jill, got her on his horse, and galloped off with her round the ring. After him went Peter, whirling a lasso, which was another trick he had learned. He neatly lassoed Dan and drew him to a standstill.

Then he snatched Jill off Dan's horse, put her on his, and rode off with her at top speed while Bobby and the rest cheered frantically at the tops of their voices.

Dan rode out of the ring after Peter. But in a second they were back again with Jill to take their bows. They leaped off their horses and bowed time and again. Then they did a series of cartwheels round their horses, leaped to their feet and vaulted on to their horses' backs. Off they went out of the ring to a perfect tornado of applause.

Peter's parents clapped madly too. They could not believe that Jill and Peter were so good. As for the circus folk they crowded round them and slapped them on the back till they were sore. Mr Martini strode up and held out his great hairy hand.

"Fine, fine! Bravo! Best act I've seen any kids do for years! If ever you want a job, you two, come along to me and I'll give you one in my circus. See! If your father and mother ever turn you out of house and home, you'll know where to come to!"

"Thanks, sir," said Peter, glowing, "but I don't think that's likely to happen somehow. All the same – it's a great feeling to go into the ring and I'll never, never forget it!"

They stayed behind to have supper with the circus folk, and their mother and father came too. After supper the camp was to start on its journey to its next camping place. It was to travel in the quiet of the night. The moon was bright, the roads were empty. In an hour's time the caravans would be on their way, and the lorries would follow after, packed with all the circus properties.

"So it's goodbye," said Mr Martini at the end of the hilarious meal. He held out his hand. "Pleased and proud to have met you. Good as any circus kids you are, and that's saying a lot. Goodbye. Look after Sam for me and send him back as soon as he's fit."

All the goodbyes were said. Jill and Peter could not help feeling a little sad as they shook hands with Tickles, the elephant man, Madame Lilliput and the rest. They patted all the horses, shook paws with the monkeys and with the performing dogs too.

"We'll come back next year," said Mr Martini, getting into his blue caravan. "See you then. And maybe you can do a Wild West act again, with Sam and Dan, if your parents will let you. Goodbye."

The line of caravans crawled out of the field gate and on to the road. The moon shone down

on the little houses on wheels. Dogs barked
and the two elephants, who were walking,
trumpeted loudly.

"They're saying goodbye too," said Jill. "Oh
Peter, do you think Bobby and the rest will

believe it was us, when we tell them next week at school?"

"We'll see," said Peter with a grin. "Old Sam will be thrilled when he hears about it, won't he?"

The next week Peter spoke to Bobby and the others at his school. "Did you see the circus on Saturday? Did you like it?"

"Oh boy! Did we like it? It was super, fantastic, tremendous!" said Bobby, beaming. "Why, weren't you there? Come to think of it, I didn't see you."

"Yes. We were there," said Peter, grinning. "You saw us all right."

"I didn't," said Bobby. "I looked all round for you. You ought to have gone, you really ought."

"What did you like the best?" asked Peter. And, of course, he got the answer he hoped for.

"The best? Why, the Wild West Kids of course!" cried Bobby, and the others yelled in agreement. "You ought to have seen them, Peter – they were amazing. I'd have loved to be them, wouldn't you?"

"Yes, I would," said Peter, grinning still more widely. "And what's more, I was one of them. What do you think of that, Bobby!" And he gave such a wild Indian yell that everyone jumped. Then he did six cartwheels round the classroom, and ended up by colliding with the headmaster who was just coming in at the door.

"Now, my boy! Do you imagine that you are a circus performer?" asked the headmaster, sarcastically.

And Peter answered at once. "Well, yes, sir – I do!"

A Night
on Thunder Rock

"Dad, we've got something to ask you," said Robert. "We do hope you'll say yes."

"Well, I'm not promising till I know what it is," said his father, cautiously. "I've been caught that way before!"

"It's something quite simple," said Rita.

"Yes, something you'd love to do yourself," said Phil. "It's this – can we spend a night on Thunder Rock?"

Thunder Rock was a tiny rocky island not far out from the coast. The three children had a small boat of their own, and were used to rowing about by themselves. They had often rowed to Thunder Rock and had a picnic there.

"So now you want to spend a night there," said their father. "Well, what does your mother say?"

"She says we must ask you," said Robert. "Say yes, Dad. Only just one night. It would be such fun to camp out there all by ourselves."

"We'd take rugs and things," said Rita.

"We'd choose a very fine warm night. It would be heavenly to go off to sleep at night with the waves beating on the rocks round us, and the stars twinkling above us."

"And waking up in the morning with the sun, and slipping into the water first thing for a swim," said Phil. "Come on, Dad – say yes."

"Well, what about that old boat of yours?" said his father. "I heard it was leaking. Is it safe?"

"Pretty safe, because we can always bale out the water," said Rita. "We don't mind. Anyway, we can all swim and we'll wear our life-jackets. But I don't think the poor old boat will last much longer, Daddy. Are new boats very expensive?"

"Very," said her father. "No hope of getting one, so don't make plans. You'll have to make the leaky old tub do for some time – but mind, if it gets too bad we'll have to scrap it. No good running into danger, and you never know!"

"Well – can we go to Thunder Rock for the night?" asked Phil. "You haven't said yet."

His father smiled. "Okay – you can go. Take your food with you, and rugs and things. You'll be all right. It is fun to camp out on a little

island like that. You feel so very much all on your own."

"Oh, thanks, Dad! We never thought you'd say yes."

In delight the three children rushed off to their mother to tell her. "Well, I do hope you'll all be all right," she said. "You're old enough to look after yourselves now – Robert is fourteen and very strong. Don't get up to any silly tricks though. And be sure that old tub of yours doesn't leak too much."

The children said nothing about their boat. It really was leaking very badly, and needed a lot of baling to keep it from sinking lower and lower! But if only it would last till they had had their night on Thunder Rock.

They made all their plans. Rita fetched a pile of old rugs and old coats. Phil went to ask for a few tins of meat and fruit to take with them, and some lemonade. Robert went to get the boat ready. They planned to set off that evening, have a picnic supper, a swim in the sun-warmed water, and then a lovely talk lying on the rugs, looking up to the starry sky.

"It will be gorgeous hearing the waves lapping round all the time," said Robert. "Fancy being all by ourselves like that, too. Nobody to send us here and there, nobody to ask what we're up to, nobody to say we're making too much noise."

They said goodbye and set off in the boat. Everything had been piled in. Had they forgotten anything? No, they didn't think so. Robert pulled at the oars and Rita and Phil baled hard.

"Bother this leak!" said Rita. "It's getting worse. I honestly don't think the poor old tub will last much longer."

"Well, Ted the fisherman says it's too old to mend," said Robert, pulling hard. "Say when you're tired of baling, Rita, and I'll have a turn and you can row."

Gulls cried loudly all round them. The sea was very calm, and only a slight swell lifted the

boat now and again. The sun shone from the western sky, and the water gleamed blue and purple and green. Lovely!

They got to Thunder Rock at last. They pulled the boat into a tiny cove, out of reach of the waves. Rita took out the rugs and old coats and spread them on a sandy place between some high rocks.

"We'll be well sheltered here," she said. "And the sand is warm and soft. Won't it be gorgeous sleeping out here? Now what about supper?"

Supper was lovely. Tinned salmon, tinned pineapple, new bread and butter, chocolate and lemonade. "Better than any meal on a table," said Phil. "Now let's have a look round Thunder Rock and then have a swim when our supper's settled a bit."

Thunder Rock was a strange little island. It was nothing but rocks and coves. Nothing grew on it at all, except seaweed. The seabirds came to it, and liked to stand on the highest rocks, gazing out to sea. They fluttered away a little when the children came near to them, but did not fly right off.

"Lovely things," said Rita, watching a big gull alight. "I wouldn't mind being a gull – swimming, flying, paddling, gliding, diving – what a nice life!"

They had their swim and then lay on their rugs in the twilight, warm and glowing. They put on pyjamas, and then Phil yawned.

"Golly, are you sleepy already?" said Rita. "I'm not. I want to enjoy every minute of this exciting evening. Don't let's go to sleep yet."

"Of course we won't," said Robert, nibbling a bar of chocolate. "The sun's quite gone now. There's not a single bit of pink cloud left in the sky. But it's still very warm."

"The waves sound nice, splashing all round Thunder Rock," said Rita, looking sleepy. They went on talking for a while, and then Phil gave another yawn, a most enormous one this time.

"I really don't believe I can keep awake," he said. "I do want to, but my eyes keep closing. I bet we'll sleep well tonight – with nothing whatever to disturb us except the sound of the sea."

"All right. We'll say goodnight then," said Rita. "I feel sleepy, too. I'm going to fix my eyes on that bright star over there and see how long I can keep awake. It's so lovely out here all alone on Thunder Rock."

It was not long before they were all asleep. The stars shone in the sky, and the sea splashed quietly on the rocks. There was no other sound to be heard.

But wait a minute – *was* there no other sound? Robert suddenly woke up with a jump. He lay there for a moment, wondering where he was. How strange to see the sky above him

311

instead of the ceiling of his bedroom. Then he remembered – of course, he was on Thunder Rock. Good!

He was just about to go to sleep again when he heard the sound that had woken him. It was an extra loud splash – and then another and another. Regular splashes.

Robert sat up. It sounded like a boat being rowed along, not far from Thunder Rock. Then he heard low voices. That really made him pay attention. A boat near Thunder Rock – and voices in the middle of the night. What did it mean?

Cautiously Robert awoke Phil and whispered in his ear. "Don't make a sound. There's a boat being rowed to Thunder Rock. I can hear it – and voices too."

The boys sat and listened. But the boat did not come to Thunder Rock after all. It went right round it and the voices died away. The splash of the oars could no longer be heard.

"The boat's on the landward side of the rock now," whispered Robert. "Let's go round and see if we can spot it. There's only starlight to see by but we might just make it out."

They walked cautiously over the rocks and round to the other side of the little island. They could see a dark mass some way off –

that must be the boat! But who was in it –
and why come rowing over the sea at this time
of night? Where to? And where from?

"It's all jolly mysterious," said Robert. "Now
let's think. Where is that boat heading for?"

"It's going towards the rocky cliffs of the
mainland," said Phil. "I should think towards
the part that is always washed by the sea – the
part we've never been able to explore properly
because you can't get round to it."

"There might be caves there," said Robert.
"I wonder where the boat came from, though.
It seemed to come from out at sea – and yet it
was only rowed."

"Do you know – I bet that it came from a motor-launch some way out," said Phil, suddenly. "They wouldn't dare to bring it right in if they were doing anything they shouldn't because the motor would be heard. I bet the boat left the launch right out at sea – and was rowed in quietly, with something illegal on board. Probably they've come from France."

"Do you mean smuggled goods?" said Robert in sudden excitement. "My word – smugglers!"

"Well, you know there are still plenty of smugglers about," said Phil. "I bet you anything you like we've just heard a boat-load of smugglers passing, with smuggled goods in the boat, and they're heading for the cliffs, where they've either got a hiding-place or friends to take the goods from them."

Robert whistled. He gazed towards the dark land which could be faintly seen as a black blur in the starlit night. "Yes. You may be right. Smugglers! I say, what are we going to do about it?"

"Let's go and wake Rita," said Phil. "We can talk about it then, all together. Well, I feel wide awake now, don't you?"

Rita was very excited when she heard the boys' news. "You might have woken me before," she said indignantly. "Do you suppose

314

the smugglers' boat will come back?"

"Well – yes – I suppose it might," said Robert. "I hadn't thought of that. We'd better keep a look-out."

They all went round to the other side of the little island and strained their eyes towards the distant cliffs. Then Robert gave an exclamation.

"Look – I'm sure I can see a light – it must be at the bottom of the cliffs, I should think."

They all stared hard, and soon Rita and Phil could see a faint light, too.

"I bet that's where the smugglers are, with their goods!" said Robert.

They sat and watched and talked for a long time. The light disappeared. Then suddenly Robert's sharp ears heard something and he clutched Rita and Phil, making them jump.

"They're coming back! Shh!" And then there came the sound of oars again, and a murmur of voices.

The boat passed in the darkness, a blur against the water. The children hardly dared to breathe. They began to whisper when the boat was out of hearing.

"They must have put the goods in a cave. Let's go tomorrow and find out."

"Shh! Listen! I believe I can hear a motor

starting up a good way out. I bet the smugglers are off back to France."

"I wish daylight would come. I want to go off and hunt for the smuggled goods!"

But day did not come. It was still only the middle of the night and the children fell asleep again and could hardly believe, in the morning, that anything had happened in the night.

"But it must have, because we all know about it," said Rita. "So it can't have been a dream. Let's have breakfast and then go and explore those cliffs. We can row quite near to them."

So after a meal they set off in their leaky old boat. They rowed towards the towering, rocky cliffs, round whose base the sea washed continually. They came nearer and nearer, and then, when they were afraid of going on the rocks, they rowed round the cliffs, examining every foot of them as carefully as they could.

And they found what they were looking for! They came suddenly to a cleft in the cliff, and guided their boat carefully towards it. A wave took them into the inlet and they found themselves in an enclosed channel, walled in by steep cliffs, with not much more room than the boat needed for itself.

On one side of the channel was a cave,

running into the cliff, quite hidden from the sea outside. "You hold the boat steady by hanging on to this rock, Phil, and I'll have a look in the cave," said Robert. He leaped from the boat on to a rock and then peered into the cave. He gave a yell.

"I say! Stacks of things! Crates and packing cases of all kinds. This is where those smugglers put their stuff. I bet someone on the mainland collects them when it's safe to do so – probably by boat."

He went back to the boat and got in. "I'd like to undo some of those crates," he said. "But I suppose I'd better not. It's a matter for the police now."

"Is it really?" said Rita, looking rather scared. "Well, come on then. Let's get back home."

They shoved the boat down through the cleft of the cliff and back to the open sea again. Robert and Phil took the oars. Phil gave a shout of dismay.

"I say! You'll have to bale like fury, Rita, the boat's awfully full of water. We'll be swimming soon! Get the baler, quick."

Certainly the boat was leaking worse than ever. Rita began to bale quickly. The boys rowed hard. But the boat was now heavy with water and it was difficult going. In the end the boys had to stop rowing and help Rita with the baling.

When they had got the boat a good bit lighter, they took the oars again.

"You'll have to hurry up," said Rita, anxiously. "It's already beginning to fill again. It must have sprung another leak. I hope we get back before it fills and sinks!"

The boat began to fill quickly again. The boys rowed hard. Just before they got to shore the boat quietly began to sink beneath them.

They had to get out and wade to shore, carrying what they could of their goods.

"That's very bad luck," said Robert, sadly. "I liked that old boat. I'm afraid it's done for now. Come on, let's go home and tell Mum what's happened. Then she can ring up the police."

Their mother was amazed at all they had to tell. She was horrified about the boat, and very glad they had got home safely, though they were very wet.

"I can hardly believe this tale of smugglers," she said. "But I suppose I'd better ring up the police. I'll do it now, while you go and put on dry things."

It wasn't long before a police inspector was round in his car. He listened with the greatest interest to all that the children told him.

"I expect they've really hit on something," he told their mother. "We know smuggling is going on all round the coast. But it's difficult to trace. I'll get a boat and go round to this cave. Perhaps I could take the children's boat and they could direct me to the place."

"It's sunk," Phil said, rather sorrowfully. "We haven't got a boat! We feel very upset about it. Ted the fisherman will lend you his. We'll come too."

The inspector found that the crates in the cave contained guns and ammunition, most certainly smuggled. "My word, this is a haul!" he said in delight. "Well, we'll remove all this tonight when nobody is likely to see us, and then we'll set a watch for the smugglers' friends, whoever they are. They are sure to come to fetch it soon. And we will also put somebody on Thunder Rock, lying in wait for the smugglers when they come again, as they are sure to do."

It all sounded very exciting indeed. The children wanted to go to Thunder Rock with the watchers, but the inspector said no. "There may be danger – shooting, for instance," he said. "You can't be involved in things like that. I'll let you know what happens, never fear!"

He kept his word, and brought them a very exciting story the next week. "We've got the men who receive the guns," he began. "We caught them rowing round to the cave to fetch them. And now we've got the smugglers too! Three of them!"

"Did you catch them in their boat?" asked Rita.

"We followed their boat when it went back to the open sea," said the inspector. "And there, sure enough, was a smart little motor-launch waiting for them. We got the whole lot – so that spot of smuggling is stopped for a little while at any rate."

"What a good thing we went to spend the night on Thunder Rock," said Phil. "It's bad luck our boat is gone, though."

"Oh, I wouldn't worry about that," the inspector said in an airy voice. "We want to give you a reward for your help – you'll find it in Ted the fisherman's charge if you care to go and look."

The children tore down to the beach and found Ted there, grinning. Beside his boat lay another one, newly-painted and smart.

"Good morning," said Ted. "Come to have a look at your new boat? Smart, isn't it? My word, you're lucky children, aren't you?"

"We are!" said Rita, in delight. "Bags I row it first! Oh, what a beauty. Come on, boys – haul it down the beach. Off we go!"

And off they went, bobbing lightly up and down on the waves. They rowed to Thunder Rock, pulled the boat up on the sand and lay down in the sun.

"Good old Thunder Rock!" said Phil, banging the sand below him with his open hand. "If it hadn't been for you we'd never have got that marvellous – wonderful – super – new boat!"

A Week Before Christmas

The Jameson family were making their Christmas plans. They sat round the table under the lamp, four of them – Mother, Robert, Ellen and Betsy. Daddy was far away across the sea and wouldn't be home for Christmas.

"Now, we haven't got much money," said Mother, "so we must spend it carefully this Christmas. We can't afford a turkey, but I can get a nice big chicken. I've made a Christmas pudding, and I shall buy as much fruit as I can for you. Perhaps I shall make mince pies for a treat!"

"Can we afford a little Christmas tree?" asked Betsy. She was ten and loved a pretty Christmas tree hung with all kinds of shiny things. "Just a little one, Mummy, if we can't afford a big one."

"Yes, I'll see what I can do," said Mother, writing it down on her list. "And I've made the cake, a nice big one. I've only got to ice it and put Christmassy figures on it. I'll see if I

325

can buy a little red Father Christmas to go in the middle."

She wrote down, *Little Father Christmas*, and then wrote something else down below. "What have you written?" asked Betsy, trying to see. But her mother covered up the words.

"No – I'm writing down what you three want for Christmas! It's not really a secret because you've all told me – and I shall try my hardest to get them."

Betsy wanted a big doll. She had never had a really big one, though she was ten. She knew she was getting a bit old for dolls now but she did so love them, and she longed to have a big one before she really was too old.

Robert wanted a model aeroplane kit. He had seen one in a shop and longed for it. It would be marvellous to put all the parts together, and at last have a model aeroplane that he could take to school for all the boys to see.

Ellen wanted a proper box of watercolours because she loved to paint and she was really very good at it.

"They're all rather expensive presents," said Ellen to Robert and Betsy, when they had discussed what they wanted. "We mustn't mind if Mummy can't get them. But she did

say we must tell her what we really wanted. I know what she wants – a new handbag. They're expensive too, but if we all put our money together we might be able to buy her the red one we saw the other day."

So they made their Christmas plans, and discussed everything together. Since their father had been away Mother had always talked over everything with the children. They knew she hadn't a great deal of money and they helped her all they could.

"Tomorrow I'm going to go out and do my Christmas shopping," Mother said. "I've got to deliver all the parish magazines for the vicar, too, because his sister who usually does it is ill. I'll do that first, then I'll go and order the chicken and the fruit and sweets – and perhaps some crackers if they're not too expensive. And I'll see if I can buy your presents too – so nobody must come with me!"

"I'll help with the magazines," said Robert. But his mother shook her head.

"No – you break up tomorrow and there will be plenty for you to do. You're one of the boys that has promised to go back in the afternoon and help to clean up the school, aren't you?"

"Yes," said Robert. His mother was proud of him because whenever there was a job to be done Robert always offered to help. "But I'll be back in good time for tea, Mum."

The girls broke up the next day too. Then there would be six days till Christmas – days to decorate the house with holly from the woods, to make paperchains to go round the walls, to decorate the Christmas tree, paint Christmas cards, and do all the jolly things that have to be done before Christmas Day.

"Ellen, you put the kettle on for tea and lay the table, because I shall be a bit late coming back from my shopping this afternoon," said

Mother, the next day. "I'll try not to be too late – but those magazines take rather a long time to deliver and I must do my shopping afterwards."

"I'll have tea all ready, Mum," said Ellen. "I'll make you some toast."

Robert went off to help at his school. Ellen sat down to draw some Christmas cards. Betsy joined her. The afternoon passed very quickly.

"Do you know it's snowing very, very hard?" Ellen said suddenly. "Just look at the enormous flakes falling down, Betsy."

They got up and went to the window. The ground was already thickly covered with snow. "Good!" said Betsy. "Snow for Christmas! That always seems right somehow. And we'll have fun with snowballs and making snowmen."

"Mum won't like shopping much in this blinding snow," said Ellen. "Good thing she's got her winter boots on. Isn't it dark, too? I suppose that's the leaden sky. It looks like evening already."

The snow went on falling all the afternoon. By teatime it was very thick on the ground. Robert came in puffing and blowing, and shook the snow off his coat. "Goodness, it's snowy! If it goes on like this we'll be snowed up in the morning!"

Ellen put the kettle on for tea and began
to cut some bread and butter. Betsy laid the
table. Then she went to the window to look for
her mother. But it was dark now and she could
see nothing but big snowflakes falling by the
window.

"I wish Mummy would come," she said.
"She *is* late. She'll be awfully tired."

Mother was late. The kettle had been boiled
two or three times before she came. She
opened the front door and came in rather
slowly. Betsy rushed to her to help her to take
off her snowy things. Ellen made the tea.

"Poor Mum! You'll be cold and hungry," she
called. Mother didn't say much. She took off
her clothes, put them to dry, and then came in
to tea. Robert looked at her in surprise. She
was usually so cheerful and happy. He saw
that she looked sad – and yes, it looked as
if she had been crying too. He got up quickly
and went to her.

"Mum! What's the matter? Has anything
happened?"

"Yes," said Mother, and sat down in her
chair. "I've lost my purse with all my
Christmas money in! Oh children, I've looked
and looked for it everywhere, and I can't find
it. I must have dropped it when I was taking

the big bundle of magazines round."

The children stared at her in dismay. "Oh, Mummy! All your money in it? Don't worry, we'll help you look for it."

They all put their arms round her. She tried to smile at them but their kindness made tears come suddenly into her eyes. She blinked them away.

"It's my own stupid fault. I should have been more careful. I can't think how it happened – and now this thick snow has come and hidden everything. I'll never find it!"

The children looked at one another in despair. If the Christmas money was gone, it meant no chicken – no sweets – no fruit – no presents! Not even a Christmas tree!

"You drink a hot cup of tea, Mum, and you'll feel better," said Ellen. "We'll manage somehow."

"We've got the cake and the pudding anyhow," said Betsy. "But, oh dear," she said secretly to herself, "I shan't have that doll now – and next year I'll be too old to ask for one." But she didn't say a word of this out loud, of course. She was much too unselfish for that.

"I'll go out and look for your purse tomorrow morning," said Robert.

"The snow will be so thick by then that you wouldn't be able to see anything – even if you knew where to look!" said his mother. "I don't mind for myself, children – but it's dreadful to think you three won't be able to have anything nice for Christmas – not even the lovely presents I had planned to give you."

"Don't bother about that," said Robert. "We

shan't mind. Come on – let's have tea and forget about it."

But, of course, they couldn't really forget about it. They pretended to talk cheerfully but inside they all felt miserable. When Mother went in to see Mrs Peters next door, they began to talk about it.

"We shall have to do something about this," said Ellen. "Mum will be awfully unhappy if she can't even buy a chicken for Christmas Day. We must make plans."

"What plans?" asked Betsy.

"Well – to earn a bit of money ourselves. Even if it's only enough to buy a chicken or a few tangerines, it will be something," said Ellen.

There was a pause. Then Robert spoke suddenly and firmly. "I know what I'm going to do. The butcher's boy is ill and can't deliver all the Christmas orders. If I offer to deliver them the butcher would pay me a wage. That will be my bit of help."

"Oh – what a very good idea!" said Betsy. "I wish I could be an errand-girl."

"You're too small," said Robert. "You can't do anything. Ellen, can you think of anything you can do?"

"Yes, I think so," said Ellen. "You know Mrs

Harris? Well, she wants somebody to take her three little children for walks each afternoon. I could do that. They're nice little children."

"Oh, good," said Robert. "Yes, that would bring in a bit of money too. It's a pity Betsy is too young to do anything."

Betsy felt sad. She didn't like being the only one who couldn't earn anything for Christmas. She wondered and wondered what she could do. She even lay awake in bed that night, wondering. And then, just before she fell asleep, she thought of something.

She remembered a blind lady who lived in the next street. What was her name? Yes, Mrs Sullivan. Mrs Sullivan had a companion who read to her each afternoon. But the companion had gone away for a week's holiday before Christmas. Had Mrs Sullivan got anyone to read to her for that week?

"I read quite well," thought Betsy. "I'm the very best in my class. I even read all the hard words without being bothered by them. I shall go tomorrow and ask Mrs Sullivan if she would like me to read to her. Then, if she pays me, I shall be doing my bit, too."

She didn't tell the others in case they laughed at her. But next morning after breakfast she went down the snowy street

334

and found Mrs Sullivan's house.

The snow was now very thick. It had snowed all night long and in places it was as high as Betsy's knees. She liked it. It was fun to

clamber through the soft white snow. She knocked at Mrs Sullivan's door.

She felt a bit frightened. Mrs Sullivan was rather a fierce-looking old lady and she wore dark glasses that made her look fiercer still. Suppose she was cross that Betsy should dare to come and ask to read to her?

Then Betsy thought of her mother's lost purse with all the money in it. This was one small way of helping. She couldn't turn back now!

Mrs Sullivan's daily woman opened the door and took Betsy into a little room where a bright fire burned. A big cat sat beside the old lady. The radio was on, and music flooded the little room. When Betsy spoke, Mrs Sullivan put out her hand, and turned the radio off.

"Well, it's little Betsy Jameson, is it?" she said. "And what do you want, Betsy?"

"Mrs Sullivan, I heard that your companion is away for a week's holiday," said Betsy, "and I didn't know if you'd got anyone to read to you in the afternoons. You see, Mummy has lost her purse with all her Christmas money in it, and we're trying to earn a bit to make up – so I thought . . ."

"You thought I might pay you for reading to

me, did you?" said Mrs Sullivan. "Well, I shall have to try you. There's a book somewhere – pick it up and read me a page."

Betsy found the library book. She began to read in her clear little voice. Mrs Sullivan listened with a smile on her face.

"Yes, you read quite well for your age – ten, aren't you? I shall be pleased to engage you. I will pay you a pound an hour for reading to me. Come at two o'clock each afternoon, starting today."

Betsy felt very proud – but a pound an hour seemed a lot of money just for reading. "I'd come for fifty pence really," she said. "I'm not as good as a grown-up at reading."

"I shall love to have you," said Mrs Sullivan. "You won't mind if we don't have reading all the time, will you? I mean, it would be nice to talk sometimes, wouldn't it?"

"Oh yes. But you wouldn't want to pay me just for talking," said Betsy.

"Well, I'll pay you for your time," said Mrs Sullivan. "Whether it's reading or talking, or just stroking my cat for me, I'll pay you for keeping me company."

"Thank you very much," said Betsy, and she stood up. "I'll come at two o'clock. I won't be late."

She went home as fast as she could through the snow. She had something to tell the others! A whole pound an hour for six days. If Mrs Sullivan kept her for two hours each afternoon, that would be twelve pounds altogether – more than enough to buy a chicken, surely!

Robert and Ellen thought it was marvellous. They had news to tell, too. "I've got the job at the butcher's," said Robert. "He asked me a few questions, and rang up my headmaster, and then said I could come till the other boy is well. I've got to deliver orders from ten to twelve o'clock each morning, and from three to five each afternoon. And he'll give me extra money on Saturdays."

"Oh, good!" said Ellen. "Considering you're only thirteen, you're jolly lucky to get a job as easily as that. You'll have to be careful not to mix up any of the orders."

"Of course I shall," said Robert, rather indignantly. "How did you get on with your job, Ellen?"

"Well, Mrs Harris was very pleased," said Ellen. "She's going to pay me five pounds each afternoon for taking all the children out. They're thrilled! I like little children, so I shall enjoy it. Between us we shall get quite a bit of money for Mummy."

"How much is Robert earning?" said Betsy.

"Five pounds a day," said Robert, "and the butcher will let me have meat at a cheaper price. Not bad considering it's only a few hours a day. By Christmas we'll have loads of money – enough for everything we need for a Christmas feast."

"And perhaps a little Christmas tree," Betsy said hopefully.

The next thing to be done was to tell Mother

what they had arranged. How they hoped she wouldn't say they mustn't. Mother listened without a word. Then she spoke in rather a shaky voice.

"Yes, you can all do your little jobs, bless you. I don't think I mind losing my purse when I know what nice children I've got. I'm proud of you all. The money will certainly help to buy the things we need."

Nobody brought Mrs Jameson's purse back to her. Robert thought that people must be very mean indeed not to take a purse back to the person who lost it. He called at the police station twice to ask if anyone had brought it in. But nobody had.

All the children began their jobs that day. Robert went off to the butcher's, and listened attentively when Mr Hughes told him about the deliveries. "The addresses are on the labels of each order," he said. "Be sure to deliver at the right house, and whatever you do, don't leave anything on the doorstep in order to be quick. If there is no one home bring it back to the shop."

Robert set off with a basket filled with orders for meat and poultry. The snow was very thick indeed, and it was a long job taking all the orders round. Everyone was very

340

surprised to see him, but when he told them why he was doing it they all smiled and nodded.

"It's a pity more children don't do things like that," said Mr George. "Helping their mothers when things go wrong."

Ellen got on very well too. The three small Harris children were delighted to see her. John, Mike and Sally all tried to cling to her hand at once. She set off very happily with them through the deep, white snow.

"We'll play snowballing. We'll build a snowman in the park and I'll try and build you a little snow-house," promised Ellen. They all had a lovely time, and when she brought them back to their mother at teatime Mrs Harris exclaimed in delight at their rosy faces and happy talk.

"Oh, Ellen, you've given them such a nice time. Here is your money. You'll come again tomorrow, won't you? The children will so look forward to it."

"I feel sorry you've got to pay me for my afternoon," said Ellen, feeling quite ashamed of taking the money. "I've had just as good a time as the children, Mrs Harris. I really have."

"Just wait a minute – I've been baking while

you've been out," said Mrs Harris. "I've got a cake for you to take home for yourself and that brother and sister of yours – what are their names – Robert and Betsy?"

And she gave Ellen a lovely chocolate cake, wrapped up in paper. Ellen was delighted. How surprised Robert and Betsy would be! She thanked Mrs Harris and hurried off home.

She met Betsy at the gate. Betsy's cheeks were red from Mrs Sullivan's bright fire, and from stumbling home through the thick snow. "Look," she said, showing Ellen her two bright coins. "That's my first wage. And isn't it lovely, Ellen, Mrs Sullivan likes just the kind of stories I like. We read a most exciting school story for a whole hour!"

Mother smiled at all the cheerful talk. She had made hot toast and butter with honey and the chocolate cake was put in a place of honour on the table. The children sat down hungrily.

"And Mrs Sullivan and I talked a lot," said Betsy. "She told me all about when she was a girl – oh, ever so long ago – and I told her about Robert and Ellen and you, Mummy. And then I had to brush the cat, Jimmy, and get him some milk. I really did have a very nice time. I can hardly wait till tomorrow to find out what happens in the story I'm reading to Mrs Sullivan."

"I bet she chose a story like that because you wouldn't be able to read a grown up one," said Robert.

"She didn't! She laughed at all the funny bits too," said Betsy. "There's a Mamselle in the book and the girls are always playing tricks on her. We laughed like anything."

"Mrs Sullivan is very kind," said Mother. "Very, very kind. I ought to pay her for having you like this."

"Oh no, Mummy – it's a job of work, really it is," said Betsy, earnestly. "Mrs Sullivan says it's not easy to be a really good companion, and she says I am. Really she does."

"You're a lovely little companion," said Mother. "Mrs Sullivan is lucky to have you. But I think she knows it. Well, as I have said before – what nice children I have got!"

"Well, we've got a jolly nice mother," said Robert, unexpectedly. "And what's more, Mum, I once heard the headmaster's wife saying to the head that she had noticed that all the nicest children were the ones that had the best mothers – so, if you think we're nice, you've got yourself to thank!"

Everybody laughed. They all felt happy and cosy. It was so nice to help and to do a job well. Really it didn't seem to matter any more that Mrs Jameson had lost her purse.

All the children went to their jobs each day, cheerfully and willingly. Mr Hughes the butcher, Mrs Harris, and blind Mrs Sullivan welcomed them and wished there were more children like them. Robert didn't deliver any

wrong orders, Ellen made the three Harris
children happy, and as for Betsy, it would be
hard to know which of the two, she or Mrs
Sullivan, enjoyed themselves the more.

"Jimmy always purrs loudly when he sees
me coming," Betsy said. "I wish I had a kitten.
Jimmy purrs like a boiling kettle. It's a pity
Mrs Sullivan can't see how nice he looks when
I've brushed him."

By the time that the day before Christmas
came the children had given their mother

quite a lot of money. Enough to buy the chicken, the fruit and a box of crackers. Marvellous!

Just as Robert was going home on Christmas Eve morning for his lunch, Mrs Toms called him. She lived in a little house in the middle of the village and she was a friend of his mother's.

"Robert! Would you have time to sweep away the snow for me before you go to the butcher's this afternoon? I did ask a man to come and do it but he hasn't turned up, and I've got my sister and her children coming for Christmas Day tomorrow. I know you're earning money for your mother and I'd be very glad to pay you for the sweeping."

"No, I'll do it for nothing," said Robert. "I'd like to. It would be nice to do something for nothing for a change, Mrs Toms. Have you got a broom and a spade? If you have I'll come along at two o'clock this afternoon, before I go to Mr Hughes, and clean up your front path for you."

"You're a kind child," said Mrs Toms. "Thank you very much. If you won't let me pay you I shall give you some of our apples and pears for Christmas instead. I had a lot from my garden this year and I've saved plenty. So you shall have a basket to take home."

Christmas was going to be good after all, thought Robert as he went home. He was out again just before two and went to Mrs Toms's house. The spade and broom were waiting for him outside the front door. Robert took the spade first. How thick and deep the snow was! Except for a little path, it had been untouched for days and was quite deep.

He began to dig, shovelling the snow away to the side. He worked hard, and soon took off his coat, he felt so hot.

When he got almost up to the front door he dug his spade into the snow, and threw aside a great heap. As the snow fell, something dark showed in it. It tumbled to the side with the snow. Robert glanced at it.

Then he looked again, more carefully. He dropped his spade and picked it up. It was a brown purse!

"Mrs Toms! I've found Mum's purse!" yelled Robert, suddenly, making Mrs Toms almost jump out of her skin. "Look, it's buried in the snow outside your front door."

Mrs Toms came hurrying out. "My goodness, is it really her purse? Yes, it is. She must have dropped it in the snow when she came

delivering the parish magazines some days ago. Would you believe it! And now you've found it! Well, well – what a good thing you're a kind-hearted lad and came to sweep the snow away for me – or someone else might have found it and taken it, when the snow melted."

"I'll just finish this," Robert said, joyfully, "then maybe I'll have time to rush home and tell Mum before I start at the butcher's. Oh, aren't I lucky. I can hardly believe it!"

He rushed home with the purse. Ellen and Betsy were not there; they had gone to their jobs. But Mother was there, and she stared in delight when Robert held out the wet purse.

"Robert! Oh, Robert, where did you find it? Is my money in it? Oh yes, everything's there, quite safe. Oh, Robert, this is wonderful. Just in time for Christmas, too! I shall go shopping this very afternoon, because now I shall be able to buy you all the presents I thought you would have to go without. It's too good to be true!"

It was a very happy and joyful Christmas for the Jameson family that year. There was plenty to eat after all, and as much fruit and chocolate and sweets as anyone wanted. There was a Christmas tree hung with all kinds of

things and topped with a lovely Father
Christmas which Mrs Sullivan gave to Betsy.
Mrs Toms sent a basket of apples and pears.
Mrs Harris gave Ellen a big box of chocolates
for everyone. And Mr Hughes presented Robert
with a big fat turkey and a pound of sausages.

"Everybody's so kind," said Ellen, happily.
"Oh, Mummy – these are wonderful paints
you've given me."

"And my model aeroplane kit is much better than I expected," said Robert. "Mum, you've bought me a more expensive one than I said – it'll make a much bigger aeroplane."

"I shall call my doll Angela Rosemary Caroline Jameson," said Betsy, hugging an enormous doll. "She's the biggest doll I've ever seen and the nicest. Oh, Mummy – we never thought Christmas would be like this, did we, when you lost your purse?"

"No," said Mrs Jameson, who was busy putting all her things from her old handbag into her new red one. "We didn't. I didn't think I'd have this lovely bag, for instance. I didn't think I'd be able to get all the things you wanted, or any nice things to eat. But you've managed it between you. I'm proud of you. There aren't many children who would do what you have done."

Isn't it marvellous how a bit of bad luck can be changed into something good if everybody helps!